A Question of Balance

A Question of Balance

The President, the Congress, and Foreign Policy

edited by

THOMAS E. MANN

THE BROOKINGS INSTITUTION
Washington

Library of Congress Cataloging-in-Publication Data

A Question of balance: the president, the Congress, and foreign
policy / Thomas E. Mann, editor.
    p.   cm.
  Includes bibliographical references.
    ISBN 0-8157-5454-X (alk. paper).—ISBN 0-8157-5453-1
(pbk.: alk. paper).
    1. United States—Foreign relations. 2. Presidents—United
States. 3. United States. Congress. I. Mann, Thomas E.
JK570.Q44 1990
353.0089—dc20   89-48523
                                                                  CIP

9 8 7 6 5 4 3 2 1

The paper used in this publication meets the minimum requirements
of the American National Standard for Information Sciences—Per-
manence of Paper for Printed Library Materials, ANSI Z39.48-1984.

Set in Linotron Janson
Composition by Monotype Composition Co.
Baltimore, Maryland
Printed by R.R. Donnelley and Sons Co.
Harrisonburg, Virginia
Book design by Ken Sabol

THE BROOKINGS INSTITUTION

The Brookings Institution is an independent organization devoted to nonpartisan research, education, and publication in economics, government, foreign policy, and the social sciences generally. Its principal purposes are to aid in the development of sound public policies and to promote public understanding of issues of national importance.

The Institution was founded on December 8, 1927, to merge the activities of the Institute for Government Research, founded in 1916, the Institute of Economics, founded in 1922, and the Robert Brookings Graduate School of Economics and Government, founded in 1924.

The Board of Trustees is responsible for the general administration of the Institution, while the immediate direction of the policies, program, and staff is vested in the President, assisted by an advisory committee of the officers and staff. The by-laws of the Institution state: "It is the function of the Trustees to make possible the conduct of scientific research, and publication, under the most favorable conditions, and to safeguard the independence of the research staff in the pursuit of their studies and in the publication of the results of such studies. It is not a part of their function to determine, control, or influence the conduct of particular investigations or the conclusions reached."

The President bears final responsibility for the decision to publish a manuscript as a Brookings book. In reaching his judgment on the competence, accuracy, and objectivity of each study, the President is advised by the director of the appropriate research program and weighs the views of a panel of expert outside readers who report to him in confidence on the quality of the work. Publication of a work signifies that it is deemed a competent treatment worthy of public consideration but does not imply endorsement of conclusions or recommendations.

The Institution maintains its position of neutrality on issues of public policy in order to safeguard the intellectual freedom of the staff. Hence interpretations or conclusions in Brookings publications should be understood to be solely those of the authors and should not be attributed to the Institution, to its trustees, officers, or other staff members, or to the organizations that support its research.

THE EXTRAORDINARY CHANGES sweeping through Eastern Europe, the accelerated globalization of economic activity, and the growing importance of new international issues such as the environment and drugs all leave little doubt about the need for a fundamental restructuring of American foreign policy. Less certain is whether our contemporary institutional arrangements for making foreign policy are up to the task. In recent years an active and aggressive Congress has often sharply disagreed with the president over the objectives and methods of foreign policy. This conflict has its roots in the constitutional partnership between the two branches, but it has been exacerbated by the modern pattern of split-party control of the branches.

This book explores the sources of the conflict, its consequences for the formulation and conduct of foreign policy, and ways to improve the relations between Congress and the president. After examining the pattern of interbranch relations on war powers, intelligence, arms control, diplomacy, and trade, the authors conclude that an effective foreign policy requires the restoration of a balance between the two branches. This will require a recognition and strengthening of each branch's comparative advantages, and must begin with an acknowledgment that neither branch can operate effectively without the other. It will entail the president's acceptance of a truly collaborative approach to foreign policy, changes in the institutional arrangements through which the branches interact, and a principled and responsible defense of both presidential and congressional prerogatives. It will also need the development of new policies that can attract broad support among foreign policy specialists and the general public.

The editor of this volume, Thomas E. Mann, is director of the Governmental Studies program at Brookings. The authors include Barry M. Blechman, president, Defense Forecasts, Inc.; Bruce W. Jentleson, associate professor of political science, University of California, Davis; Robert A. Katzmann, president, the Governance Institute, and visiting fellow at the Brookings Institution; Pietro Nivola, associate professor of political science, University of Vermont, and visiting fellow at the Brookings Institution; and Gregory F. Treverton, senior fellow, the Council on Foreign Relations.

The editor wishes to thank Robert J. Kurz, James M. Lindsay, Norman J. Ornstein, Harry Howe Ransom, and Joseph White for their comments on the manuscript; Pamela A. Humbert, Julia F. Kogan, David I. Lublin, and Rebecca L. Noah for their research assistance; Renuka D. Deonarain, Vida R. Megahed, Teresita V. Vitug, Eloise C. Stinger, and Susan L. Woollen for preparing the manuscript; and Sandra Z. Riegler for her assistance in managing the project. Nancy Davidson edited the manuscript; Linda Keefer verified factual statements and citations; and Max Franke prepared the index.

Brookings and the Governmental Studies program also wish to gratefully acknowledge the generous support of the Dillon Fund.

The interpretations and conclusions presented here are solely those of the authors and should not be ascribed to the persons whose assistance is acknowledged above, to any group that funded research reported herein, or to the trustees, officers, or other staff members of the Brookings Institution.

BRUCE K. MAC LAURY
President

November 1989
Washington, D.C.

Contents

A Question of Balance

Making Foreign Policy: President and Congress

THOMAS E. MANN

CONGRESS began to assert itself as an active and consequential player in the making of American foreign policy in the late 1960s, as public doubts about the wisdom of U.S. involvement in Vietnam increased. It soon became commonplace to speak of foreign policy by Congress.[1] After bitter confrontations and dramatic reversals of policies espoused by Presidents Nixon and Ford, however, many observers began to question whether Congress could play both an active and a constructive role in foreign policy making. Careful chroniclers noted that before the 1970s ended "much of the bloom had left the congressional rose,"[2] and that the pendulum had begun to swing back—at least partly—to the White House.[3]

Yet the pace of congressional involvement actually accelerated during the presidency of Ronald Reagan, which featured pitched battles between the executive and legislative branches on such issues as aid to the contras, arms control, war powers, trade, and congressional "micromanagement" of the conduct of foreign policy. This renewed congressional activism has spawned its own critics, who argue that congressional overreaching in foreign policy has upset the balance between executive and legislative power intended by the Constitution's Framers and has weakened this country's ability to defend its interests around the globe. Indeed, the opposition to the new role of Congress has recently gathered strength, buoyed by the publication of books bemoaning the constraints on the modern presidency and excoriating the excesses of the contemporary House and Senate and by the portrayal of Congress in the popular press as corrupt and irresponsible.[4]

1. Thomas M. Franck and Edward Weisband, *Foreign Policy by Congress* (Oxford University Press, 1979).
2. I. M. Destler, "Executive-Congressional Conflict in Foreign Policy: Explaining It, Coping with It," in Lawrence C. Dodd and Bruce I. Oppenheimer, eds., *Congress Reconsidered*, 3d ed. (Washington: Congressional Quarterly Press, 1985), p. 344.
3. James L. Sundquist, *The Decline and Resurgence of Congress* (Brookings, 1981).
4. See L. Gordon Crovitz and Jeremy A. Rabkin, eds., *The Fettered Presidency: Legal*

It is not a coincidence that this spirited debate about the constitutional authority and institutional competence of the president and Congress in the realm of foreign policy is occurring in the midst of an extraordinary period of divided government. The normal tensions that arise in the U.S. system of separate institutions sharing power have been exacerbated by the contemporary pattern of split-party control of the two branches. Republicans have become the party of the White House, Democrats the party of Congress. Under these circumstances, substantive differences and partisan rivalries are routinely escalated into institutional warfare, and members of the executive and legislative branches have an even greater interest in protecting and expanding their institutional prerogatives.

This is not to say that divided government is the sole or even primary source of interbranch conflict on foreign policy. The seeds of today's tensions were planted over 200 years ago in a Constitution that compelled a partnership between the executive and legislative branches. That partnership was built upon the distinctive competencies of each branch: for the presidency, "decision, activity, secrecy, and dispatch";[5] for Congress, democracy, deliberation, and the development of consensus. But when substantive differences between the president and Congress over the ends and means of foreign policy are sharp, each has the incentive to use its powers under the Constitution to press its views upon the other, even at the cost of violating the principles underlying that partnership.

Executive-legislative conflict on foreign policy escalates when policy disagreement is pronounced and when the constraints, both formal and informal, on institutional assertiveness are weakened. These are precisely the conditions that have shaped foreign policy making in recent years. The bipartisan consensus that allowed presidents to control American foreign policy from Pearl Harbor to the early stages of the Vietnam War gave way to ideological polarization on the substance of policy and an erosion of trust among policymakers in Washington. Substantive differences on policy, both within and between the branches, became the rule rather than the exception. And

---

Constraints on the Executive Branch (Washington: American Enterprise Institute for Public Policy Research, 1989); Gordon S. Jones and John A. Marini, eds., *The Imperial Congress: Crisis in the Separation of Powers* (Heritage Foundation and Claremont Institute, 1988); and "The World of Congress," *Newsweek*, April 24, 1989, pp. 28–34.

5. *The Federalist No. 70* (New York: New American Library, 1961), p. 424.

those different views about the proper course of American foreign policy, rather than being stifled in a deferential, closed, policymaking system, were fully vented in a transformed environment featuring many more pressure groups with foreign policy agendas, a vastly expanded and more ideological foreign policy establishment, an aggressive and suspicious press, and an assertive, decentralized, resource-rich Congress.

In many respects this recent politicization of foreign policy is closer to the norm in American history than the "golden era" of bipartisanship. The scope and character of congressional involvement is unusual, but the level of conflict is not. But the world and America's role in it have changed fundamentally since the days when presidents' foreign policy aspirations were routinely constrained by domestic political pressures, so it is important to identify the consequences of this renewed tension. On the one hand, conflict between the president and Congress over the objectives and methods of American foreign policy is not ineluctably harmful to the national interest nor even injurious to the president's program. Second-guessing by Congress can keep presidents from pursuing ill-conceived policies. Initiatives from Capitol Hill can also prompt presidents to consider new policies or new ways of thinking about old ones. Aggressive "bad cop" behavior by Congress can actually strengthen the bargaining position of "good cop" presidents in dealing with other countries. Open debate in Congress can help build the public support needed to sustain foreign policies over the long term and to adjust those policies to better serve the interests and values of the American people.

Yet with conflict often comes stalemate, irresolution, or inaction. From the executive's perspective, the president's ability to formulate and conduct foreign policy—to respond to military threats to the national security, to fashion arms control negotiating positions, to authorize covert action in support of American interests, or to engage in diplomacy with friends and foes—is compromised by Congress's determination to play an active role at each stage of the process. The costs flow from two types of congressional behavior. On some occasions, Congress makes a collective decision to explicitly reject a presidential policy. These are the dramatic encounters between the branches that capture the most public attention. Much more frequently, what frustrates the executive is the ability of an individual member or committee to impede or redirect American foreign policy. An administration necessarily consumed with diplomatic relations along Pennsylvania Avenue may find itself drained of creative energies and overly tentative in its diplomacy around the world.

There are clearly both costs and benefits from a Congress determined to assert itself in foreign policy and from the executive-legislative conflict that follows. As one scholar has argued, "Americans want two things that often prove incompatible in practice: *democratic government* (involving ongoing competition among a range of U.S. interests and perspectives) and *effective foreign policy* (which requires settling on specific goals and pursuing them consistently)."[6] The question is whether current arrangements for making American foreign policy provide an acceptable balance between competing values and interests. Strong partisans of the executive branch, who nod approvingly when Oliver North and his compatriots state flatly that "the president makes foreign policy," see the problem as not one of achieving balance but rather of unshackling the president from unconstitutional restrictions imposed by Congress. Similarly, balance is not a concern of those who take the primary lesson of the Iran-contra affair to be that the president's virtually unlimited discretion to pursue his foreign policy objectives must be reduced or preferably eliminated by statute and constant vigilance. Neither will find much solace in the pages that follow. The authors of this volume believe that an effective foreign policy requires the restoration of a balance between Congress and the president—a clearer identification of the areas where each has a comparative advantage over the other, and a renewed effort to strengthen those roles.

Constitutional Arguments

While it is commonplace for combatants in struggles between the branches to lay claim to the moral authority of the Framers, it is also largely fruitless. In its specific grants of authority in foreign policy, the Constitution favors Congress, the first branch of government. In addition to its exclusive authority to make laws and to tax and spend for the common defense and the general welfare, Congress was given the power to declare war, to raise and support armies, to provide and maintain a navy, to make rules for the government and regulation of

6. Destler, "Executive-Congressional Conflict in Foreign Policy," p. 344 (emphasis in original).

the armed services, to grant letters of marque and reprisal, to define offenses against the law of nations, to advise and consent on treaties and ambassadorial appointments, and to regulate foreign commerce. The president, by contrast, was specifically authorized only to receive foreign envoys, to negotiate treaties and appoint ambassadors, and to serve as commander in chief of the armed forces.

But if Congress was given a more generous grant of specific authorities in foreign and military affairs, the executive was nonetheless expected to play a central role. The architecture of the Constitution and the debates surrounding the Constitutional Convention and ratification period show "that the Founders intended to create two vigorous, active and combative branches with significant overlapping roles in foreign policy."[7] They produced, in the famous phrase of Edward Corwin, "an invitation to struggle for the privilege of directing American foreign policy."[8]

The ambiguities, omissions, and overlapping grants of authority in the constitutional blueprint do not mean that the struggle is unbounded. Congress neither makes treaties nor appoints ambassadors. It leaves to the president the management of diplomatic relations with other countries and the conduct of authorized military operations. Presidents, on the other hand, ordinarily acknowledge the constitutional imperatives that they may spend no funds without congressional appropriations, conclude no treaty without Senate consent, and declare or wage no full-scale war without congressional authorization. These are largely settled questions. Moreover, it is generally accepted that neither branch may use its powers to trample on the exclusive constitutional authority of the other. For example, Congress is constitutionally bound to appropriate necessary funds to pay for an embassy in a country the president has recognized,[9] although it feels no reticence about reversing presidents' decisions to close consular offices.

But many important foreign policy matters fall in Justice Robert H. Jackson's famous twilight zone, in which the president and Congress

---

7. Norman J. Ornstein, "The Constitution and the Sharing of Foreign Policy Responsibility," in Edmund S. Muskie, Kenneth Rush, and Kenneth W. Thompson, eds., *The President, the Congress and Foreign Policy* (Association of Former Members of Congress and Atlantic Council of the United States, 1986), p. 44.

8. Edward S. Corwin, *The President: Office and Powers, 1787–1957*, 4th rev. ed. (New York University Press, 1957), p. 171.

9. Louis Henkin, "Foreign Affairs and the Constitution," *Foreign Affairs*, vol. 66 (Winter 1987–88), pp. 295–97.

have concurrent authority or the distribution of authority is uncertain.[10] Many of the controversies that have arisen in this twilight zone—the deployment of military forces, the use of executive agreements, the regulation of covert action, claims of executive privilege, and congressional control of foreign policy through the power of the purse—are expressed in constitutional terms but must be resolved or at least accommodated in the political arena. Since the primary interpreters of the foreign policy powers of the president and Congress are not the courts but the two branches themselves, it is perfectly natural for each to make its strongest case, to test the limits of what the other is willing to tolerate. The form of their partnership, the balance of institutional interests and prerogatives, is subject to constant competition and negotiation.

Through much of American history, beginning with George Washington, presidents pushed the limits of their constitutional authority and found Congress largely acquiescent.[11] Washington established the precedent that the president plays an active and assertive role in foreign policy and military affairs, and subsequent occupants of the White House followed suit. Managing the day-to-day relations with foreign nations, reaching agreements with other governments without resort to a formal treaty (and, therefore, the advice and consent of the Senate), and deploying military forces without explicit authorization by Congress became the normal wont of presidents, as Congress implicitly acknowledged the comparative advantage of the executive to act quickly, informally, knowledgeably, and secretly.

It would be a mistake, however, to infer from these developments that strong and assertive presidents based their leadership in foreign and military affairs on claims of constitutional primacy or that Congress acknowledged its own position of powerlessness. After unilaterally declaring neutrality for the United States in the war between England and France, Washington provided a full explanation to Congress when it reconvened later in the year and conceded that he had no power to keep Congress from charting a different course in the war. After sending naval forces to the Mediterranean to fight the Barbary pirates, Jefferson sought congressional sanction; he also invoked John Locke's doctrine of emergency prerogative (the law of self-preservation), not

---

10. *Youngstown Sheet and Tube Co.* v. *Sawyer*, 343 U.S. 579, 635–38 (1952).
11. See Henkin, "Foreign Affairs and the Constitution"; and Ornstein, "The Constitution and the Sharing of Foreign Policy Responsibility."

constitutional authority, to justify his unilateral foreign policy actions that went beyond congressional authorization. Much the same can be said of the emergency policies of Lincoln and Franklin Roosevelt. Both presidents acknowledged that the extraordinary powers they claimed for the presidency were temporary, subject to ratification by Congress, and based not on a routine presidential right under the Constitution but rather on the doctrine of emergency prerogative.[12]

Although Congress was often content through tacit concurrence or explicit delegation to let the president take the initiative in foreign policy, it reserved the right to object, which it did in a sporadic but telling fashion throughout the nineteenth and twentieth centuries. Congress has had few doubts about the breadth of its own powers:

> Congress has insisted that, whatever the president may do on his own initiative when Congress is silent, he may not act contrary to the wishes of Congress when they are expressed by law in the exercise of the legislature's broad powers over war and commerce with foreign nations and its power to spend for the common defense and general welfare.[13]

Against this broadly accepted understanding of constitutional design and development, there has emerged in recent years an argument that presidents have inherent powers under the Constitution that guarantee them the primary role in conducting the foreign policy of the United States. This position is presented most explicitly and coherently in the minority report of the congressional committees that investigated the Iran-contra affair, where it undergirds the assertion that however unwise some of his actions may have been, President Reagan exercised constitutionally protected powers.[14]

The case for inherent presidential powers in foreign policy is based on a string of arguments. Powers are separated between the branches according to underlying principles of institutional competence; the need for energy in the executive led the Framers to place the deployment

12. Arthur Schlesinger, Jr., "The Legislative-Executive Balance in International Affairs: The Intentions of the Framers," *Washington Quarterly*, vol. 12 (Winter 1989), pp. 103–04.

13. Henkin, "Foreign Affairs and the Constitution," pp. 294–95.

14. *Report of the Congressional Committees Investigating the Iran-Contra Affair with Supplemental, Minority, and Additional Views*, H. Rept. 100-433, S. Rept. 100-216, 100 Cong. 1 sess. (Government Printing Office, 1987), sec. 2, pt. 2. (Hereafter *Minority Report.*)

and use of force, together with negotiations, intelligence gathering, and diplomatic communications, at the center of the president's foreign policy powers. The general grant of executive power to the president (which for Alexander Hamilton included all foreign affairs powers not expressly provided to the Congress), combined with his role as the "sole organ of the nation in its external relations, and its sole representative with foreign nations" (declared by John Marshall while a member of the House of Representatives), provides a basis for presidential prerogatives well beyond the powers enumerated in Article II.[15] Early constitutional history affirmed the executive's broad foreign policy authority: presidents engaged in secret diplomacy and intelligence activities, established military and diplomatic policy with other countries, and deployed military forces without congressional approval. Finally, the president's inherent powers in foreign policy were explicitly recognized by the courts, most importantly in *U.S.* v. *Curtiss-Wright*, which referred to "the very delicate, plenary and exclusive power of the President as the sole organ of the federal government in the field of international relations."[16]

The Iran-contra minority report concludes that the Constitution gives the president power to act on his own in foreign affairs—as the "sole organ" of the government in negotiation, intelligence sharing, and other forms of communication with the rest of the world—and to protect the lives and interests of American citizens abroad. While neither the president nor Congress can accomplish very much over the long term by trying to go it alone, "neither branch can be permitted to usurp functions that belong to the other."[17]

Some of these arguments are consistent with the constitutional framework I identified at the outset. Surely the Framers recognized that the legislative and executive branches had distinctive institutional strengths and weaknesses and sought to separate and combine powers to maximize their comparative advantage. They also intended the president to be more than a clerk or agent of Congress, and events throughout U.S. history underscore the value of a strong presidency, particularly in foreign and military affairs. It is also generally accepted, as I argued above, that neither branch may use its powers to deprive the other of its exclusive constitutional authority.

15. See *Minority Report*, p. 464; and Henkin, "Foreign Affairs and the Constitution," p. 292.
16. *U.S.* v. *Curtiss-Wright Export Corp.*, 299 U.S. 304 (1936).
17. *Minority Report*, p. 478.

But the signers of the Iran-contra minority report go well beyond these sensible formulations to embrace a constitutional construction that enlarges the president's domain of exclusive authority well beyond what is expressly provided in the Constitution. There is no compelling reason to believe that Hamilton is a more reliable witness to the founding than James Madison, who vigorously contested Hamilton's expansive reading of presidential power. And it seems most unlikely that this view will ever be anything but a minority dissent or that Congress or the Supreme Court will ever accept such an executive-centered interpretation of the Constitution. The fact remains that many of the most important questions of foreign policy fall in the twilight zone of concurrent authority or uncertainty. The case for a redistribution of authority and responsibility for foreign policy between the president and Congress must perforce rest on other than constitutional grounds.

The Two Presidencies

The constitutional argument that the president has the primary authority and responsibility for the conduct of American foreign policy fits well with the empirical observation that the president invariably has his way on major issues of foreign affairs. Over two decades ago Aaron Wildavsky argued that foreign and domestic policy are shaped in very different political processes.

> The United States has one President, but it has two presidencies; one presidency is for domestic affairs, and the other is concerned with defense and foreign policy. Since World War II, Presidents have had much greater success in controlling the nation's defense and foreign policies than in dominating its domestic policies.[18]

Wildavsky portrayed foreign policy making as largely insulated from the pluralistic pressures that characterize the domestic policy process. Instead of the normal battle of interest groups, parties, and bureau-

18. Aaron Wildavsky, "The Two Presidencies," *Trans-Action*, vol. 4 (December 1966), reprinted in Aaron Wildavsky, ed., *Perspectives on the Presidency* (Little, Brown, 1975), p. 448. Wildavsky and his colleague, Duane Oldfield, have recently revisited this argument. See Duane M. Oldfield and Aaron Wildavsky, "Reconsidering the Two Presidencies," *Society*, vol. 26 (July–August 1989), pp. 54–59. Much of the following discussion is drawn from the latter article.

Thomas E. Mann

cracies, foreign policy making was seen as an apolitical, technical realm of presidential problem solving. Presidents dominated foreign policy because the new international role taken on by the United States after World War II made foreign policy extremely important to them and attracted a substantial share of their resources, foreign policy was largely outside the realm of partisan conflict, and presidents' competitors in the foreign policy arena were weak.

The intervening years have not been kind to the two-presidencies thesis; Wildavsky is the first to admit that it has limited utility in an age of political dissensus. There is little evidence to suggest that recent presidents have succeeded in pressing the view that "politics stops at the water's edge." As a description of and explanation for the president's comparative advantage in foreign and defense policy during the 1950s, and as a conceptual tool for differentiating the Truman and Eisenhower years from the periods before and after, however, the concept of the two presidencies continues to serve a useful purpose. What was distinctive about foreign policy making in the post–World War II era was the success of presidents in attracting support from the opposition party in Congress, starting with the Truman administration's alliance with Republican Senator Arthur Vandenberg, chairman of the Foreign Relations Committee, and continuing through northern Democrats' favorable treatment of Eisenhower's internationalist policies.

However, the key to this anomaly is not presidential deference, but policy agreement.[19] The conversion of Vandenberg from midwestern isolationism to an internationalist position that embraced the Marshall Plan, the Greece-Turkey aid program, and NATO was based on a genuine change in his view of the U.S. role in the world under the threat of Soviet expansionism. It also involved a partnership between the legislative and executive branches that went well beyond deference to presidential wishes and required intensive political bargaining to achieve victory on Capitol Hill. (Vandenberg's leadership in forging a bipartisan foreign policy did not prevent his Republican colleagues from bitterly criticizing the Truman administration on other foreign policy issues, including "the loss of China.") This new conservative internationalism initiated by Truman and Vandenberg provided the basis for cooperation on foreign policy between President Eisenhower

19. George C. Edwards III, "The Two Presidencies: A Reevaluation," *American Politics Quarterly*, vol. 14 (July 1986), pp. 247–63; and Bert A. Rockman, "Mobilizing Political Support for U.S. National Security," *Armed Forces and Society*, vol. 14 (Fall 1987), pp. 17–41.

and the Democratic Congress. Eisenhower won the strong support of northern Democrats largely because he espoused foreign policies with which they agreed.

Presidents since Eisenhower have not enjoyed a clear foreign policy advantage in dealing with Congress, at least as measured by levels of support on domestic and foreign policy roll call votes. The difference has been the withdrawal of support from members of the opposition party: no president since Eisenhower has consistently won a majority of the opposition party on foreign policy votes.[20] This is the result of fundamental disagreement along ideological and partisan lines about the proper policy course. The consequences of the loss of opposition party support for the president are especially pronounced under divided government. Republican presidents Nixon, Ford, Reagan, and now Bush have all been forced to seek majorities in a Democratic House or Senate when there was no longer a presumption of bipartisanship in foreign policy.

Public Opinion and Foreign Policy

There is little doubt that changes in public opinion about foreign policy were the root cause of the weakening of the president's leadership position and of the chronic conflict between the executive and legislative branches that began in the late 1960s. Moreover, public opinion continues to be a prime determinant of the level of cooperation or conflict between the president and Congress. An administration that sails against the tide of public opinion invites a more active congressional role; a president who succeeds in bringing foreign policy and public opinion into closer conformance—either by adjusting his policy or by reshaping public opinion—will be more successful in diffusing opposition on Capitol Hill.

The bipartisan foreign policy consensus that prevailed for almost two decades after World War II was sustained by a leadership stratum that shared an internationalist and interventionist view of the U.S. role in world affairs, an attentive and educated group of citizens who followed and supported this leadership, and a poorly informed and largely inert mass public that tolerated official policy as long as it

20. Edwards, "The Two Presidencies," pp. 253–57.

appeared to be working.[21] The new elite consensus, which reflected the special challenges and opportunities posed by the postwar world, signaled the demise of both left-wing and right-wing isolationism among American leaders. This left the largely isolationist public without any stimulus to oppose presidential initiatives in foreign policy, except for real-world events that called into question the efficacy of those initiatives.

William Schneider has provided a persuasive account of how this "followership" model of American foreign policy making broke down after 1964.[22] Growing disenchantment with the Vietnam War led to an ideological polarization over foreign policy within the attentive public, while broader societal forces stimulated antiestablishment sentiments at both the mass and elite levels. Liberal internationalists harbored a deep suspicion of the use of military force as an instrument of foreign policy. They looked to a new world order based on global interdependence, and stressed détente with the Soviets, economic and humanitarian aid, and multilateralism in world politics. Conservative internationalists viewed the world primarily in East-West terms: they continued to believe that military power and the containment of communism should be the cornerstone of U.S. foreign policy. These ideological divisions on foreign policy became institutionalized within the party system as insurgent forces within both political parties successfully challenged their establishments. The parties became more internally consistent across economic, social, and foreign policy issues, reinforcing differences that had arisen out of the Vietnam experience, and the bipartisan consensus was shattered. The polarization of foreign policy opinion also coincided with changes taking place in Congress, where junior Democrats, sympathetic to the ideology of liberal internationalism, sought to wrest power from their more conservative senior colleagues.

The traumatic events of the 1960s and 1970s, made all the more vivid by their coverage on television, also had an effect on the general public. Mass opinion became less passive and more distrustful, prone to swing left or right unpredictably in response to current fears and concerns. The larger public did not internalize the ideological views

21. John E. Mueller, *War, Presidents and Public Opinion* (Wiley, 1973).

22. William Schneider, "Public Opinion," in Joseph S. Nye, Jr., ed., *The Making of America's Soviet Policy* (Yale University Press, 1984), pp. 11–35. The following discussion draws heavily on Schneider's analysis.

of the more attentive citizenry; it remained essentially pragmatic and hoped to achieve both goals sought by the contending elites: peace and strength. As the relative salience of these two concerns has shifted over time in response to events and debates at the elite level, so has the substance of public opinion—and in turn the dominant ideological position in Congress on foreign policy issues.

Broad currents in mass opinion shape the context of presidential-congressional relations on foreign policy. Between 1964 and 1974 the primary concern of the public was peace, which provided political sustenance to the liberals. After 1975, concerns about Soviet global adventurism and American military weakness gave support to conservative forces advocating increased defense spending and a tougher foreign policy posture. The Soviet invasion of Afghanistan was the coup de grace. These shifting public sentiments did not go unnoticed or unheeded by the Carter administration in its last two years or by Congress in the first year of the Reagan presidency. Yet by 1982 public support for increased defense spending had collapsed as strong anti-Soviet feelings gave way (or gave rise) to a renewed fear of war and a consequent desire for arms control. The nuclear freeze movement embodied these public fears and had no small part in the unprecedented and influential role Congress came to play on arms control issues in the 1980s. Finally, in the wake of the dramatic moves of Gorbachev and Reagan to improve U.S.-Soviet relations and reduce the perception of a Soviet threat, by the end of the 1980s the public came to view national security increasingly in economic as well as military terms, underscoring to politicians of both parties the potential appeal of economic nationalism.

While the relative salience of peace and strength has shifted back and forth over the past fifteen years, the public has remained deeply skeptical of substantial and extended American involvement abroad and suspicious of foreign policy leaders. These attitudes provide fertile ground for critics of administration policy seeking to mobilize opposition. Presidents have a difficult time building and maintaining public support for their foreign policies because the public hears dissenting voices and is inclined to listen to them. The polarization of opinion among political activists and the rise of antiestablishment feeling in the mass public "have weakened the political preconditions that enable any president to exercise independent foreign policy leadership."[23]

23. Schneider, "Public Opinion," p. 34.

The New Foreign Policy-making Process

The changes in mass and elite opinion contributed to a transformation of the foreign policy-making process. The old foreign policy establishment of relatively homogeneous, pragmatic, and mostly bipartisan East Coast diplomatic and financial figures was replaced by a much larger, more diverse, and often ideological elite of foreign policy professionals.[24] Dozens of research organizations and thousands of specialists joined the conversation on American foreign policy, providing ideas and information to politicians engaged in policy wars within and between the branches.

At the same time, the number of interest groups with a foreign policy agenda soared. Some of the growth was due to the globalization of the American economy. Some reflected the heightened political involvement of traditional interests (ethnic constituencies, businesses, farmers) drawn to the more open and decentralized policy process. But much of the increase came from groups concerned more with championing values than with protecting interests. On issues ranging from Vietnam to Central America, from détente to the nuclear freeze, liberal and conservative groups sought to advance their goals in Washington by bringing public pressure to bear on policymakers.

The media also became an important player in this altered process. The new-style pressure groups adopted lobbying strategies modeled on political campaigns, with major emphasis on the mobilization of public support or opposition through the mass media. Foreign policy specialists discovered that the best way to influence policymakers in an open process is through public argument (on op-ed pages and television and radio shows), not private advice. Ambitious politicians found television irresistible as a means for identifying with popular foreign policy sentiments. But the media are more than a passive vehicle through which the many players in the foreign policy process communicate with one another. A skeptical and aggressive press amplifies the policy differences that exist among elites and sharpens the criticisms that are leveled against those with responsibility for conducting foreign policy. At the same time, television, which has created a vast, inadvertent audience for news about foreign affairs, reinforces and intensifies the public's opposition to America's involve-

24. I. M. Destler, Leslie H. Gelb, and Anthony Lake, *Our Own Worst Enemy: The Unmaking of American Foreign Policy* (Simon and Schuster, 1984), chap. 2.

ment around the world and its cynicism about its leaders' motives in promoting such policies.[25]

The most noticeable, and perhaps significant, changes in the policy process occurred within Congress. It is by now a familiar story that the 1970s witnessed the most sweeping reforms in the history of Congress.[26] Stimulated by the twin concerns of strengthening the legislative branch vis-à-vis the executive and breaking down the old congressional power structure, Congress moved dramatically to transform the way business was conducted on Capitol Hill. Power was taken from senior, often elderly, committee chairmen and shifted both down to aggressive junior subcommittee chairmen and rank-and-file committee members and up to the full party caucus. Committee meetings were opened to the public, roll call votes were permitted on key floor amendments, and House (and eventually Senate) sessions were televised. The staff capabilities of Congress were greatly expanded—in members' offices, committees and subcommittees, and support agencies like the Congressional Budget Office, the General Accounting Office, the Congressional Research Service, and the Office of Technology Assessment. And finally, new statutes were enacted to restrict the president's discretion over war powers, impoundments, arms sales, covert action, and human rights violations. Congress became more decentralized and democratized, stronger in its policymaking capabilities, and assertive in its dealings with the executive branch.

These changes coincided with a rapid turnover in the membership of both House and Senate, so that by the end of the 1970s Congress was dominated by members whose formative political experiences were Vietnam and Watergate. The new members were active and entrepreneurial at home and in Washington, adept at generating favorable publicity for themselves, and determined to advance their substantive interests, which more often than not were in conflict with those of the president. Unlike their elders, they were unwilling to wait for the seniority system to empower them, and they were less inclined to heed the call of presidential leadership. They had both the incentives and the resources to challenge the president on foreign policy, whatever his party, and they did so with obvious energy and relish.

25. Schneider, "Public Opinion," p. 19.
26. See Sundquist, *The Decline and Resurgence of Congress*; Thomas E. Mann and Norman J. Ornstein, eds., *The New Congress* (Washington: American Enterprise Institute for Public Policy Research, 1981); and Ornstein, "The Constitution and the Sharing of Foreign Policy Responsibility."

The executive branch was not immune to the changes that swept through the foreign policy-making process in the wake of the collapse of the postwar bipartisan consensus. The general trend toward the centralization and politicization of executive power in the White House staff has been especially pronounced in the foreign policy arena.[27] In most recent administrations the National Security Council staff has eclipsed the State Department, and the antipathy of the president's political advisers toward the foreign service and other parts of the bureaucracy has been exacerbated. The growth in the White House staff and its aggrandizement of executive power have put a premium on loyalty to the president. Helping the president achieve his foreign policy agenda, often over the opposition of Congress and experienced hands in the bureaucracy, takes precedence over dispassionate determination of what those foreign policies should be. The White House has assumed day-to-day management of foreign policy, and in extreme cases, such as the Iran-contra affair, "the White House staff is asked to carry out a major operational mission that the departments (State, Defense, CIA) are thought to be too clumsy, rule-bound—or astute— to attempt."[28] As both products and shapers of the new politicized foreign policy environment, recent presidents (Carter and Reagan in particular) have often fanned the ideological fires rather than dampened them. And a more vigilant press and active Congress have provided ample outlets for executive branch officials who dissent from the president's views and hope to force a change in policy through embarrassing leaks.

In sum, the more open and ideological foreign policy-making process now encompasses the public, political parties, elections, media, experts, interest groups, Congress, *and* the executive branch. Conflict between the president and Congress must be seen as a consequence of a broader set of developments affecting America's place in the world and domestic political interests and processes. It is no wonder that the president today occupies a less than dominant position in American foreign policy. In terms of the concept of the two presidencies, foreign policy now attracts a substantial share of the resources of Congress and other interested parties as well as of the president, it is very much within

27. For a discussion of the general trend, see John E. Chubb and Paul E. Peterson, eds., *Can the Government Govern?* (Brookings, 1989), pp. 20–24. For its application in the foreign policy arena, see Destler and others, *Our Own Worst Enemy*, chaps. 4–5.

28. Chubb and Peterson, *Can the Government Govern?*, p. 24.

the realm of partisan conflict, and the president's competitors in the foreign policy arena are strong.

But to conclude that the president no longer dominates foreign policy is not to deny that he retains substantial advantages or continues to enjoy a high degree of success in putting his personal imprint on policy. In some areas of foreign policy, to be sure, the configuration of political forces and the allocation of policy instruments between the branches limit the president's authority. For example, decisions about military installations and selected weapons procurement are made largely in the manner of domestic distributive policies, with constituency benefits and pork barrel politics leaving a distinctive mark on the ultimate policies.[29] Similarly, the intensity of feelings among ethnic interest groups and the unquestioned authority of Congress to appropriate funds for military assistance powerfully constrain the president's ability to restructure foreign aid programs. But presidents have impressive resources—from unilateral actions to public appeals—with which to overcome obstacles and transform public debate. It has long been recognized that presidents enjoy extraordinary powers in times of crisis, based on their constitutional role as commander in chief and in response to the expectations of elites and the mass public. Presidential initiatives in response to a perceived national security threat can overcome statutory and political inhibitions and negate congressional influence.[30] The relative weakening of America's global stature and the incentives of a plebiscitary presidency to find popular solace in foreign policy crises may be responsible for a growing trend toward executive initiative in foreign policy.[31]

Thus, while a transformed foreign policy-making process certainly requires a change in strategy and tactics, it hardly renders the president powerless. The degree of success a president enjoys and the character of executive-legislative relations depend on several factors: the nature of the policy in question (the type of action required, the level of substantive disagreement, the amount of pressure from interest groups and public opinion, and the policy instruments available to each

29. Rockman, "Mobilizing Political Support"; and Thomas L. McNaugher, *New Weapons, Old Politics: America's Military Procurement Muddle* (Brookings, 1989).

30. Rockman, "Mobilizing Political Support."

31. Harold Hongju Koh, "Why the President (Almost) Always Wins in Foreign Affairs: Lessons of the Iran-Contra Affair," *Yale Law Journal*, vol. 97 (June 1988), pp. 1292–97; and Theodore J. Lowi, *The Personal President: Power Invested, Promise Unfulfilled* (Cornell University Press, 1985).

branch), the political division between the branches (unified or divided government), and the approaches to governance adopted by the president and Congress. In the chapters that follow, the authors examine how these factors have influenced foreign policy making on war powers, intelligence, arms control, diplomacy, and trade. They seek to understand the sources of the often bitter conflict between the branches during the Reagan years, the consequences of that conflict for the formulation and conduct of foreign policy, and the ways in which relations between the president and Congress might be improved.

War Powers

No area of foreign policy better reflects the tension between presidential discretion and congressional authority than the power to make war short of formal declaration. American history is replete with instances in which presidents deployed military forces without prior authorization by Congress.[32] And Congress largely acquiesced to these presidential initiatives, praising the president when the operations were successful and criticizing him when they were not. For example, Congress made no move to formally endorse or question the authority of President Truman to send troops to Korea, but it felt free to attack him when the conflict became increasingly frustrating and unpopular. In 1973, after years of symbolic and largely ineffectual moves to challenge the administration's policy on Vietnam (and after American troops had been withdrawn and prisoners of war returned home), Congress finally cut off funds for American military operations in Indochina and then overrode Nixon's veto to enact the War Powers Resolution.[33]

As Robert A. Katzmann explains in his chapter, the War Powers Resolution was an attempt by Congress to prevent presidents from gradually moving the country into war without a formal legislative declaration. Its objective is to "insure that the collective judgment of both the Congress and the President will apply to the introduction of United States Armed Forces."[34] The key provisions of the resolution require the president to consult with Congress before introducing U.S.

---

32. *The War Power after 200 Years: Congress and the President at a Constitutional Impasse,* Hearings before the Special Subcommittee on War Powers of the Senate Committee on Foreign Relations, 100 Cong. 1 sess. (GPO, 1989).

33. Destler and others, *Our Own Worst Enemy,* pp. 133–34.

34. 87 Stat. 555 (1973), sec. 2, para. a.

armed forces into hostilities, or into situations in which imminent involvement in hostilities is clearly indicated, or under certain other conditions. He also must submit a report to the Speaker of the House and president pro tempore of the Senate within forty-eight hours after doing so. The president is required to terminate the involvement of U.S. forces within sixty calendar days (with a possible thirty-day extension) unless Congress specifically declares war or extends the time period. The language is crafted to permit Congress to trigger the sixty-day clock if the president fails to submit the requisite report. Moreover, the original language allowed Congress to require the president to withdraw U.S. forces at any time by passing a concurrent resolution, which does not require a presidential signature. In the aftermath of the Supreme Court's decision in *Chadha* to outlaw the legislative veto,[35] this later step now requires a joint resolution, which is subject to a presidential veto.

The history of executive-legislative relations pertaining to the use of American military force since the enactment of the War Powers Resolution is not substantially different from that in earlier years. Presidents have continued to deploy U.S. military forces on their own initiative, in almost all cases without consulting Congress before deployment and without citing the provision of the resolution that triggers the sixty-day clock. Congress has been unwilling to use its authority under the resolution to invoke the key sanction of automatic withdrawal of forces after sixty days. Presidents have refused to acknowledge the constitutionality of the resolution, but have complied with its least threatening reporting provisions so as to avoid a court test or a constitutional crisis. Members of Congress have pleaded with the president and demanded that he implement the main provisions of the resolution and have even filed suit in federal court seeking judicial enforcement of the resolution, but they have not mustered majorities in both houses declaring that the sixty-day clock shall begin to tick. The overriding political reality is that Congress wants to be visibly involved but not held responsible if something goes wrong. Katzmann's description of the tortuous 1987 war powers debate on the Persian Gulf crisis underscores the dominance of blame avoidance as a motivation for congressional behavior.[36] Congress refused to take

35. *Immigration and Naturalization Service* v. *Chadha*, 462 U.S. 919 (1983).
36. The seminal analytic treatment of blame avoidance is found in R. Kent Weaver, *Automatic Government: The Politics of Indexation* (Brookings, 1988).

responsibility either for approving the president's actions or for compelling the withdrawal of American forces from the gulf.

The War Powers Resolution has proven unworkable because it fails to accommodate presidential *and* congressional interests in war-making decisions. Presidents insist on retaining the discretion to act quickly and decisively to protect American security interests; that ability is lost if legislative inaction can force troops to withdraw. Members of Congress want to be consulted by the president before military forces are deployed; they also want a practical means of terminating military actions whose costs outweigh their benefits. But the resolution provides neither the mechanism for consultation nor a politically feasible way for Congress to reverse the president's course in those rare instances when it might seek to do so. However modestly the resolution might constrain presidents and encourage consultation, its main effect is to exacerbate conflict between the branches and undermine the legitimacy of the president's use of force. Both the president and Congress have good reason to renegotiate the statutory framework under which they share war powers.

Intelligence

If the War Powers Resolution has largely failed to establish an acceptable balance between presidential and congressional responsibilities and interests, the new mechanisms for congressional oversight of intelligence have been more successful. This conclusion may seem absurd in light of the open warfare that was waged between the branches over aid to the contras in Nicaragua and the extraordinary revelations of the Iran-contra affair. No one can reasonably deny that years of struggle between the president and Congress led to a vacillating and ineffective policy toward Nicaragua. The intensity of the policy dispute between the Reagan administration and congressional Democrats and the close division on the issue within Congress worked to exacerbate conflict and prevent any accommodation of opposing views.[37]

37. The Senate, under Republican control for the first six years of the Reagan presidency, consistently supported the president, often by narrow margins, while the House, where the balance of power was held by three dozen members whose votes swung back and forth depending upon the immediate context, lacked a stable majority opposing the president. Michael J. Malbin, "Legislative-Executive Lessons from the Iran-Contra Affair," in Lawrence C. Dodd and Bruce I. Oppenheimer, eds., *Congress Reconsidered*, 4th ed. (Washington: CQ Press, 1989), pp. 375–92.

Nor is there any serious dispute that the Iran-contra affair represented a complete breakdown in relations between the branches. President Reagan's failure to notify Congress before his ill-fated operation to sell arms to Iran deprived him of some much-needed advice from Capitol Hill. Certainly his failure to inform the Intelligence committees in a timely fashion after the operation was launched violated the clear intent of the law. And the well-documented efforts of the National Security Council staff to resupply the contras while American aid was prohibited by law involved blatant deception of Congress and contempt for its role in foreign policy making.

But, as Gregory F. Treverton argues, one important lesson of the Iran-contra fiasco is that there are limits to the role process can play in imposing wisdom on the making of American foreign policy. The procedures in place for the initiation and oversight of covert activities, both within and between the branches, were adequate; the problem was the president's decision to circumvent the requirements of that process. Even in this most glaring of failures, the process produced warning signals that the policy was unwise, which unfortunately went unheeded. In Treverton's words: "If presidents are determined to do something stupid, they will find someone, somewhere, to do it."

In virtually every other instance of the use of covert action during the Reagan years, the system worked about as well as could be expected—that is, it provided a secure setting for consultation and the management of policy disputes. As anticipated by the Intelligence Oversight Act of 1980, the Reagan administration notified the Intelligence committees before undertaking significant operations. The committees had an opportunity to persuade the administration to change its mind or to use the annual budget review to terminate operations with which they disagreed. The president retained his authority to initiate covert operations without the prior approval of Congress. He also succeeded in building political support on Capitol Hill for a substantial expansion of covert activity. His interests were protected because he accepted the legitimacy of the congressional role in intelligence oversight and provided Congress with the timely information it needed to discharge its responsibilities. The Iran-contra affair was a dramatic and devastating exception to the pattern of largely constructive relations between the branches on intelligence matters. One key question is whether the political punishment imposed on the Reagan administration was sufficient to discourage future presidents from evading these mechanisms for congressional oversight of covert action. Another is whether the Reagan administration's failure to keep its part of the institutional bargain will lead Congress to redefine the terms of their relationship regarding covert operations in ways that prove unacceptable to George Bush and his successors.

Whatever the outcome of that debate, Treverton's analysis makes clear that the transformation of the intelligence policy-making process, in which authority, responsibility, and information are now shared by the executive and legislative branches, is irreversible. Largely through its Intelligence committees, Congress has become a (sometimes uneasy) partner with the president in covert operations, an insatiable consumer of intelligence analysis, and an influential patron of the intelligence community. Intelligence agencies have come to look more and more like their domestic counterparts at Commerce and Agriculture, with congressional oversight committees providing protection as well as criticism. In this relatively open and democratic process, the potential for conflict is unlimited: the president versus Congress, Republicans versus Democrats, House versus Senate, the Intelligence committees versus the Foreign Affairs (Relations) and Armed Services committees and the full membership of each chamber. What is remarkable is the extent to which the conflicts have been contained, the leaks limited, the self-promotional behavior of members circumscribed, the president's initiatives largely supported, and the intelligence community strengthened. Presidents are well advised to embrace a process that balances the institutional strengths and interests of the two branches.

Arms Control

Congress is most likely to be assertive in its role and insistent on its views when it believes the president is out of step with strong public sentiment. At the beginning of the Reagan administration, members of Congress perceived a disjuncture between the harsh anti-Soviet rhetoric of President Reagan and growing public concerns about superpower confrontation. Many rushed to champion the cause of the nuclear freeze movement. The political incentives for visible involvement in arms control issues persisted well beyond the movement's demise as liberal arms control groups joined established public interest groups to form a formidable grass-roots lobby.

As Barry Blechman recounts, Congress moved beyond its traditional instruments of influence on arms control policy—ratifying treaties and confirming appointments—and used its authorizing and appropriating authority to press its views on the administration. As the center of Democratic opposition during the first six years of the Reagan presidency, the House of Representatives took the lead in Congress in trying to pressure the administration to resume negotiations on long-range strategic forces, to alter its negotiating posture on both intermediate-range and strategic forces, to impose a moratorium on tests of antisatellite weapons, and to adhere to the terms of the unratified Strategic Arms Limitation Treaty (SALT II). After the Senate returned to Democratic hands in the 1986 elections, the House continued to attach arms control amendments to defense authorization bills, with the Democratic leadership playing a crucial role in developing legislative strategy and tactics.

Just how consequential these congressional initiatives were is a matter of some dispute. Former Reagan administration officials emphasize that increased defense spending, resolve in deploying intermediate-range missiles in Europe, and advocacy of the strategic defense initiative (SDI) were crucial to the successful completion of the intermediate-range nuclear force treaty and the moderation in Soviet aggression around the world. Arms control activists in Congress argue that political pressure from Capitol Hill pushed Reagan into a less confrontational stance toward the Soviet Union and thus a better position to respond to economically driven changes in Soviet policy. Whatever the merits of each of these assertions, two points are perfectly clear. First, Congress has the ability to influence nuclear weapons policy and every administration must reckon with this ability. Second, presidents are well positioned to undercut congressional opposition by moving boldly to redefine U.S. policy in ways that ease public concerns. Republican presidents facing a Democratic Congress, the norm in contemporary American politics, are in a particularly strong position to confound their opposition by doing the opposite of what is expected of them on ideological grounds.[38] President Reagan's dramatic diplomatic encounters with Mikhail Gorbachev palpably altered the public mood and thereby reduced, though not eliminated, the influence of arms control activists on Capitol Hill.

Public opinion is by no means the only source of tension between the executive and legislative branches on arms control policy. Problems also arise when one branch believes its own constitutional authority is being usurped by the other. Perhaps the most serious confrontation

38. Schneider, "Public Opinion," p. 33.

came in the aftermath of the administration's announcement in the fall of 1985 that the testing of space-based antiballistic missile weapons was not barred by the 1972 U.S.-Soviet antiballistic missile (ABM) treaty. This broad interpretation, which ran counter to the traditional understanding of the pact's limits on space-based weapons, drew a storm of protest from Congress. The pitched battle between the branches reached a boiling point in 1987, when both the House and Senate adopted language legally restricting the administration's reinterpretation of the ABM treaty.

At one level, the struggle over the interpretation of the ABM treaty was merely a cover for an intensely ideological and partisan struggle over the president's SDI program. But the administration's tactic, by challenging so directly the Senate's authority as ratifier and thus ultimate arbiter of treaties, forced a more process-based opposition led by Senate Armed Services Committee Chairman Sam Nunn. Nunn's opposition to the president's reinterpretation of the ABM treaty attracted support from a wide range of senators precisely because it was based on issues of process, not substance. Lacking a credible case on the merits of the ABM treaty reinterpretation and facing a Congress that could impose its will by slashing funds for the SDI, the administration had no realistic chance of prevailing on this constitutional confrontation.

Blechman concludes that presidents must adapt to the new congressional role in arms control by accepting that role as part of the normal course of setting policy and by reaching out to moderate forces in both parties in Congress to develop policies that have broad political support. In this way presidents can limit Congress's use of binding instructions on ongoing negotiations and achieve a more satisfactory balance between executive and legislative strengths.

Diplomacy

The stereotype of congressional overreaching in foreign policy is in the domain of diplomacy, where critics conjure up the image of 535 secretaries of state operating from Capitol Hill. The criticism is not without foundation. As Dick Cheney has observed, "Senators and representatives from both parties have crossed the line separating . . . legitimate legislative fact finding from the realm of diplomatic communication."[39] For example, although Speaker Jim Wright was praised

39. Dick Cheney, "Congressional Overreaching in Foreign Policy," in Robert A.

by his Democratic colleagues for taking the initiative as mediator and negotiator to advance the peace process in Nicaragua, his actions clearly undermined the president's constitutional authority as the "sole organ" of diplomatic communication with other countries. The White House is not without blame in this matter: administration officials worked to coopt the Speaker into embracing a Reagan-Wright peace plan. Nonetheless, the frustration of House Democrats over the failure of the Reagan administration to pursue a diplomatic solution to the conflict, combined with their growing sense of separation from an executive branch dominated by the Republican party, led them to embrace a congressional usurpation of an executive branch responsibility. In other cases, rank-and-file members of Congress have attempted to influence foreign governments to act contrary to official U.S. policy. One frequent offender, Senator Jesse Helms, was reported to have engaged in his own personal diplomacy to advance the cause of the contras in Nicaragua.[40]

The line between appropriate activities by members of Congress and interference with the formal communication between governments is not always easy to draw. As influential participants in the making of American foreign policy, members of Congress, not surprisingly, are consulted and lobbied by foreign governments and private interests within countries that are increasingly affected by decisions made on Capitol Hill. A generation ago embassy staff in Washington directed the vast preponderance of their energies toward executive branch officials; today no self-respecting diplomatic mission is without a stable of congressional liaison officials and well-cultivated friendships among congressional members and staff. In a world of global economic interdependence and instant communication and in an open and fragmented political system, it is naive to imagine that the executive branch can monopolize diplomatic exchanges with foreign representatives. Nonetheless, individual members of Congress must be careful not to overstep their authority as representatives and legislators and set themselves up as alternative diplomats. Presidents are well advised to challenge them when they do.

While this stereotype of congressional interference in a quintessentially executive activity is based on a kernel of truth, it misses the

Goldwin and Robert A. Licht, eds., *Foreign Policy and the Constitution* (Washington: American Enterprise Institute for Public Policy Research, 1990), p. 106.

40. Cheney, "Congressional Overreaching," p. 108.

larger reality that Congress increasingly draws on its legitimate authority to shape American diplomacy around the world. And, as Bruce Jentleson relates, the pattern of interbranch relations that emerges from this congressional activism is highly variable, depending on such factors as the degree and intensity of substantive disagreement over U.S. interests, the nature of domestic political pressures, and the institutional resources and strategies of the two branches. Relations between the Reagan administration and Congress ranged from outright confrontation (on Nicaragua, South Africa, and Arab arms sales) to bipartisan cooperation (on China, Afghanistan, and, increasingly, the Soviet Union). In between was the enervating institutional competition over the day-to-day conduct of diplomacy (manifest in battles over State Department authorization and foreign aid bills), but also areas of constructive compromise (for example, El Salvador and the Philippines) in which conflict between the branches produced better policies.

At its worst, Congress is a collection of individual political entrepreneurs, claiming credit and avoiding blame, conducting private negotiations with foreign leaders, and using procedural devices to press their personal agendas on administration officials. But much more consequential for American foreign policy are actions taken by Congress as a collective body, responding to strong currents in American public opinion, involving serious and informed disagreement about the best policy course, and based on institutional authority firmly rooted in the Constitution. The challenge for presidents is to manage diplomatic relations along Pennsylvania Avenue in ways that strengthen the hand of responsible forces in Congress and thereby constructively channel the energies of those would-be secretaries of state.

Trade

When it comes to assigning responsibility for foreign economic policy, the Constitution is unambiguous: the power to "regulate commerce with foreign nations" is given to Congress. The president's authority over trade policy exists only insofar as Congress chooses to delegate to the executive branch. And, following the disastrous consequences for the international economy of the protectionist policies of the Tariff Act of 1930 (better known as "Smoot-Hawley"), Congress decided to do precisely that.[41] It gave the executive new trade powers

41. I. M. Destler, *American Trade Politics: System under Stress* (Washington: Institute for International Economics; New York: Twentieth Century Fund, 1986), chap. 2.

as a way of protecting itself from domestic political pressure for trade restrictions. It gave the president authority to negotiate tariff revisions and to grant relief to individual claimants, thereby deflecting pressure from the logrolling environment of Capitol Hill to administrative institutions better suited to promote both trade liberalization and selective protection. Congress retained the ability to oversee and guide the executive. And "individual members also remained free to make ample protectionist noise, to declaim loudly on behalf of producer interests that were strong in their states or districts . . . secure in the knowledge that most actual decisions would be made elsewhere."[42]

By most accounts, the trade system that evolved from this institutional bargain was successful, particularly in the quarter century following World War II. The United States became a powerful force for free trade around the globe, and the nation's and the world's economic welfare increased as a consequence. During the last fifteen years, however, political and economic changes have increased protectionist pressures and weakened the system's ability to resist those pressures. By the end of the 1980s, the tone of American trade policy had shifted from promoting free trade to ensuring fair trade.

Pietro Nivola argues that the trade policy system designed to channel, and presumably contain, demands for protection has gradually, almost imperceptibly, become a regime for doing just the opposite. Regulation of unfair trade practices has often stimulated the appetite of firms and industries for protection rather than quenched it. The costs of this new policy—in the form of retaliatory sanctions and "voluntary" trade restraints—are high. And these costs are borne despite politicians' full realization that policies designed to crack down on other countries' unfair trading practices do little to correct the U.S. trade deficit and to address the broader problem of the vulnerability of the American economy in a more competitive world.

Nivola does not tie the preoccupation with fair trade to unrestrained conflict between the president and Congress, commonly seen as the source of policy failure in other areas of foreign policy, but rather ascribes it to a subtle form of collusion between the branches. Just as Congress sought to duck responsibility for potentially harmful consequences of trade policy yet claim credit for delivering selective benefits, so too were presidents increasingly drawn to policy devices that permitted credit claiming and blame avoidance. Under the banner of

42. Destler, *American Trade Politics*, p. 13.

fair trade, the legislative and executive branches discovered they could respond to powerful domestic economic and political interests without incurring too many conspicuous costs.

Nivola argues that the traditional distinction between a parochial Congress clamoring for import bars and an internationalist president struggling to preserve free trade is simplistic. The politicization of trade policy extends to both ends of Pennsylvania Avenue, and giving presidents enhanced trade authority is no guarantee of steady trade liberalization. The challenge is to structure choices on trade policy so that the general costs and benefits are not obscured by fair trade rhetoric and administrative arrangements that blur lines of responsibility. Active leadership by both the president and Congress, not delegation to administrative agencies, will be needed to resist self-destructive protectionism and attend to the crucial macroeconomic and structural problems that plague the U.S. economy.

Striking a Balance

Any serious effort to strike a more productive balance between the executive and legislative branches in making foreign policy must take into account several crucial developments in contemporary American politics. First, divided government has become the norm, not the exception, in national politics, and White House Republicans and congressional Democrats are growing accustomed to their separate roles. Split-party control of the two branches encourages an institutionalized partisanship, which often frustrates policymaking, but it also facilitates bargaining arrangements that diffuse political responsibility and allow each branch to avoid blame for unpopular but necessary policies.

Second, the trend toward congressional involvement in foreign policy, itself a part of a broader transformation of the process of foreign policy making, is irreversible. The institutional legacy of Vietnam, Watergate, and the Iran-contra affair; the political incentives for foreign policy activism; and the culture of Capitol Hill all ensure a resurgent Congress for the forseeable future, whatever the partisan makeup of the national government.

And third, foreign policy is losing its distinctiveness as a domain of governmental activity and as a unique responsibility of the president. The central role of economic performance in national security, the declining utility of military force, the changing shape of Western and Eastern Europe, and the rising importance of new international issues such as the environment and drugs all work to blur the differences between domestic and foreign policy and to move the latter into the maelstrom of American politics. Moreover, the restructuring of American foreign policy that must follow the extraordinary changes taking place in world affairs will certainly entail broad discussion and debate that extend well beyond the White House.[43]

At the same time, it is important not to exaggerate the fragmentation and parochialism in Congress or the erosion of presidential authority over foreign policy. Members of Congress are genuinely ambivalent about their role in foreign policy: they often want to be involved and influential but not always held responsible or accountable. This may result in a bias toward inaction in the face of ambiguous threats to the national security. But Congress is much more than a collection of 535 election-obsessed individuals. Members are, in many cases, experienced foreign policy hands who have been weathered by years of confrontation and crisis. They have strong policy motivations, they are capable of being moved by new information and persuasive argument, and they are not indifferent to appeals by respected colleagues. With the support of key party and committee leaders, choices can be structured in ways that weaken incentives for parochialism and irresponsibility on major foreign policy questions and that diffuse partisan opposition to presidential initiatives.

While Congress has the capacity, if not the natural instinct, to take responsible collective action, presidents retain substantial advantages in leaving their personal mark, for good or ill, on American foreign policy. A review of the foreign policy record of the Reagan administration argued that "the autonomy of the modern American President: his capacity to set the public agenda; his day-to-day operational leeway on issues where executive agencies have the action; his effective veto over compromises that involve a sharing of pain" means that policy persistence can be enormously consequential.[44] In the face of these presidential resources, members of Congress often feel their own policy levers are woefully inadequate.

43. John D. Steinbruner, ed., *Restructuring American Foreign Policy* (Brookings, 1989).
44. I. M. Destler, "Reagan and the World: An 'Awesome Stubbornness,' " in Charles O. Jones, ed., *The Reagan Legacy: Promise and Performance* (Chatham, N.J.: Chatham House, 1988), p. 243.

All of these considerations suggest an approach to managing foreign policy conflict between the president and Congress and strengthening each branch's comparative advantages. Because this is an approach particularly well suited for a Republican president confronting a Democratic Congress, it is no surprise that George Bush embraced some of its central elements during the first year of his administration. It begins with an acknowledgement of reality: the president and Congress are partners in the making of American foreign policy, each has a legitimate and important role to play, and no foreign policy can be sustained over the strong opposition of either. The starting point for negotiations on the appropriate responsibilities of each branch is an admission that neither can do without the other. Making the partnership normal and routine will require the president's acceptance of a genuinely collaborative approach to foreign policy, an adjustment in the organizational and statutory environment of interbranch relations, and a principled and responsible defense of presidential and congressional prerogatives in foreign policy making. It also will require the development of new policies that can attract broad support among foreign policy elites and the public at large.

Collaboration entails consultation with Congress before executive action. It requires the initiation of serious discussions on Capitol Hill with key members of both parties before policies are set in stone. It means the president must provide timely information to Congress on major foreign policy developments and demonstrate a capacity to change his mind in the face of reasonable opposition. By dealing honestly and openly with influential and knowledgeable legislators, the president can strengthen the hand of responsible forces in Congress and thereby increase his chances of attracting majority support for his policies and preserving as much discretion as possible over the conduct of foreign policy.

No formal mechanisms can guarantee collaboration between the branches: presidents will pursue this approach only when they believe it will advance their interests. But some changes in law and organization would make consultation a more routine feature of presidential-congressional relations. The spirit, if not the letter, of laws and mechanisms presently in place for the oversight of intelligence activities could well be applied to war powers, arms control, diplomacy, and foreign economic policy. The Select Intelligence committees give the administration a secure setting for advice and criticism but also for support of covert activities. When used in the manner that was intended, these procedures provide the benefits of democratic accountability without compromising the president's ability to act quickly and decisively on behalf of American security interests.

These virtues are noticeably absent in the spheres of war powers and arms control. As Katzmann recommends, the War Powers Act should be amended by substituting an explicit consultation mechanism for the provision requiring the withdrawal of troops as a consequence of congressional inaction. And in line with Blechman's advice, the president would strengthen his position in arms control policy and reduce the maneuvering room for congressional initiatives on the details of negotiating positions by devising informal arrangements whereby Congress can help shape negotiating objectives and strategies.

The same general strategy of reform—seeking to substitute early congressional involvement in the setting of broad policy goals for a reliance on detailed, restrictive, often punitive measures after the fact— can be pursued fruitfully in other areas of foreign policy. The Hamilton-Gilman initiative to revamp the foreign assistance program, discussed by Jentleson, is a good case in point. Another attractive proposal recently advanced calls for new congressional select oversight committees on the dollar and the national economy to focus attention on exchange rate policy and its connection with fiscal, monetary, and trade issues.[45]

Reformers should be wary of reorganization plans that put a premium on simplification and hierarchy. Despite the surface appeal of joint oversight committees in foreign policy (less burden on executive officials, fewer leaks), separate House and Senate committees provide significant policymaking advantages. Competition between the chambers and their committees can energize congressional oversight and keep collaboration and consultation from degenerating into cooptation. Increased opportunities for service on the committees help build a critical mass of knowledgeable and experienced members in each chamber. Separate committees have more credibility in their respective chambers and thus are in a better position to facilitate more constructive and predictable involvement by the full House and Senate in foreign policy. By the same token, mechanisms for consultation can be effective

45. I. M. Destler and C. Randall Henning, *Dollar Politics: Exchange Rate Policymaking in the United States* (Washington: Institute for International Economics, 1989).

only insofar as those being consulted can speak for the full Congress. While contemporary congressional leaders are necessarily sensitive to and solicitous of rank-and-file opinion, it would be wise to include some less senior members, particularly the relevant subcommittee chairs, in formal and informal discussions between the branches.

Another trap that reformers on Capitol Hill should avoid is the "never again" genre of statutory restriction that, like generals' tendency to fight the last war, follows episodes in which the executive branch fails to honor the letter and spirit of its foreign policy partnership with Congress. While it was perfectly natural for Congress to move to close possible loopholes in existing law following the revelations of the abuse of White House power in the Iran-contra affair, efforts to codify limits and criminalize executive behavior can be counterproductive to inter-branch relations. Examples of legislative overkill include proposals requiring notice of all covert operations within forty-eight hours and making it a crime for any government official to try to provide aid indirectly to any foreign country or group that is prohibited by law from receiving direct U.S. aid. Remedies of this sort, designed to prevent the recurrence of what was almost certainly the exception, not the norm, in executive behavior, are of dubious constitutionality and certain to provoke opposition from any occupant of the White House. Instead, Congress should replace its passive-aggressive syndrome in foreign policy with a steadier, more mature posture toward the president. Congress should monitor executive behavior vigilantly and punish presidents for clear transgressions of law and procedure, but not rewrite the rules that govern their normal interactions.

An acceptance of a partnership and a commitment to collaboration between the president and Congress in the making of foreign policy do not require an overly solicitous, institutionally timid posture by each branch toward the other. A clear, credible, and consistent defense and exercise of each branch's foreign policy prerogatives and respon-sibilities is essential to a healthy policy process. Presidents should avoid the tendency, manifest throughout the Reagan years, to careen between grandiose pronouncements of executive supremacy in foreign policy and a willingness to compromise the principles of separation of power for short-term policy objectives. A prototype of the latter flaw is an informal congressional committee veto provision in President Bush's contra aid agreement with Congress. The agreement was otherwise commendable in its bipartisan approach that combined nonlethal aid with the active pursuit of diplomatic solutions to the problems in Central America.

The starting point for a president determined to protect the powers of his office is the public embrace of a reasonable position on the constitutional division of labor and sharing of powers by the two branches. Congress is more likely to take claims of presidential prerogative seriously if it believes the president seeks balance and comparative advantage, rather than dominance, in their relations. Then the president and Congress could profitably follow the advice "to arrive at an informal, mutual understanding of what constitutes procedural cooperation and then encourage each side to protect its own interest."[46] Rather than rely solely on trust or statute, cooperation can evolve through a system of mutually reinforced rewards and sanctions.

The character of executive-legislative relations in foreign policy can be altered by changing the strategies and tactics of the two branches' leaders, especially the president, and by reshaping the institutional arrangements through which they interact. Both factors make a difference, and efforts to improve executive-legislative relations properly focus on the motivations and incentives of the participants and the formal and informal rules by which they play the foreign policy game. But as is evident in each of the chapters of this book, what drives the relationship inside Washington are forces largely outside. No president can hope to maintain a productive working relationship with Congress in the absence of some general agreement in the country on the central ends and means of American foreign policy. By embracing and articulating ideas responsive to changing international conditions and consonant with American values and interests, presidents can help build the consensus that is an essential underpinning of a sustainable foreign policy. Dramatic developments within the Soviet Union and Eastern Europe may well diminish the ideological polarization among elites that has conditioned American foreign policy making over the last two decades. But there is no guarantee that a more consensual politics will follow in its wake. There are already stirrings of a resurgent conservative isolationism among political activists. And the inevitable strains between an increasingly global economy and domestic political forces heighten the challenge of building public support for an enlightened foreign policy.

46. Malbin, "Legislative-Executive Lessons," p. 391.

The point is to neither stifle disagreement nor avoid conflict. Substantive differences, constructively expressed and channeled, can lead to wiser policies. The restoration of a balance between the president and Congress in the making of foreign policy will increase the likelihood that wise and sustainable foreign policies are a more regular product of our political system.

War Powers:
Toward a New Accommodation

ROBERT A. KATZMANN

FEW ISSUES so graphically illustrate the problems of allocating responsibility between Congress and the executive as the power to make war. Few pieces of legislation testify to the difficulties of defining the balance of authority as much as the War Powers Resolution of 1973, which seeks to ensure a congressional role in the decision to dispatch the military to combat.[1] In 1990, only one year past the 200th anniversary of the convening of the First Congress, the core issues surrounding war powers are still very much alive: the discretion of the president to commit armed forces without congressional participation; when and how Congress should become involved in such decisions; and what the legislature can do if relations with the executive break down.

A growing consensus maintains that the War Powers Resolution has not worked as Congress envisioned. Presidents have refused to invoke the law in ways that could limit their freedom of action; indeed, they have not even conceded its constitutionality. Congress, for its part, has been reluctant to challenge the president.

At present, three perspectives characterize the war powers debate: the resolution should be retained in its present form, with perhaps a strengthened provision for judicial enforcement; the law should be modified to make it more likely that the president will comply; or the War Powers Resolution should be repealed.

In evaluating the War Powers Resolution, it is necessary to examine the constitutional framework in which any statute must fit; analyze the language of the statute to discern the problems in interpretation and implementation that flow from it; assess how the resolution has operated thus far, particularly with regard to how Congress and the

The author wishes to thank Thomas Thornburg for research assistance, Robert J. Kurz for his comments, and Marc E. Smyrl for discussions on the War Powers Resolution.

1. 87 Stat. 555 (1973).

presidency have each viewed their own interests; and consider proposals for reform in the search for a new accommodation between the branches.

The Constitutional Framework

Article I of the Constitution—the legislature's charter—speaks to the congressional role in matters of war. It states that Congress shall have the power "to declare war, grant letters of marque and reprisal, and make rules concerning captures on land and water." The legislative branch is to "raise and support armies," "provide and maintain a navy," "make rules for the government and regulation of the land and naval forces," "provide for calling forth the militia to execute the laws of the Union, suppress insurrections and repel invasions," and, more generally, "to make all laws which shall be necessary and proper for carrying into execution the foregoing powers, and all other powers vested by this Constitution in the government of the United States, or in any department or officer thereof."

Article II—the president's principal guide—vests "the executive power" in the president. It further declares that the president shall be "commander in chief of the Army and Navy of the United States" and have the power, by and with the advice and consent of the Senate, to make treaties and to appoint ambassadors, other public ministers and consuls.

For as long as these constitutional phrases have been part of this country's heritage, they have spurred debate about their meaning. The context in which these matters were considered was important, of course. The experience of the Articles of Confederation, which had lodged all executive power in one representative unit, had been an unhappy one.[2] At the same time, those engaged in governance were reluctant to accede to the prevailing practice of vesting the executive with virtually sole military power. The Framers who met in the heat of Philadelphia thus sought to strike a balance between these divergent conceptions, in which the executive and the legislature would share power. But how precisely the line should be drawn is as elusive today as it was then.

Historians and constitutional scholars have struggled mightily with

2. See W. Taylor Reveley III, *War Powers of the President and Congress: Who Holds the Arrows and Olive Branch?* (University Press of Virginia, 1981), pp. 57–59; and Marc E. Smyrl, *Conflict or Codetermination? Congress, the President, and the Power to Make War* (Cambridge, Mass.: Ballinger, 1988), p. 6.

the effort to discern the meaning of war power in the charter of nationhood.[3] But the task is not an easy one. The records of the Constitutional Convention are hardly complete, as James Hutson has noted.[4] Much has been made of a change in the draft, advanced by James Madison and Elbridge Gerry, which, by a vote of 7–2, charged Congress with the power to "declare war" rather than "make war." In his notes, Madison wrote that this change meant that Congress would have the power to initiate war, though the president could act immediately to repel sudden attacks without congressional authorization.[5]

But even in the few short years following the adoption of the Constitution, two of the convention's most prestigious participants, Alexander Hamilton and James Madison, would argue about the allocation of war-making responsibilities. In defense of the Neutrality Proclamation of 1793, in which President George Washington determined that the treaty of alliance of 1778 did not require the United States to defend French territory in America, Hamilton argued that the chief executive, not Congress or the judiciary, is responsible for conducting the foreign relations of the nation. In exercising its authority to declare war, Congress could and should ascertain whether the treaties with France obligated the United States to make war.[6] However, before Congress made such a determination, the president had the right to conduct the foreign relations of the nation. Put another way, although "only Congress can move" the country to "public, notorious,

3. See, for example, Louis Henkin, *Foreign Affairs and the Constitution* (Mineola, N.Y.: Foundation Press, 1972); Abraham D. Sofaer, *War, Foreign Affairs, and Constitutional Power: The Origins* (Cambridge, Mass.: Ballinger, 1976); Francis D. Wormuth and Edwin B. Firmage, *To Chain the Dog of War: The War Power of Congress in History and Law*, 2d ed. (University of Illinois Press, 1989); Eugene V. Rostow, " 'Once More unto the Breach:' The War Powers Resolution Revisited," *Valparaiso University Law Review*, vol. 21 (Fall 1986), pp. 1–52; David Gray Adler, "The Constitution and Presidential Warmaking: The Enduring Debate," *Political Science Quarterly*, vol. 103 (Spring 1988), pp. 1–36; and Michael J. Glennon, *Constitutional Diplomacy* (Princeton University Press, forthcoming).

4. James H. Hutson, "The Creation of the Constitution: The Integrity of the Documentary Record," *Texas Law Review*, vol. 65 (November 1986), pp. 1–39.

5. Max Farrand, ed., *The Records of the Federal Convention of 1787*, vol. 2 (Yale University Press, 1911), pp. 182, 318–19; and Charles A. Lofgren, "War-Making under the Constitution: The Original Understanding," *Yale Law Journal*, vol. 81 (March 1972), pp. 672–702.

6. See Henry Cabot Lodge, ed., *The Works of Alexander Hamilton*, vol. 4 (Putnam, 1904), pp. 432–89.

and general war," the president can use armed forces in all other situations in which international law permits such use, in time of peace.[7]

In response, Madison contended that the Neutrality Proclamation could not be valid because it conferred upon the president the legislative power to decide between a state of peace or a state of war. He wrote:

> Every just view that can be taken of this subject, admonishes the public of the necessity of a rigid adherence to the simple, the received, and the fundamental doctrine of the constitution, that the power to declare war, including the power of judging of the causes of war, is *fully* and *exclusively* vested in the legislature; that the executive has no right, in any case, to decide the question, whether there is or is not cause for declaring war; that the right of convening and informing Congress, whenever such a question seems to call for a decision, is all the right which the constitution has deemed requisite or proper; and that for such, more than for any other contingency, this right was specially given to the executive.[8]

If Madison and Hamilton, so soon after the Constitutional Convention, could not agree about the allocation of war power responsibility, it is perhaps hardly a surprise that there should be uncertainty today about what the Framers intended. John Quincy Adams stated in his eulogy of Madison that the boundary between executive and legislative power in foreign affairs was as yet undetermined and perhaps could never be delineated.[9]

The words of the Constitution and the historical materials surrounding its adoption may provide ambiguous support for those who would hope to appeal to history. But at the same time, that ambiguity has provided some justification for the variety of normative frameworks that have sought to set the balance between the presidency and Congress in war powers. Although categorizations are inherently artificial, three schematas characterize much of the discussion: the "presidentialist," which holds that the president should have virtually

7. Rostow, " 'Once More unto the Breach,' " p. 15.
8. Gaillard Hunt, ed., "Letters of Helvidius, No. 1," in *The Writings of James Madison*, vol. 6 (Putnam, 1900–10), p. 174 (emphasis in original).
9. Eugene Rostow refers to the Adams eulogy (" 'Once More unto the Breach,' " p. 5, n. 9).

exclusive control over war powers short of the declaration of war;[10] the "congressionalist," which maintains that Congress has the authority to regulate war powers as it sees fit;[11] and the "shared power," which argues that the presidency and Congress both have important roles to play.[12]

The most sweeping expression of the first view, that of presidential power, is found in the case of *United States* v. *Curtiss-Wright Export Corp.*, in which the Supreme Court cited approvingly the notion that "the President is the sole organ of the nation in its external relations, and its sole representative with foreign nations." Writing for the Court, Justice Sutherland stated that in the vast realm of foreign affairs, "with its important, complicated, delicate and manifold problems, the President alone has the power to speak or listen as a representative of the nation." Moreover, Justice Sutherland averred that the president's "very delicate, plenary and exclusive power . . . as the sole organ of the Federal government in the field of international relations . . . does not require as a basis for its exercise an act of Congress." In adhering to the premise that all of foreign policy is within the president's inherent authority, *Curtiss-Wright* denied a role for Congress, even with regard to consultation. Its language supports the presumption that sanctions executive activity:

It is quite apparent that if, in the maintenance of our international relations, embarrassment . . . is to be avoided and success for our aims achieved, congressional legislation which is to be made effective through negotiation and inquiry within the international field must often accord to the President a degree of discretion

10. See, for example, Robert F. Turner, *The War Powers Resolution; Its Implementation in Theory and Practice* (Philadelphia: Foreign Policy Research Institute, 1983); and Kenneth M. Holland, "The War Powers Resolution: An Infringement on the President's Constitutional and Prerogative Powers," in R. Gordon Hoxie, ed., *The Presidency and National Security Policy* (New York: Center for the Study of the Presidency, 1984), pp. 378–400.

11. See, for example, Jacob K. Javits with Don Kellermann, *Who Makes War: The President versus Congress* (Morrow, 1973); Thomas Eagleton, *War and Presidential Power: A Chronicle of Congressional Surrender* (1974); and Harold Hongju Koh, "Why the President (Almost) Always Wins in Foreign Affairs: Lessons of the Iran-Contra Affair," *Yale Law Journal*, vol. 97 (June 1988), pp. 1255–1342.

12. See the remarks of Senators Byrd, Nunn, Warner, and Mitchell in *Congressional Record*, daily ed., May 19, 1988, pp. S6173–78.

and freedom from statutory restriction which would not be admissible were domestic affairs alone involved.[13]

Although the decision itself did not immunize executive actions in foreign policy from judicial scrutiny—in fact, the Court reviewed and upheld the president's actions as authorized by Congress—its thrust has gradually been held to support court deference to executive decisions.

Scholars have long disputed the historical analysis of *Curtiss-Wright*. Charles Lofgren, for example, concludes that if one "tests the historical accuracy of Sutherland's evidence, *Curtiss-Wright* does not support the existence of an extra-constitutional base for federal authority, broad independent executive authority, or laxness in standards governing delegation. . . . The history on which [it] . . . rest[s] is 'shockingly inaccurate.' "[14]

Whatever the merits of the underlying historical argument, much of *Curtiss-Wright*, as Justice Jackson noted in *Youngstown Sheet & Tube Co.* v. *Sawyer*, is "dictum."[15] Congress had, in fact, authorized the executive action under review through a joint resolution. Although courts and commentators have echoed Justice Jackson's pronouncement, *Curtiss-Wright* retains some vitality as a justification for those who would allow the president maximum leeway in the conduct of foreign affairs. The Supreme Court cites the case to sanction presidential power when it defers to the executive branch in external affairs.[16] Moreover, the Court incants *Curtiss-Wright* when it interprets statutes as constituting congressional acquiescence.[17] That is, legislative inaction

13. 299 U.S. 304, 320 (1936).

14. Charles A. Lofgren, "*United States v. Curtiss-Wright Export Corporation*: An Historical Reassessment," *Yale Law Journal*, vol. 83 (November 1973), p. 32. Others have reached similar judgments; see, for example, Julius Goebel, Jr., "Constitutional History and Constitutional Law," *Columbia Law Review*, vol. 38 (April 1938), pp. 555–77; David M. Levitan, "The Foreign Relations Power: An Analysis of Mr. Justice Sutherland's Theory," *Yale Law Journal*, vol. 55 (April 1946), pp. 467–97; Louis Fisher, "Understanding the Role of Congress in Foreign Policy," *George Mason University Law Review*, vol. 11 (Fall 1988), pp. 153–68; and C. Perry Patterson, "*In Re the United States v. The Curtiss-Wright Corporation*," *Texas Law Review*, vol. 22 (1943–44), pp. 286–308.

15. 343 U.S. 579, 635–36 n. 2 (1952).

16. See, for instance, *Regan* v. *Wald*, 468 U.S. 222, 243 (1984).

17. See, for example, *Haig* v. *Agee*, 453 U.S. 280, 291 (1981); and *Dames & Moore* v. *Regan*, 453 U.S. 654, 661, 675–88 (1981), which makes even greater use of Justice Jackson's typology, discussed below, to maximize presidential authority.

is taken as approval of executive action. If Congress does not expressly disapprove the president's action and previously had not sought to stop the president, then the Court is inclined to determine that Congress endorsed the president's action. By equating legislative inaction with approval, the Court's test effectively enhances executive power. In so doing, the Court increases the burden on Congress to express itself unambiguously. At the same time, this line of cases does not preclude Congress from restricting executive behavior; the Court may very well sustain a statute that explicitly provides such curbs.

A second framework, the congressionalist perspective, maintains that the Framers intended to vest the power to commit the country to war solely in Congress, leaving the president only the power to repel sudden attacks and to wage war as commander in chief once Congress has declared war. According to this view, neither the president's responsibility to conduct foreign affairs nor his duty as commander in chief gives him the power to make war without the consent of Congress.

Proponents of the congressionalist view argue that the constitutional text decidedly points to Congress. Most of the specific grants of authority, they note, are given to Congress. Moreover, "the sequence in which the text assigns authority to each branch, the location of certain provisions relative to others, and the simple weight of the words devoted to Congress as opposed to the President are as telling as is the precise language of the grants." As Taylor Reveley writes, in presenting the congressionalist case (though not accepting it in total), the provision for suspending habeas corpus during military emergency is part of the legislative rather than the executive article of the Constitution, and state war powers are grouped with congressional grants, rather than in Article IV with other state concerns.[18]

In addition, with regard to the few specific grants of power to the president, "two of the most important (over treaties and major federal appointments) he shares with the Senate." In other words, in situations where authority is not committed to Congress, it is held jointly by the president and the Senate, "except for certain ministerial functions most efficiently left to one person, for instance, military command and law

18. William Taylor Reveley III, "Prepared Statement," in *The War Power After 200 Years: Congress and The President At a Constitutional Impasse,* Hearings before the Special Subcommittee on War Powers of the Senate Committee on Foreign Relations, 100 Cong. 2 sess. (Government Printing Office, 1989), p. 501. (Hereafter *War Powers Hearings.*)

enforcement, and, except for powers of limited war or peace importance, such as granting pardons and commissions."[19]

More generally, according to this perspective, the capacity of Congress to check and override the president suggests that the legislative branch has a preeminent role in such matters as war powers. Congress can overcome presidential vetoes, reject executive initiatives, and investigate the executive branch. Moreover, the legislature, through either or both houses, can impeach and remove the president "and all Civil Officers of the United States." Through the appropriations and authorizations processes, Congress can very much affect the shape and direction of executive policy.[20]

A third framework, that seeking balance between the president and Congress, finds support in Justice Jackson's concurring opinion in *Youngstown Sheet & Tube Co.* v. *Sawyer.* In that case, the Supreme Court struck down President Truman's attempt, on the basis of "emergency powers," to seize steel mills in the midst of a nationwide strike during the Korean War.[21] "Presidential powers," wrote Justice Jackson in an opinion that has had a greater legal influence than the majority opinion, "are not fixed but fluctuate, depending upon their disjunction or conjunction with those of Congress." The Constitution "enjoins upon its branches separateness but interdependence, autonomy but reciprocity."[22] Under this scheme, according to Justice Jackson, presidential powers can be set in terms of three different circumstances:

> 1. When the President acts pursuant to an express or implied authorization of Congress, his authority is at its maximum, for it includes all that he possesses in his own right plus all that Congress can delegate. In these circumstances, and in these only, may he be said (for what it may be worth), to personify the federal sovereignty. . . .
>
> 2. When the President acts in absence of either a congressional grant or denial of authority, he can only rely upon his own independent powers, but there is a *zone of twilight* in which he and Congress may have concurrent authority, or in which its distribution is uncertain. Therefore, congressional inertia, indif-

---

19. Reveley, *War Powers Hearings*, p. 501.

20. Reveley, *War Powers Hearings*, pp. 501–02.

21. See Alan F. Westin, *Anatomy of a Constitutional Law Case: Youngstown Sheet and Tube Co. v. Sawyer* (Macmillan, 1958); and Maeva Marcus, *Truman and the Steel Seizure Case: The Limits of Presidential Power* (Columbia University Press, 1977).

22. 343 U.S. at 635.

ference or quiescence may sometimes, at least as a practical matter, enable, if not invite, measures on independent presidential responsibility. In this area, any actual test of power is likely to depend on the imperatives of events and contemporary imponderables rather than on abstract theories of law.

3. When the President takes measures incompatible with the expressed or implied will of Congress, his power is at its lowest ebb, for then he can rely only upon his own constitutional powers minus any constitutional powers of Congress over the matter. Courts can sustain exclusive Presidential control in such a case only by disabling the Congress from acting upon the subject. Presidential claim to a power at once so conclusive and preclusive must be scrutinized with caution, for what is at stake is the equilibrium established by our constitutional system.[23]

These three normative visions of relations between Congress and the executive are useful for at least three reasons. First, they stimulate thinking about the kinds of structures and processes the Constitution sanctions in the pursuit of governance. Second, they aid evaluation of the constitutionality of existing legislation. Third, they provide reference points for the design of new legislation.

In any situation, differences may arise as to which of the three classifications of the Jackson typology apply. To say that the branches should engage in dialogue consistent with the powers assigned to them cannot end the inquiry. Some may disagree, for example, about whether Congress has expressed its will, or about what that expression is. Disputes may surface as to whether the president's actions are incompatible with the expressed or implied will of Congress. There may be differences as to what constitutes the zone of twilight; some may argue that the fact of twilight cannot erase the difference between night and day. But Justice Jackson's scheme presumes that any such analyses must take into account the constitutionally assigned roles for *both* the president and Congress; indeed, the scheme is presented in the context of the interdependent powers of the branches.

I start from the premise that the Constitution created separated institutions sharing powers. The balance of power may shift from one branch to another, depending upon the issue. But the presumption is that even in those situations in which one branch has the power to act or lead, the other has a role—even if it is only to check after the fact.

23. 343 U.S. at 635–38 (emphasis added).

The Constitution envisioned a process, a dialogue among the branches. In the realm of war powers, that dialogue is to be primarily between the executive and the legislature. The substance of such a dialogue is peculiarly within the province of these two branches. Under appropriate circumstances, the constitutionality of war powers legislation may be challenged in court. But it is beyond the competence of the judiciary to become part of the substantive dialogue between the executive and the legislature, to judge the wisdom of particular actions, or to assume the role of the presidency or the Congress. The court's limited role should be to ensure that the dialogue takes place, as the statute suggests.

The process of dialogue in the context of war powers involves consultation and participation. How those terms are defined and what the roles of Congress and the executive are will depend on the particular situation. Their definitions may differ, depending upon whether the president is seeking a formal declaration of war, on whether national security demands immediate action, or on circumstances that fall in between.

The first two frameworks—the presidentialist and congressionalist—are not consistent with this view of dialogue and shared power. They do not envision either one. For the most part, they vest in one branch—the legislative or the executive—the power of pronouncement and action, with little left to the other. The third framework—that of shared power, as enunciated in Justice Jackson's opinion in *Youngstown Sheet & Tube*—calls for a process of dialogue.

As proposals for reform of the War Powers Resolution are considered, it is important to underscore that any such measure must adhere to a vision consistent with constitutional values. That a measure is judged unworkable may be enough grounds to change it. But that a new measure is thought expedient or workable (however defined) is not enough to sustain it. The measure must fit within the contours of the Constitution. However, one might conclude that a particular piece of legislation should be revised or even scrapped without resort to the constitutional framework. The measure may be impractical or imprudent in ways that argue against its retention in its current form for reasons distinct from constitutional questions. Indeed, apart from whether the War Powers Resolution is constitutional—a question that has engaged many scholars—its operational problems call for a fresh look. It is through the prism of practice that the current War Powers Resolution will be discussed.

The War Powers Resolution of 1973

In enacting the War Powers Resolution of 1973, Congress sought to provide a process that would strengthen its role in war-making decisions. Throughout U.S. history, presidents have committed military forces without a congressional declaration of war. In more than 200 cases of the use of armed forces, Congress has declared war in only four instances—the War of 1812, the Spanish-American War, World War I, and World War II—and in a fifth—the Mexican War—passed a joint resolution. The executive branch, in short, has dominated decisions to send forces abroad.

Much attention has been paid to the events leading up to the passage of the War Powers Resolution, and I will not attempt to travel familiar ground.[24] But it is important to note the combination of forces that led to its enactment. In one sense, Congress reacted against what was perceived to be the unrestrained use of executive power. As the Vietnam War continued through the 1960s, many legislators came to feel that it was not always practical or politically feasible for the legislative branch to curb military action once it had begun. What was needed was a structure that would affirmatively define the congressional role from the start, when the president first contemplated military activity. Opponents of the Vietnam War were not the only ones to hold that view. There were also many who supported American involvement in the Southeast Asian conflict but believed that Congress needed institutional mechanisms to exercise its prerogatives in the future. And thus was forged a consensus that something should be done, with Chairman Clement Zablocki of the Foreign Affairs Committee assuming a major role in the House of Representatives and Jacob K. Javits, ranking minority member of the Foreign Relations Committee, doing the same in the Senate. The House Foreign Affairs Committee and the Senate Foreign Relations Committee held exhaustive hearings, with the former beginning the process that would result in the War Powers Resolution. The diminished power of the presidency in the midst of the Watergate debacle and Democratic control of both legislative chambers facilitated passage of the resolution over President Richard Nixon's veto. Only 18 Senators and 135 representatives voted to sustain the president's action.

24. For a very good discussion, see Smyrl, *Conflict or Codetermination?* pp. 19–29.

THE STATUTORY FRAMEWORK

The War Powers Resolution consists of ten sections, with the first merely citing the title and the last the effective date. Section 2, setting out the resolution's purpose and policy, states that the objective is to "insure that the collective judgment of both the Congress and the President will apply to the introduction of United States Armed Forces into hostilities, or into situations where imminent involvement in hostilities is clearly indicated by the circumstances, and to the continued use of such forces in hostilities or in such situations." The authority of the president to introduce armed forces "into hostilities, or into situations where imminent involvement in hostilities is clearly indicated by the circumstances," is to be exercised "only pursuant to (1) a declaration of war, (2) specific statutory authorization, or (3) a national emergency created by attack upon the United States, its territories or possessions, or its armed forces." The meat of the resolution, sections 3 to 5, is concerned with consultation, reporting, and congressional action.

Consultation. Under the terms of section 3, the president is required "in every possible instance" to consult with Congress "before introducing United States Armed Forces into hostilities or into situations where imminent involvement in hostilities is clearly indicated." Moreover, the chief executive "shall consult regularly with the Congress until United States Armed Forces are no longer engaged in hostilities or have been removed from such situations."

Reporting. Section 4 states that in the absence of a declaration of war the president shall submit a report within forty-eight hours to the Speaker of the House of Representatives and the president pro tempore of the Senate in any case in which armed forces are introduced: (1) "into hostilities or into situations where imminent involvement in hostilities is clearly indicated by the circumstances; (2) into the territory, airspace or waters of a foreign nation, while equipped for combat, except for deployments which relate solely to supply, replacement, repair, or training of such forces; or (3) in numbers which substantially enlarge United States Armed Forces equipped for combat already located in a foreign nation." That report, in writing, is to set forth the circumstances of the introduction of forces, the constitutional and legislative authority supporting the president's action, and the estimated scope and duration of the hostilities or involvement. In cases involving hostilities, additional reports are to be made in intervals not less than once every six months for as long as the circumstances continue.

Congressional Action. Section 5(a) provides that if the president transmits a report pursuant to section 4(a)(1) during a congressional adjournment, the Speaker of the House and the president pro tempore of the Senate, when they deem it advisable or if they are petitioned by at least 30 percent of the members of their respective houses, "shall jointly request the President to convene Congress in order that it may consider the report and take appropriate action."

The succeeding section, 5(b), at the heart of the congressional mechanism, provides for a sequence of events within sixty calendar days "after a report is submitted or is required to be submitted pursuant to section 4(a)(1)." It requires the president to terminate the use of U.S. armed forces unless Congress has declared war or authorized the action; extended the period by law; or "is physically unable to meet as a result of an armed attack upon the United States." If the president certifies that "unavoidable military necessity respecting the safety of United States Armed Forces" requires their continued presence in the course of effecting their removal, the sixty days can be extended by thirty days. The language, "after a report is submitted or is required to be submitted pursuant to section 4(a)(1)," is significant because it means that Congress does not have to rely upon the president to trigger the sixty-day clock; the legislative branch could presumably vote that circumstances require the submission of a report, in which case the sixty-day clock would begin to tick.

Section 5(c) states that by concurrent resolution Congress can require the president to remove forces at any time. Because of the Supreme Court's decision in *Chadha* outlawing the legislative veto,[25] and thus possibly section 5(c), Congress adopted in 1983 a freestanding measure, attached as an amendment to a State Department authorization bill, that substitutes a joint resolution for the concurrent resolution.[26] The procedures provided in that legislation, which did not formally amend the War Powers Resolution, could be invoked if the Supreme Court were to strike down section 5(c). How the judiciary would, in fact, interpret section 5(c) has been the subject of debate. Some have argued that section 5(c) is not a legislative veto, where Congress delegates

25. *Immigration and Naturalization Service* v. *Chadha*, 462 U.S. 919 (1983).
26. 97 Stat. 1062-63 (1983).

certain powers to the executive but reserves the right to veto the executive exercise of that delegation. According to this view, Congress has not delegated power, but has sought "to approximate the accommodation reached by the Constitution's framers, that the President could act militarily in an emergency but was obligated to cease and desist in the event Congress did not approve as soon as it had a reasonable opportunity to do so."[27] The shift from a concurrent resolution to a joint resolution has important implications for the operation of the War Powers Resolution. The former, unlike the latter, is not subject to a presidential veto; if the president vetoes a joint resolution, Congress must muster a two-thirds majority in each house to overturn it.

Sections 6 and 7 provide respectively for expedited procedures for congressional consideration under section 5(b) of a joint resolution or bill introduced to authorize the use of armed forces and of a concurrent resolution to withdraw forces.

Section 8 is the interpretive provision of the War Powers Resolution. In order to ensure that appropriations measures, security treaties, or broadly worded resolutions such as the Tonkin Gulf Resolution not be used as authorization for the introduction of troops, section 8(a) declares that "authority to introduce . . . Forces into hostilities or into situations wherein involvement in hostilities is clearly indicated by the circumstances shall not be inferred . . . from any provision of law (whether or not in effect before the date of the enactment of this joint resolution) . . . unless such provision specifically authorizes the introduction of . . . Forces into hostilities or into such situations and states that it is intended to constitute specific authorization within the meaning of this joint resolution."

Section 8(b) seeks to make clear that the War Powers Resolution is not intended to prevent "high-level military commands which were established prior to . . . this joint resolution and pursuant to the United Nations Charter or any treaty ratified by the United States prior to such date" from participating in those joint military exercises. Those "high-level" military commands are the United Nations command in Korea, the North American Air Defense Command, and the North Atlantic Treaty Organization.

Section 8(c) holds that "the term 'introduction of United States

Armed Forces' includes the assignment of members of such armed forces to command, coordinate, participate in the movement of, or accompany the regular or irregular military forces of any foreign country or government when such military forces are engaged, or there exists an imminent threat that such forces will become engaged, in hostilities." Its objective, according to a Senate Foreign Relations Committee report on the bill, was to "prevent secret, unauthorized military support activities and to prevent a repetition of many of the most controversial and regrettable actions in Indochina."[28]

To make clear that the resolution does not change constitutional arrangements, section 8(c) declares that "nothing in this joint resolution . . . is intended to alter the constitutional authority of the Congress or of the President, or the provisions of existing treaties." Moreover, the section provides that nothing in the resolution should be construed as granting any authority to the president with respect to the intro-duction of forces that he would not have had without the joint resolution.

PROBLEMS IN THE STATUTORY FRAMEWORK

Given the diversity of interests and perspectives surrounding the war powers issue, it is perhaps remarkable that Congress enacted any legislation at all. That it was able to do so reflects the strength of the system. But the lawmaking process is hardly precise. Ambiguity, as Herbert Kaufman has observed, may be a solvent of disagreement;[29] but the ambiguity that politics requires to secure the votes for a bill's passage ultimately leads to problems of interpretation later. In part, these problems arise because of the failure to anticipate various difficulties. The pressure of time sometimes prevents legislative con-sideration of the ramifications of adding or subtracting particular phrases. To one degree or another, all of these problems have afflicted the War Powers Resolution. Indeed, simply by reading the statute and its accompanying legislative history, one could predict many of the difficulties that would later appear.

One such problem is found in section 2(c) of the resolution, which declares that the president exercises his constitutional powers as commander-in-chief "only" pursuant to three situations: a declaration of war, specific statutory authorization, or a national emergency created by attack upon the United States, its territories or possessions, or its

28. *War Powers*, S. Rept. 93-220, 93 Cong. 1 sess. (GPO, 1973), p. 27.
29. Letter from Herbert Kaufman to author, October 5, 1989.

armed forces. But those circumstances appear to exclude others where the commitment of forces might be appropriate, for instance, in the rescue of American citizens. In fact, reports filed by Presidents Ford, Carter, and Reagan all involved the rescue of U.S. citizens. That the rescue circumstance is not included in section 2(c) was not an oversight; Congress, especially the House, believed that presidents might construe "rescue" too broadly and enter into situations the legislature did not intend.

The question of whether to enumerate specifically those circumstances in which the president could exercise his power as commander in chief occupied much debate in Congress. Ultimately, the forces that feared the president would view such a list as a loophole prevailed. For that reason, section 2(c) is part of the "purpose and policy" section of the resolution, separate from the succeeding operational sections. In other words, the statement—although phrased in rather definitive language—was meant to reflect almost the lowest common denominator of agreement as to when the president can act, rather than a complete enumeration of such authority. But the subtlety of that compromise has spawned considerable confusion about what Congress intended.

The resolution's reporting requirements in section 4 are hardly the model of precision. They classify activities in three ways: (1) when forces are introduced into "hostilities or into situations where imminent involvement in hostilities is clearly indicated by the circumstances," (2) when troops "equipped for combat" are introduced into situations where hostilities are not considered imminent, and (3) when the U.S. military presence in a foreign nation is "substantially enlarge[d]."

The differences in these classifications are important. The first, that of imminent hostilities, triggers the sixty-day time clock in section 5, while the other two do not obligate the president to do anything but report. A president who thus seeks to avoid the sixty-day clock, which could result in the removal of troops, would report under the other two sections. Had Congress tied all of the reporting provisions to the sixty-day clock, the action-forcing mechanism in the resolution would arguably have been more difficult to evade, especially before the *Chadha* decision cast doubt on section 5(c). The drafters of the resolution should have anticipated that its effect would be to shift the onus to Congress to decide whether to trigger the sixty-day clock, rather than to the president—as the spirit of the resolution intends.

Another source of difficulty is the references to troops "equipped for combat" in section 4. Read literally, the resolution does not cover unarmed forces, even if used for military missions. A commander in chief could thus immunize forces from the scope of the resolution by asserting that they were not "equipped for combat."

The term "hostilities" and the clause "situations where imminent involvement in hostilities is clearly indicated by the circumstances" have fostered much disagreement. The report of the House of Representatives on its war powers bill seeks to provide some definition:

> The word *hostilities* was substituted for the phrase *armed conflict* during the subcommittee drafting process because it was considered to be somewhat broader in scope. In addition to a situation in which fighting actually has begun, *hostilities* also encompasses a state of confrontation in which no shots have been fired but where there is a clear and present danger of armed conflict. "*Imminent hostilities*" denotes a situation in which there is a clear potential either for such a state of confrontation or for actual armed conflict.[30]

It was foreseeable, and perhaps inevitable, that disagreements would arise as to when there was "a clear and present danger" or "a clear potential either for such a state of confrontation or for actual armed conflict."

Similarly, the legislation is unclear as to the meaning of "substantially enlarge" in section 4(a)(3), which requires the reporting of the introduction of troops "in numbers which substantially enlarge United States Armed Forces equipped for combat already located in a foreign nation." Although the House report seeks to provide some broad parameters, it acknowledges that the word "substantially" is designed to provide a flexible criterion.[31] One could predict that such flexibility, however necessary, would lead to disagreement about the "commonsense understanding of the numbers involved."

Not only the sections on reporting are fraught with difficulties that could frustrate implementation of the resolution, but also those on consulting. First, there is the problem of definition. To be sure, the

30. *War Powers Resolution*, H. Rept. 93-287, 93 Cong. 1 sess. (GPO, 1973), included in *The War Powers Resolution: Relevant Documents, Correspondence, Reports*, Committee Print, Subcommittee on International Security and Scientific Affairs of the House Committee on Foreign Affairs, 98 Cong. 1 sess. (GPO, 1983), p. 23. (Hereafter *War Powers Reports*.)
31. *War Powers Reports*, p. 24.

House report seeks to provide some direction, noting: "Rejected was the notion that consultation should be synonymous with merely being informed. Rather, consultation in this provision means that a decision is pending on a problem and that Members of Congress are being asked by the President for their advice and opinions and, in appropriate circumstances, their approval of action contemplated."[32] But the failure to provide such a definition in the legislation itself was bound to provide the executive with some discretion as to the meaning of consultation. Even the language of the House report does not define "appropriate circumstances."

Second, in stating that the president shall "in every possible instance" consult with Congress before introducing U.S. armed forces into situations of actual or imminent hostilities, the legislature presented a president who wished to evade the spirit of the resolution with some license to do so. It could have been anticipated that a commander in chief might assert that the exigencies of the moment prevented such consultation, that it was not possible in that particular instance.

Third, the resolution does not provide a mechanism for consultation. It does not specify *who* should be consulted. A president could thus state with some credibility that because it was impossible to consult every member of Congress, the provision made little sense. It would be better, he might contend, to focus on those sections that offer standards or guidelines for implementation.

The War Powers Resolution in Operation

It is perhaps axiomatic that a statutory framework riddled with problems causes difficulties for those charged with implementing it. But those difficulties can ultimately be overcome when there is a shared commitment of the branches to execute the law. When such a consensus does not exist, however, then one or another branch can take advantage of the flaws in the statutory framework in ways that arguably frustrate the implementation of the law. That has been the experience with the War Powers Resolution. How the resolution has operated cannot be understood without first looking at the way each branch has perceived its interests and role.

Across administrations, the executive branch has rather consistently opposed the resolution. Although acknowledging the need to cooperate

32. *War Powers Reports*, p. 23.

with Congress, presidents have resisted any efforts that encroach upon their freedom to maneuver. As a matter of strategy, the executive has been careful not to do anything that might be construed as an acknowledgment of the constitutionality of the War Powers Resolution. Moreover, presidents have proceeded in ways that test congressional tolerance for their military initiatives, generally calculating that the legislature will ultimately acquiesce to the decisions of the commander in chief. At the same time, they have skillfully avoided constitutional confrontations with Congress.

Presidents since Richard Nixon have cast their arguments on constitutional as well as practical grounds.[33] With respect to the Constitution, chief executives have contended that the meat of the resolution—section 5—concerning the withdrawal of U.S. forces from a situation of actual or imminent hostilities, violates the presentment clause (Article I, section 7, clause 2). That clause holds that every bill passed by Congress "shall, before it becomes a law, be presented to the president of the United States." But under the terms of the War Powers Resolution, Congress could, through inaction during the sixty-day period, compel the withdrawal of troops without enacting a bill for the president's consideration. Similarly, presidents have challenged as unconstitutional the concurrent-resolution part of section 5, stating that to the degree that Congress can impose restrictions on military action, it can do so only by legislation subject to a presidential veto. Since the Supreme Court's ruling in *Chadha* striking down the legislative veto, the executive branch has based its argument on that judicial ruling.

Presidents have also contended that as the repository of the executive power of the United States, commander in chief of the armed forces, and the officer in charge of the diplomatic and intelligence resources of the United States, they are "responsible for acting promptly to deal with threats to U.S. interests, including the deployment and use of U.S. forces where necessary in defense of the national security," in the words of the Reagan administration's State Department legal adviser, Abraham Sofaer. He added that "Congress should not, as a matter of sound policy, and cannot, as a matter of constitutional law, impose statutory restrictions that impede the President's ability to carry out these responsibilities."[34]

33. See, for example, text of President Richard M. Nixon's veto of war powers bill, reprinted in *Congressional Quarterly Almanac, 1973*, vol. 29 (1974), pp. 90-A–91-A.
34. *War Powers Hearings*, p. 1052.

In their critiques of the War Powers Resolution, chief executives have all alluded to the problems in the statutory scheme discussed above, regarding the enumeration of presidential authority, consultation, and reporting. Moreover, they have asserted that as a practical matter, the resolution has several adverse consequences for the conduct of foreign policy. Presidents have alleged that the deadlines interfere with the completion of initiatives and that the very existence of limits may signal to the enemy that the United States is divided. Adversaries may feel that the president will be forced to desist; if the enemy has the patience to wait sixty days, then American troops might be compelled to withdraw due to legislative inaction. The executive has further maintained that the time limits place U.S. forces at risk in the field, especially if they are forced to withdraw under fire. Also, allies might be less willing to commit their forces if they know that the U.S. commitment is tentative.

In terms of legislative-executive relations, the resolution's critics maintain it is deleterious because it increases conflict between the branches. In an address at the University of Virginia in the waning days of his administration, President Ronald Reagan remarked that "where Congress and the President have engaged each other as adversaries, . . . U.S. policies have faltered and our common purposes have not been achieved. . . . Sometimes congressional actions in foreign affairs have had the effect of institutionalizing that kind of adversarial relationship. We see it in the War Powers Resolution."[35] Consistent with this view is the charge that the resolution encourages congressional irresponsibility because the automatic nature of the deadline could result in the end of executive protection of the national interest without the necessity of legislative action. Moreover, the deadline lessens the likelihood that Congress can play a useful role "by placing unnecessary pressure on Congress to act where the President has not sought specific legislative approval to continue an action beyond the designated time limits."[36]

Apart from arguing that the War Powers Resolution is unconstitutional or imprudent, presidents have claimed that it is unnecessary. No commander in chief, they assert, can engage in military action for long without popular support. Congress already has the means to

35. *Weekly Compilation of Presidential Documents*, vol. 24 (December 19, 1988), p. 1633.
36. Statement of Abraham Sofaer, presenting the Reagan administration's position, in *War Powers Hearings*, p. 1060.

impose constraints on executive action through the power to declare war, to raise and support armies, to tax and spend, to regulate foreign commerce, and to adopt measures necessary and proper to implement its powers. The Vietnam War may have led to the War Powers Resolution. But that war would not have continued for as long as it did without congressional appropriations and authorizations. Once Congress denied funds for certain military activities, the argument continues, the president complied—before the War Powers Resolution became a reality.

If the executive position has been consistent from one administration to the next, the congressional perspective has been harder to discern. Put another way, it is difficult to pronounce a single view from Capitol Hill. Congress does not speak with one voice; it has no unitary position or statement of institutional interest. That has been true from the outset, from the time that Congress first considered appropriate means to increase its role in the decision to make war. The War Powers Resolution itself reflects the difficulties that Congress had in striking the right balance between presidential and legislative powers. The lengthy congressional deliberations were in large measure about the extent to which presidential discretion should be curbed. Although Congress concluded that limits were appropriate, it was uncertain about its own institutional role. The gaps and ambiguities in the resolution were the product of the effort to secure enough votes from a diversity of interests to ensure passage. As a consequence, such thorny issues as the enumeration of presidential powers were not as definitively resolved as they might have been. By not providing mechanisms that would help crystallize its positions and interests—for example, in the consultation process—the legislative branch further exacerbated its difficulties in defining its role in war powers.

As a result of the problems in achieving a consensus about congressional power, legislators have frequently grounded their defense of the War Powers Resolution in terms of the inadequacy of other laws and procedures. As the late Senator Jacob K. Javits, an architect and forceful proponent of the resolution, commented:

> It has been argued that Congress could cut off appropriations or statutorily prohibit certain actions, like the bombing of Cambodia during the Vietnam War, and accordingly had adequate power to stop the President from continuing a war or war situation with which the Congress disagreed. But the Vietnam War clearly

indicated the inadequacy of these remedies. The Congress can hardly cut off appropriations when 500,000 American troops are fighting for their lives, as in Vietnam, and the voting on such a cutoff demonstrated its inadequacy. And the inability to apply a statutory mandate to the secret bombing of Cambodia clearly indicated the inadequacy of that remedy.[37]

Even when Congress has provided authority to assert war-making responsibilities, the legislature has hardly been eager to exercise it. For instance, on only one occasion, during the 1983 Lebanon incursion, did Congress invoke section 4(a) of the War Powers Resolution, triggering the sixty-day clock. But this was only after a deal had been struck with the White House assuring that troops could remain for eighteen months. In the absence of Congress's desire to make use of the powers afforded by the resolution, some legislators have almost plaintively appealed to the president to invoke those sections that trigger the resolution. Thus Senator Joseph R. Biden, Jr., chair of the Special Subcommittee on War Powers of the Committee on Foreign Relations, inquired:

I have always wondered why has no President asked at the outset of his action to make it a 4(a)(1) and to ask for authorization? Can any of you think of any time . . . where a President has taken the action of committing U.S. forces anywhere that the Congress has not, if asked or having participated in it, immediately after the action was taken, that the Congress has not supported it? . . . Can any of you imagine . . . a President saying he was committing troops for the withdrawal of students from Grenada, or he was committing troops for saving anyone in Panama, that a congressional body of 535 women and men, if asked in the immediate aftermath of that for their support, would not give it?[38]

Similarly, during the 1987 Persian Gulf crisis, Representative Stephen J. Solarz, a member of the Foreign Affairs Committee, urged President Reagan to invoke the resolution, in part because "both houses of

---

37. Jacob K. Javits, "The War Powers Resolution and the Constitution: A Special Introduction," in Demetrios Caraley, ed., *The President's War Powers: From the Federalists to Reagan* (New York: Academy of Political Science, 1984), p. 3.

38. *War Powers Hearings*, pp. 119–20.

Congress would undoubtedly adopt, by substantial majorities, a resolution approving our military presence in the gulf, since even many
legislators who opposed the original policy of reflagging the Kuwaiti
tankers would be reluctant at this point to order our fleet home."[39]

A variety of explanations account for the reluctance of Congress to
trigger the War Powers Resolution. First, many presidential actions,
because of their quickness and brevity, are completed before Congress
has a chance to respond. Second, in the earliest days of a military
engagement, legislators, reflecting their constituencies, are loath to
second-guess the president or to do anything that might be perceived
as undercutting American forces, especially if the administration could
blame them for the loss of life. Indeed, the tendency is to support the
president's decision, rather than to challenge it. Third, although
Congress wants some role—however undefined it may seem—in the
war-making process, it is inclined to defer to executive claims of
competence in making such military decisions. Congress is not equipped
organizationally to make tactical military decisions or to direct operations. Rather, its strength lies as a participant in the process of
formulating and overseeing the policies that might lead to military
action.

Whatever the reasons for Congress's general unwillingness to contest
the president through the War Powers Resolution, the legislature's
difficulty in clearly presenting its interests has given a distinct advantage
to the executive. As evidence, I summarize the experience under the
War Powers Resolution with respect to the key sections on reporting
and consultation and offer a brief review of the Persian Gulf affair.

REPORTING

Since 1973 presidents have submitted twenty reports under the War
Powers Resolution. Three of those occasions, during the Ford administration, dealt with the use of combat forces, helicopters, and tactical
air elements to assist with the evacuation from Vietnam and Cambodia
in 1975. In addition, President Gerald Ford reported on his order to
rescue the crew of the *Mayaguez* and retake it from Cambodian naval
patrol boats that had seized the vessel. President Jimmy Carter reported
the use of military force in the failed effort to rescue American hostages

39. Stephen J. Solarz, "Missing the Point on War Powers," *New York Times*, October
28, 1987, p. A31.

in Iran in 1980; the report was filed, in part, "consistent with the
reporting provisions" of the War Powers Resolution.[40]

The Reagan administration submitted fourteen reports. Three in
1982 were tied to activities in the Middle East. Two of those reports
related to the deployment of U.S. troops to multinational forces in
Beirut and a third to the use of troops as part of the multinational
force created by the Israeli-Egyptian peace treaty. In 1983 the administration filed three more reports. One dealt with sending two AWACS
electronic surveillance planes, eight F-15 fighter planes, and ground
and logistical forces to Sudan to aid Chad against Libyan and rebel
forces. Another report was submitted after marines who were part of
the multinational force in Lebanon were fired upon, two fatally.
President Reagan also reported in 1983 that American forces were
being dispatched to Grenada.[41] In 1986 the administration reported
that U.S. forces had responded to a Libyan attack in the Gulf of Sidra
and had engaged in air raids against terrorist and military targets in
the Libyan cities of Tripoli and Benghazi.[42] Military action in the
Persian Gulf, as will be discussed below, prompted six more reports.
In December 1989 President Bush reported on the use of American
military force against Panama's Manuel Noriega.

It is important to note that on only one occasion has a president
reported under section 4(a)(1), which triggers the sixty-day clock. And
in that incident, involving the *Mayaguez*, President Ford submitted the
report after the ship had been retaken and the U.S. forces had been
withdrawn. The general pattern has been for the president to file the
report, citing section 4 (without reference to a particular subsection)
or simply noting that report is "consistent with the War Power
Resolution," but without reference to any specific provision. The
executive branch will also note authority under the Constitution and
international law.

The executive's decision not to cite section 4(a)(1) has been part of
a strategy that has anticipated that Congress would ultimately not vote
on its own authority to trigger the sixty-day clock. If Congress wants
to invoke the resolution, it can always do so. But, as has been noted,
it has done so on only one occasion, during the Lebanon crisis. In that
case, President Reagan submitted a report in August 1983, following

40. See *War Powers Reports*, pp. 40–49.

41. *War Powers Reports*, pp. 57–66, 84–85.

42. *Weekly Compilation of Presidential Documents*, vol. 22 (March 31, 1986), p. 423;
and (April 22, 1986), pp. 499–500.

the death of two marines. The report made note of section 4, but did not specifically cite section 4(a)(1). The failure to refer to this section openly enraged even Republican legislators. The chair of the Foreign Relations Committee, Republican Senator Charles H. Percy, commented: "We have people up in helicopters, we're shooting rockets and artillery—if that isn't imminent hostilities, I don't know what is."[43] As opposition mounted within the legislative branch, the Republican leadership convinced the Reagan administration that the White House would have to reach some accommodation with Congress. In the end, with the critical support of House Speaker Thomas P. "Tip" O'Neill, the executive and legislative branches engineered a compromise.[44]

The resulting Multinational Force in Lebanon Resolution declared that "significant hostilities" had occurred and that section 4(a)(1) was triggered on August 29, 1983, when the first marine died. At the same time, the resolution authorized the president to keep U.S. troops in Lebanon for eighteen months, unless he or Congress determined that they should be withdrawn. Under the terms of the resolution Congress could choose to extend the deadline or could require by joint resolution that forces be withdrawn during that eighteen-month period.[45] Some liberal senators objected that by granting the president eighteen months, the resolution's enactment constituted "a dereliction of Congressional responsibility to uphold the principles and procedures of the War Powers Resolution of 1973" and "an 18-month 'blank check' under which the Administration could pursue hitherto unspecified military objectives in Lebanon while asserting that it is operating with full Congressional sanction."[46] For its part, the Reagan administration took some pains to make clear that it was not acknowledging the constitutionality of the War Powers Resolution. In his signing statement, President Reagan stated that his acceptance of the Multinational Force in Lebanon Resolution "should [not] be viewed as any acknowledgment that the President's constitutional authority can be impermissibly infringed by statute, that congressional authorization would be required

43. John Felton, "Congress Wants Greater Role on U.S. Presence in Lebanon," *Congressional Quarterly Weekly Report*, September 3, 1983, p. 1876.
44. See Hedrick Smith, *The Power Game: How Washington Works* (Random House, 1988), pp. 550.
45. *War Powers Reports*, pp. 78–83.
46. *Multinational Force in Lebanon*, S. Rept. 98-242, 98 Cong. 1 sess. (GPO, 1983), p. 16.

if and when the period specified in Section 5(b) of the War Powers
Resolution might be deemed to have been triggered and the period
had expired."[47]

At times, conflict between the branches has arisen not only when
the president has cited the War Powers Resolution without reference
to section 4(a)(1), but also when the president did not submit any
report at all. Generally, such tension has been of brief duration because
the military initiatives were themselves limited and quickly accomplished without the loss of life. Two actions, however, did bring to
the fore some problems in the resolution's statutory framework.

With regard to the first, President Reagan stated in July 1983 that
the United States would participate in "two joint training exercises"
in the Caribbean and Central America. The exercises involved the use
of army and marine combat troops in Honduras and ocean maneuvers
of the U.S. fleet. Several thousand ground troops were used, and
military facilities were constructed. President Reagan did not report
the exercises under the War Powers Resolution; the executive branch
noted that section 4(a)(2) requires the reporting of troops equipped for
combat, but not deployment relating solely to training.[48] By labeling
the exercises as training maneuvers, the administration thus sought to
skirt the War Powers Resolution.

The second incident involved the commitment of U.S. military
advisers to El Salvador. The Carter administration made the initial
decision, and by March 1981 the Reagan administration had added
thirty-five such experts to the nineteen that were already in place. The
State Department asserted that the War Powers Resolution did not
apply because the advisers were not being introduced into hostilities
or situations of imminent hostilities.[49] Although the administration's
decision not to report under the War Powers Resolution upset many
in Congress, especially after some military advisers were killed, the
legislative branch did not formulate a response. The lack of congressional action has probably been due largely to the fact that the
administration has kept the number of military advisers within limits
acceptable to the legislative branch. Still, eleven legislators, joined later
by eighteen colleagues, filed suit in federal court alleging that the

47. *Weekly Compilation of Presidential Documents*, vol. 19 (October 17, 1983), pp.
1422–23.

48. Ellen C. Collier, "The War Powers Resolution: Fifteen Years of Experience,"
Congressional Research Service, August 3, 1988, pp. 24–25.

49. Collier, "The War Powers Resolution," pp. 21–24.

president's action had violated the Constitution and the War Powers Resolution. The judiciary dismissed the suit, determining that it was for Congress, not the courts, to decide whether U.S. forces in El Salvador were involved in hostilities or situations of imminent hostilities.[50]

CONSULTATION

The absence of clarity in the statutory framework as to the "consultation" provision—the definition of consultation, when consultation should occur, who should be consulted—has exacerbated difficulties between the legislative and executive branches. For the most part, the executive branch has interpreted "consultation" to mean "inform," whereas Congress had hoped that the term would require the president to seek the advice of and even in "appropriate circumstances" the "approval of action contemplated."[51]

Typically, the executive informs the legislative branch after a decision is made. For instance, in the case of the Grenada invasion, President Reagan had a meeting with congressional leaders two hours after he had signed the order for the landing the next morning.[52] In the case of the Libyan air raids, the president met with about a dozen legislative leaders at around 4 P.M. and informed them that airplanes had already been dispatched from Great Britain and would begin bombing at about 7 P.M.[53] In the matter of Panama, a military operation much larger and more complex than the Grenada invasion, President Bush informed some key congressional leaders of his not unexpected decision to commit troops only a few hours before the first shots were fired and well after the military action had been set in motion.

At times presidents have taken advantage of the statute's directive to consult "in every possible instance" and argued that in the particular circumstance in question it was not "possible" to consult. For example, in the case of the failed attempt to rescue American hostages in Iran, the Carter administration chose not to consult with congressional leaders out of concern that such exchanges would jeopardize the

---

50. *Crockett* v. *Reagan,* 558 F. Supp. 893 (D.D.C. 1982).

51. *War Powers Reports,* p. 23.

52. See Michael Rubner, "The Reagan Administration, the 1973 War Powers Resolution, and the Invasion of Grenada," *Political Science Quarterly,* vol. 100 (Winter 1985–86), pp. 627–47.

53. See generally, *War Powers, Libya, and State-Sponsored Terrorism,* Hearings before the Subcommittee on Arms Control, International Security and Science of the House Committee on Foreign Affairs, 99 Cong. 2 sess. (GPO, 1986).

mission.[54] As acting Secretary of State Warren Christopher later explained, congressional leaders would have been consulted "at a time so late that the compromise of secrecy would not have been as great."[55] The Iran mission prompted the Senate Foreign Relations Committee to hold hearings. Although Chairman Frank Church suggested that the incident pointed to the need for Congress to clarify what consultation means, the legislative branch has yet to formally do so.

THE PERSIAN GULF CRISIS

The Persian Gulf crisis vividly showed the unwillingness of both the president and Congress to invoke the key operative provisions of the War Powers Resolution. Congress's failure to do so has led to rethinking the War Powers Resolution.

In 1987 President Reagan decided to provide U.S. naval escorts for Kuwaiti oil tankers through the Persian Gulf.[56] Through "reflagging," Kuwaiti tankers were registered in the name of an American company and thus entitled to fly the flag of the United States and to have the protection of the U.S. government. During 1987 U.S. naval forces significantly increased their military presence in the gulf.

In providing support for Kuwait, the United States was indirectly assisting Iraq in its war with Iran, because Iraq depended upon Kuwait for much of its oil. A critical question that soon surfaced within Congress was whether the Iran-Iraq war had caused the Persian Gulf to become an area of hostilities or imminent hostilities for U.S. forces and whether, therefore, the president should be required to report under the War Powers Resolution.

The administration did not submit any report until an Iraqi aircraft fired a missile on the U.S.S. *Stark* on May 17, 1987, killing thirty-seven U.S. sailors. But that report did not mention the resolution itself. Similarly, the president did not file a report after other incidents, such as when a naval ship struck a mine and a U.S. F-14 fighter plane fired two missiles at an Iranian aircraft.

In September 1987 the administration did begin to file reports "consistent with" the War Powers Resolution; by mid-1989 six had

54. *War Powers Reports*, p. 50.

55. *The Situation in Iran*, Hearing before the Senate Committee on Foreign Relations, 96 Cong. 2 Sess. (GPO, 1980), p. 4.

56. For an account, see *Congressional Quarterly Almanac, 1987*, vol. 43 (1988), pp. 252–64.

been filed, although none cited section 4(a)(1).[57] Not coincidentally perhaps, only one month before the president submitted the first report, Representative Mike Lowry and 110 other members of Congress filed suit in federal district court contending that the reporting requirement of section 4(a)(1) was triggered on July 22, 1987, by the use of U.S. navy ships to escort the reflagged Kuwaiti tankers. In December 1987 Judge George H. Revercomb dismissed the suit because of the "constraints of the equitable discretion and political question doctrines." The court concluded that the plaintiffs' dispute was "primarily with [their] fellow legislators."[58] With regard to that point, Judge Revercomb quoted Senator Brock Adams, who along with Senators Paul Simon and Spark Matsunaga was for a brief time a plaintiff in the case:

> We are blocked on every one of these [bills] and we are going into a congressional recess and I am concerned about attacks on our allies, attacks such as occurred at Mecca, attacks on our ships, the difficulties we have. I want the country united.
>
> We could not get it through before the recess, so yesterday along with Senators Simon and Matsunaga and over 100 Members of the House, I joined as a plaintiff in a suit to seek judicial relief and enforcement of the requirements of the War Powers Act, saying it was triggered by this reflagging of vessels.[59]

By the time the case was reviewed by the U.S. Court of Appeals for the D.C. Circuit, the Iran-Iraq cease-fire was in place. The appeal was ultimately dismissed on October 17, 1988, on grounds of nonjusticiability and mootness.[60]

Apart from resorting to the judiciary, Congress considered legislation addressing the Persian Gulf policy without triggering the War Powers Resolution. For example, Congress enacted provisions mandating the secretary of defense to submit a report before executing any agreement between the United States and Kuwait for American military protection

---

57. See *Weekly Compilation of Presidential Documents*, vol. 23 (September 28, 1987), p. 1066; vol. 23 (October 19, 1987), pp. 1159–60; vol. 23 (October 26, 1987), p. 1206; vol. 24 (April 25, 1988), pp. 493–94; vol. 24 (July 11, 1988), pp. 896–97; and vol. 24 (July 18, 1988), p. 938.

58. *Lowry v. Reagan*, 676 F. Supp. 333, 338 (D.D.C. 1987).

59. *Congressional Record*, daily ed., August 7, 1987, p. S11567.

60. *Lowry v. Reagan*, No. 87-5426 (D.C. Cir. 1988).

of Kuwaiti shipping. That report was filed on June 15, 1987.[61] But such measures did not satisfy those legislators who believed the War Powers Resolution should be invoked. Several senators, particularly Adams, Lowell Weicker, Mark Hatfield, and Dale Bumpers, still sought to invoke the resolution on a number of occasions. Adams declared: "I cannot believe that there is anyone in the Senate of the United States who does not believe that our troops and our sailors who are in the Persian Gulf are in an area of imminent hostilities." Weicker queried: "How can anyone in this Nation . . . say that there are no hostilities or the situation is not imminent of hostility? The mines . . . certainly are not beachballs with which people play. The warships of the U.S. Navy are not cruise ships. It reeks of hostility. It is a definition of the word 'hostility' in and of itself." Hatfield argued that the higher "imminent danger" pay that the secretary of defense authorized for troops in the Persian Gulf indicated that imminent hostilities existed. "But still the administration insists the war powers resolution does not apply," Hatfield lamented.[62] In the end, despite many procedural wranglings on the question of the War Powers Resolution, the Senate did not invoke it, largely because it acquiesced in the Persian Gulf policy. Majority leader Robert C. Byrd, Armed Services Committee Chairman Sam Nunn, and the committee's ranking minority member, John Warner, all opposed triggering the War Powers Resolution. To fortify them, the administration sought to upgrade its consultation with congressional leaders. On the House side, the effort to invoke the War Powers Resolution, led by Representative Peter A. DeFazio, withered once 111 members resorted to the judiciary for redress.

By the summer of 1987, the War Powers Resolution seemed somewhat an empty shell. In exasperation, Senator Adams declared: "If we do not want to apply this War Powers Act, then let us get it off the books. But if it is there, each of us, under our oath that we have undertaken . . . should apply the statute as it is there." "What we have not seen is the Congress accept its role and responsibility under the Constitution and under the War Powers Act," he declared. Remarked Representative DeFazio, "The War Powers Resolution

61. Collier, "The War Powers Resolution," p. 43.
62. *Congressional Record*, daily ed., September 18, 1987, pp. S12336–37; and September 22, 1987, p. S12486.

doesn't work. It's that simple."[63] Still, the resolution was a reminder to Congress of the need to assess its role in war powers decisions. It began to do so with the creation in 1988 of a special Subcommittee on War Powers of the Senate Foreign Relations Committee, chaired by Senator Joseph Biden, and through an examination of the issue by the House Foreign Affairs Committee.

Repairing the Resolution

In enacting the War Powers Resolution, Congress sought to claim a role in the decision to commit troops to combat. The measure's very existence provides an outlet for legislators who seek to challenge executive action. Moreover, the resolution has served to create an institutional memory of interbranch debates about the wisdom of various military actions. In the view of some observers, the War Powers Resolution has set the outer boundaries for the presidential commitment of armed forces short of a formal declaration of war. That presidents seek to anticipate congressional reaction as part of their political calculations is undoubtedly true. Even so, it would be hard to make the case that the War Powers Resolution has deterred chief executives bent on engaging troops.

Indeed, a growing sentiment in Congress maintains that the War Powers Resolution needs repair. According to this view, presidents do not adhere to its provisions, largely because of constitutional objections, but also because of concern about the law's sixty-day troop withdrawal provisions. Since 1973 chief executives have filed twenty reports pursuant to the War Powers Resolution; on only one occasion did a president cite section 4(a)(1), and then only when the military action had ended (the *Mayaguez* incident). One can state with reasonable confidence that chief executives are unlikely to invoke section 4(a)(1), especially if they believe that troops may have to be committed beyond sixty days and if there is a risk that Congress will not vote to approve the action during that period. Even when a president could probably have secured such affirmation—for instance, the Persian Gulf episodes—he chose not to seek it.

For its part, the legislative branch has been largely unwilling to

63. *Congressional Record*, daily ed., September 22, 1987, p. S12487; August 7, 1987, p. S11567; and March 1, 1988, p. E423.

challenge the president, particularly in those situations in which the chief executive could rally public opinion—as is almost always the case in the early phases of military confrontation. In the one instance in which Congress on its own authority invoked section 4(a)(1), the Multinational Force in Lebanon Resolution, the legislature authorized the continued role of the marines in the multinational force for another eighteen months. The judiciary, quite prudently, has steadfastly avoided the attempts of some legislators to trigger the War Powers Resolution's sixty-day cutoff procedure. If Congress will not do what it has the power to do, then why should the courts?

Any amendments to the War Powers Resolution must be grounded in an appreciation of the institutional interests of the executive and Congress. Presidents, as discussed earlier, have perceived their interests in terms of maximizing discretion over foreign policy. That has meant a reluctance to involve Congress in war-making decisions. In reality, the executive will have difficulty sustaining extended military action without popular approval and congressional support. That argues for some legislative involvement in the decisionmaking process.

There is no single congressional view. A few would grant the president virtually absolute discretion and call for repeal of the resolution. Some argue that the resolution should be basically preserved with some mechanism for judicial enforcement. Still others would call for parity with the executive branch. However, the emerging consensus appears to be that even if the president is to have primacy in the decision to commit troops, Congress should be consulted and involved in the decisionmaking process in a meaningful way. This perspective concedes the president discretion to commit forces, but only after legislative involvement. Implicitly, this position acknowledges that Congress is generally unwilling to challenge the president, so if Congress is to have a role, the law must be changed to make it more likely that the president will comply.

It is within the context of these institutional interests that the political viability of various proposals can be assessed. In the current climate, some are nonstarters. It is hard to imagine that President George Bush would sign legislation shortening the period he could keep forces in hostile situations without congressional authorization. Similarly, no president is likely to approve such legislation, even if it enumerates exceptions for emergency use, such as response to or forestalling of an armed attack against the United States or its forces or the protection of U.S. citizens while evacuating them. Within

Congress, the exceptions clause is likely to provoke the same reaction as when it was first proposed: a fear that such a provision could provide blanket authorization for a president determined to abuse it.

Efforts to repeal the War Powers Resolution are likely to fail as well. Not long before his nomination as secretary of defense, Dick Cheney called for repeal, arguing not only that the War Powers Resolution is "based on wrongheaded constitutional assumptions that produce mischievous and dangerous results," but also that Congress already "has plenty of constitutional and political power to stop a president whenever it wants to."[64] However, outright repeal is unlikely, if for no other reason than it would symbolize to many in Congress a surrender of its role in war-making decisions.

Similarly, the proposal that the courts be given authority to start the sixty-day clock when the president fails to file a section 4(a)(1) report and Congress declines to trigger the withdrawal provision is predicated on the assumption that the legislature lacks the institutional will to participate in the decision to make war. That proposal, moreover, would require the courts to render judgments about military situations that they are not equipped to make.

Perhaps, given the diversity of perspectives, a promising approach is that advanced by Senators Byrd, Warner, Nunn, George Mitchell, David Boren, William Cohen, and John Danforth, with growing support in the House (though not from Foreign Affairs Chairman Dante Fascell).[65] Stripped to its bare essentials, the amendment would repeal the automatic requirement for withdrawal of troops sixty days after the president submits a section 4(a)(1) report. Through a joint resolution that would receive expedited attention, Congress could either authorize the military action or require withdrawal. In other words, the presumption would be reversed: troops would be allowed to stay unless Congress voted otherwise. At the core of this approach is consultation. As Representative Lee Hamilton recently wrote:

The first priority in reform efforts is improved communications. A foreign-policy crisis is no time to discover that the channels of communication do not work. The executive must recognize that

64. Dick Cheney, "Congressional Overreaching in Foreign Policy," in Robert A. Goldwin and Robert A. Licht, eds., *Foreign Policy and the Constitution* (Washington: American Enterprise Institute for Public Policy Research, 1990), p. 120.

65. See, for example, S. 2, "A Bill to Amend the War Powers Resolution," *Congressional Record*, daily ed., January 25, 1989, p. S167.

Congress is not an obstacle to be overcome but a valuable source
of opinion, support and feedback. In turn, Congress must be
sensitive to legitimate security concerns that are raised by broader
consultations.[66]

The approach described above would require that the president consult
regularly with a group of six: the majority and minority leaders of
both houses, plus the Speaker of the House and the president pro
tempore of the Senate. Following a request from a majority of this
group, the commander in chief would consult with an expanded group
of eighteen, consisting of the leadership and the ranking and minority
members of the Committees on Armed Services, Foreign Affairs (and
Relations), and Intelligence. That group would also have the authority
to ascertain whether the president should have reported the introduction
of forces, and then to introduce a joint resolution of approval or one
requiring withdrawal.

From the perspective of the executive branch, this approach has the
virtue of eliminating the provision that troops would have to be
withdrawn as a consequence of congressional inaction. With this
problem removed, a chief executive might find it in his interest to
invoke the War Powers Resolution with the objective of securing
congressional support. To be sure, Congress still would have the
authority to require the withdrawal of troops. But the president could
veto a joint resolution requiring disengagement; Congress would rarely
be able to muster the two-thirds vote needed to override the veto. To
the extent that the measure encourages presidential compliance, it also
restores legitimacy to the law.

From the vantage point of Congress, this kind of reform gives the
legislative branch what it seeks most: meaningful consultation, along
with some responsibility. A statute enacting any such reform should
be clear as to two points. First, it should define "consult" as not merely
"inform," but also as "engage in discussion with" and "seek the advice
of" legislators. Second, the legislation should specify which members
of Congress should be consulted. Perhaps the consultative mechanism
should provide seats for not only the leadership, but also for some
junior members on a rotating basis, as a means of securing wider
support.

66. Lee H. Hamilton, "War Powers: Revise Resolution to Make It Work," *Wall
Street Journal*, March 20, 1989, p. A14.

The Constitution may be, in the oft-quoted phrase, an "invitation to struggle" over foreign policy. But it is more than that. The constitutional vision calls for the interplay of diverse interests, responding to their own incentives, to achieve national purposes. Governmental institutions are the medium through which energies are absorbed and outcomes realized. Accommodation can flow from constructive tension. The Constitution, in short, is also an invitation to comity. The debate about the War Powers Resolution bears with it the hope of a healthier relationship between the executive and the legislature.

Intelligence:
Welcome to the
American Government

GREGORY F. TREVERTON

CONGRESS WAS deeply engaged in intelligence at the beginning of the Republic: in 1775 the Second Continental Congress set in motion covert operations to secure French supplies for Washington's army. The next year Thomas Paine, the first congressional "leaker," was dismissed for disclosing information from the Committee of Secret Correspondence. For the next century and a half, however, the congressional role lapsed. A disengaged America had little need for foreign intelligence, and for the first thirty years after World War II the preeminence of the president and the imminence of the cold war induced Congress to leave intelligence to the executive, for better or worse.

Events of the 1970s changed that. Since then, the role of Congress in intelligence matters has increased dramatically, and the intelligence community has become like the rest of the government. In the intelligence agencies' relations with Congress, especially, they are coming to resemble the Agriculture or Commerce departments. The House and Senate Intelligence committees have become, like other committees on Capitol Hill, the patrons as well as the overseers of "their" government agencies.

Intelligence officials are finding, as have other members of the executive branch before them, that congressional patrons who control purse strings are also tempted to tell them how to run their business. For their part, members of Congress find secret oversight politically awkward. In the words of Republican Senator William Cohen, then vice-chairman of the Senate Intelligence Committee: "It's not exactly a Faustian bargain, . . . But if we wish to have access, we are bound."[1]

This chapter draws on but greatly expands chap. 7 of Gregory F. Treverton, *Covert Action: The Limits of Intervention in the Postwar World* (Basic Books, 1987). The author thanks Loch Johnson and Robert J. Kurz for comments on earlier versions of this chapter; his colleagues in the Harvard Project on Intelligence and Policy, Ernest May and Richard E. Neustadt, for discussion that shaped the chapter; and William E. Kline for his Philippine case study.

1. Quoted in Susan F. Rasky, "Walking a Tightrope on Intelligence Issues," *New York Times*, October 11, 1988, p. A26.

The paradox of secret oversight by the branch of government meant to be characterized by open debate is sharpest in the realm of covert action. There, intelligence officials are tempted to see their congressional overseers as potential leakers, while the overseers fear being misled or deceived or becoming responsible, in secret, for covert actions they cannot easily stop even if they oppose them.

Yet the oversight process has not worked badly even for covert action; ironically, the recent Iran-contra debacle is testimony to that judgment even as it also testifies to the limits whereby process can impose wisdom on the making of American public policy. This grappling over secret *operations* gets the headlines; as a vexing constitutional question, it merits them.

However, covert action is only a small part of oversight, and despite the publicity accorded it, the balance between executive and Congress in the making of foreign policy is probably more affected by a related change: Congress now receives virtually the same intelligence *analysis* as the executive. One senior Central Intelligence Agency (CIA) official described the agency as "involuntarily poised equidistant between the executive and legislative branches."[2] Asking whether intelligence agencies can serve both masters is shorthand for a wider question about the implications of intelligence joining an American government in which the fault lines sometimes divide along the executive-legislative gap but often cut across it.

"Plausible Denial" and the "Buddy System"

Since its first serious investigations of intelligence in the mid-1970s, Congress has become steadily more involved in secret operations. Its most recent investigations into the Iran-contra affair, however, testify to the continuing puzzles, constitutional and procedural. These questions run through all of foreign affairs but are sharper in the realm of intelligence.

The investigations in the mid-1970s began very much in the shadow of Watergate; the press was full of intimations that intelligence agencies had acted outside the law, beyond the ken of Congress and the control even of presidents. Democratic Senator Frank Church, the chairman of the Senate investigating committee, likened the CIA to a "rogue

2. Quoted in "Taking Toshiba Public," Case C15-88-858.0, Harvard University, Kennedy School of Government, 1988, p. 5.

elephant on the rampage."[3] In the event, the committees did not find
much evidence of rogue elephants in the CIA or other agencies involved
in foreign intelligence, like the National Security Agency or the
Defense Intelligence Agency.[4]

Yet the committees did find a troubling looseness in the control of
covert action. Part of the problem was CIA abuse of so-called plausible
denial, a practice intended to protect the American government, a
practice also abused by Oliver North and John Poindexter during the
arms sales to Iran in the 1980s. A second part of the problem was a
kind of "buddy system" in which oversight consisted of informal
conversations between the director of central intelligence (DCI) and a
few senior members of Congress. Neither plausible denial nor the
buddy system emerged because the CIA had broken free of its political
masters. Rather, they emerged because that was how successive
administrations and Congress had wanted it.

In 1975, testifying before the Senate committee—often called the
"Church committee" after its chairman—about charges that the CIA
had tried to kill Fidel Castro, former DCI Richard Helms was vivid
in describing plausible denial and almost plaintive in drawing its
implications:

> It was made abundantly clear . . . to everybody involved in the
> operation that the desire was to get rid of the Castro regime and
> to get rid of Castro . . . the point was that no limitations were
> put on this injunction. . . . one . . . grows up in [the] tradition
> of the time and I think that any of us would have found it very
> difficult to discuss assassinations with a President of the U.S. I
> just think we all had the feeling that we're hired out to keep
> those things out of the Oval Office.[5]

If he had ever thought he would later have to testify before Congress

3. At a press conference at the Capitol, July 19, 1975, quoted in Gregory F.
Treverton, *Covert Action: The Limits of Intervention in the Postwar World* (Basic Books,
1987), p. 5.

4. The committees did find some rogue elephants in domestic intelligence activities,
especially those of the Federal Bureau of Investigation.

5. *Alleged Assassination Plots Involving Foreign Leaders*, An Interim Report of the
Senate Select Committee to Study Governmental Operations with Respect to Intelligence
Activities, S. Rept. 94-465, 94 Cong. 1 sess. (Government Printing Office, 1975),
p. 149. (Hereafter cited as *Assassination Report*.)

about what he had done, Helms reflected, he would have made sure that his orders were clear and in writing.

By their own testimony, not a single member of the National Security Council (NSC) outside the CIA knew of, much less authorized, those plots.[6] Even inside the CIA, officials spoke with each other about these operations only in riddles. And if they spoke of them at all with those outside the CIA charged with approving covert operations, they did so indirectly or in circumlocutions. Thus, in 1975 the Church committee spent hours trying to unravel whether terse references in documents to "disappear" or "direct positive action" or "neutralize" referred to assassination. It could not be sure. And that was precisely the point of plausible denial. Those CIA officials who spoke in circumlocutions could feel they had done their duty as they understood it. Their political superiors could understand what they would, ask for more information if they desired, but also forebear from asking. If things went awry, they could, if they chose, disclaim knowledge and do so more or less honestly.

These effects of plausible denial are extreme in the instance of the Cuban assassination plots, but similar effects ran through covert actions of the 1950s and 1960s. Dean Rusk, who served Presidents Kennedy and Johnson as secretary of state, observed that he routinely knew little of CIA operations: "I never saw a budget of the CIA, for example."[7] Of thousands of covert action projects between 1949 and 1968, only some 600 received consideration outside the CIA by the National Security Council body then charged with reviewing covert operations.

For its part, the American Congress was more interested in making sure the CIA had what it needed in the fight against communism than in overseeing its operations. The fate of several congressional initiatives for improving oversight that came to naught in these early years is eloquent testimony to the mood of the time and the temper of Congress. In early 1955 Democratic Senator Mike Mansfield, later chairman of the Foreign Relations Committee, introduced a resolution calling for a joint oversight committee. The resolution had thirty-five cosponsors. It also had the strong opposition not only of the executive but also of

6. See *Assassination Report*, p. 108ff.
7. Richard B. Russell Library, Oral History No. 86, taped by Hughes Cates, February 22, 1977, University of Georgia, Athens, Georgia, cited in Loch K. Johnson, *America's Secret Power: The CIA in a Democratic Society* (Oxford University Press, 1989), p. 108.

the "club" of senior senators. In hearings on the resolution, Mansfield
elicited the following comment from Senator Leverett Saltonstall, the
ranking Republican on the Armed Services Committee:

> It is not a question of reluctance on the part of the CIA officials
> to speak to us. Instead, it is a question of our reluctance, if you
> will, to seek information and knowledge on subjects which I
> personally, as a Member of Congress and as a citizen, would
> rather not have, unless I believed it to be my responsibility to
> have it because it might involve the lives of American citizens.[8]

In April 1956 the resolution was voted down, 59-27, with a half dozen
cosponsors voting against it.

The debate did, however, result in the creation of formal CIA
subcommittees in both Armed Services committees. Yet the buddy
system remained largely unchanged. Allen Dulles, the near legend,
was DCI until the Bay of Pigs fiasco in 1961; relaxed and candid with
senior members, he had their absolute trust. In the Senate Armed
Services Committee, Senator Richard Russell appointed to the formal
subcommittee those senators with whom he had been meeting informally on CIA matters—Saltonstall and Harry Byrd. Later he added
Lyndon Johnson and Styles Bridges. When, in 1957, the Appropriations
Committee formed a subcommittee for the CIA, its members were
Russell, Byrd, and Bridges. They both authorized and appropriated,
often at the same meeting. Most CIA business continued to be conducted
as before—by Dulles and Russell, meeting informally.

The Climate Changes

The Bay of Pigs marked the end of an era for the CIA. It was a
stunning defeat for an agency known only for success. Dulles and his
deputy, Richard Bissell, were eased out of their jobs. Yet neither
executive procedures for, nor congressional oversight of, intelligence
changed all that much.

A decade later, with the big expansion in covert action in Asia as

8. Quoted in "History of the Central Intelligence Agency," in *Supplementary Detailed
Staff Reports on Foreign and Military Intelligence*, bk. 4, *Final Report*, S. Rept. 94-755,
Senate Select Committee to Study Governmental Operations with Respect to Intelligence
Activities, 94 Cong. 2 sess. (GPO, 1976), p. 54.

the war in Vietnam heated up, the executive branch undertook somewhat more formal procedures. For instance, the NSC body charged with reviewing covert action (after 1970 called the 40 committee) considered operations in Chile on twenty-three separate occasions between March 1970 and October 1973, the period surrounding the presidency of Salvador Allende. Still, in numbers, most covert action projects continued not to be approved by anyone outside the CIA. By the early 1970s only about a fourth of all covert actions came before the NSC review body.[9]

During the 1960s more committees of Congress were receiving more information from the CIA than in the early days; however, about clandestine operations the CIA did not often volunteer information and Congress did not often ask. The role of Congress had not moved from receiving information to overseeing operations. In 1961 after the Bay of Pigs, and again in 1966, Democratic Senator Eugene McCarthy attempted unsuccessfully to revive the idea of a CIA oversight committee.

Watergate and Chile, coming on the heels of the war in Vietnam, changed all that. So did the passing of a congressional generation and the enacting of internal reforms that dispersed authority away from committee chairmen. The buddy system, smooth and private, had depended on a handful of congressional barons. Thus, as a former CIA director of congressional liaison put it, "When Chairmen Russell, [Carl] Hayden, [Mendel] Rivers, and [Carl] Vinson retired between 1965 and 1971, CIA's congressional constituency retired with them."[10] Or as William Colby, the DCI at the time of the first congressional investigations, later recalled:

> There had been a time when the joint hearing held by the Senate's intelligence subcommittees would have been deemed sufficient [to end the matter]. Senators with the seniority and clout of [John] McClellan and [John] Stennis then could easily

9. *Covert Action in Chile, 1963–1973*, Committee Print, Senate Select Committee to Study Governmental Operations with Respect to Intelligence Activities, 94 Cong. 1 sess. (GPO, 1975), pp. 41–42.

10. David Gries, "The CIA and Congress: Uneasy Partners," *Studies in Intelligence* (September 1987), p. 77. This is an unclassified article in a CIA journal. In the original, "Vinson" is rendered "Vincent," a typographical error that is, perhaps, inadvertent testimony to just how foreign the Congress was to the CIA.

have squelched any demands for further action on the part of their junior colleagues. But this was no longer the case.[11]

Congress's disinclination to ask about secret operations was the first change. Neither reticence nor deference were hallmarks of the congressional class of 1974, elected as Watergate played out on the nation's television screens. Congress passed the Hughes-Ryan act of 1974, the operative paragraph of which reads:

> No funds appropriated under the authority of this or any other Act may be expended by or on behalf of the [CIA] for operations in foreign countries, other than activities intended solely for obtaining necessary intelligence, unless and until the President finds that each such operation is important to the national security of the United States and reports, in a timely fashion, a description and scope of such operation to the appropriate committees of the Congress.[12]

From the verb "finds" came the noun "finding"—a written document bearing the president's signature. As was often the case, Congress sought to change the pattern of executive action not by making specific decisions but rather by changing the process by which decisions were made. The Hughes-Ryan act was intended to end the abuse of plausible denial displayed in the Cuban assassination plots, which seemed to have confused procedures within the executive—and deluded Congress—more than it protected anyone.

Hughes-Ryan required the president to put his name and his reputation on the line. It was meant to ensure that there would be no future wrangles such as those over assassinations. Covert actions, wise or stupid, would reflect presidential decision; there would be no doubt that someone was in charge. It also meant that members of Congress would find it harder to assert that they had been kept in the dark. Less often could they speechify in professed ignorance of covert action. The "appropriate committees" now became six: the Intelligence subcommittees of Armed Services and Appropriations in both houses plus the Foreign Affairs and Foreign Relations committees.

11. William Colby and Peter Forbath, *Honorable Men: My Life in the CIA* (Simon and Schuster, 1978), pp. 402–03.

12. Officially, Foreign Assistance Act of 1974, sec. 32 (88 Stat. 1804).

Tending the "Government's" Secrets

A year later Congress established the Church committee and a parallel investigating committee in the House, chaired by New York Democrat Otis Pike. Those committees, the Church committee in particular, represented an innovation in constitutional relations between the executive and Congress.[13] At the heart of the wrangling between the committees and the Ford administration over access to classified documents lay a constitutional issue: were those secret documents, written and classified by the CIA or State, the property of the executive only? Or were they the "government's" documents, to which Congress should have access on terms decided by it and which could be declassified by its decision as well as that of the executive? Popular usage mirrors ambiguity about what constitutes "the government," particularly in foreign affairs. Constitutionally, Congress is a coequal branch of the government, yet people often speak of "the government" more narrowly to refer to a particular administration in power.

The committees did not resolve the question of who controlled documents. In the nature of the system, they could not. But Congress and the executive did move a long way toward the view that even in matters of clandestine operations, Congress has its own right to the "government's" secret documents and that it bears the responsibility that goes with that right.

The Ford administration was a grudging partner in adjusting the constitutional bargain. A few in the administration, Colby foremost among them, believed the changes were fundamentally correct; others felt that, given the public mood, the administration simply had no choice. The administration had something of a dual approach to the Church committee. At one level, that of executive prerogatives in foreign affairs, it was opposed to the investigation and its results. It held, thus, that publication of an interim report on assassinations was not only wrong but also a mistake that would harm the reputation of the United States.

At another level, however, it was prepared to work with the committee, particularly to protect intelligence sources and methods. In that regard the administration and the committee shared an interest;

13. For an intriguing account of the Senate Select Committee, see Loch K. Johnson, *A Season of Inquiry: The Senate Intelligence Investigation* (University Press of Kentucky, 1985).

the committee had no reason to want to endanger intelligence methods or agents' lives. In the case of the assassination report, the issue boiled down to whether the committee would publish the names of some thirty-three CIA officers. The administration argued that publishing the names would tarnish reputations and might, in one or two instances, endanger the individuals in question. Colby even took the issue to district court.

In the end, the committee and the administration reached a sensible compromise. The committee agreed to delete the names of twenty of the officers, required for neither the substance nor the credibility of the report. The remaining names were left in. Most were those of senior officers and were already in the public domain. The committee felt, moreover, that senior officials should be held publicly accountable for their actions. Like most compromises, it pleased neither side fully but was one with which both could live.[14]

In seeking to establish its position, the Church committee was assiduous about leaks. Not a single secret worth mention got out.[15] The same could not be said of the Pike committee, whose entire final report leaked into the press in 1976 after the full House had voted not to release it until the president certified that it did not contain information that would harm U.S. intelligence activities.[16]

When the House, like the Senate, later decided to establish a permanent intelligence committee, the Pike committee experience, which had created acrimony not only between the committee and the administration but within the House as well, was much on the House's collective mind. As one sophisticated former staffer observed: "The message from the House was clear: no more fiascos. The new . . . committee would have to stay in line; the honor of the House was at stake."[17]

The House did not agree to a permanent committee until 1977, a year after the Senate. The vote was closer—227–171 in the House, compared with 75–22 in the Senate; and the House committee was

---

14. For instance, Colby regards the outcome as "not unreasonable." See Colby and Forbath, *Honorable Men*, p. 429.

15. The Church committee was more often the victim of leaks than the perpetrator. See Johnson, *Season of Inquiry*, pp. 206–07.

16. It was published by the *Village Voice* as "The CIA Report the President Doesn't Want You to Read," February 16 and 23, 1976.

17. Loch Johnson, "The U.S. Congress and the CIA: Monitoring the Dark Side of Government," *Legislative Studies Quarterly*, vol. 5 (November 1980), pp. 491–92.

granted less autonomy and control over classified information. For instance, the Senate committee was authorized to disclose classified information over the president's objection, while in the House that right rested with the full body. The House committee was also smaller and more partisan—13 members, 9 of them Democrats, in a House of 435, compared with 15, 8 Democrats, in a Senate of 100. The House Democrats were chosen by the Speaker, not the majority caucus, evidence of a desire to retain control. By contrast, the Senate committee, following the relatively bipartisan approach of the Church committee, made the ranking minority member the vice-chairman, a unique arrangement in Congress.

Initially, the two congressional investigations resulted only in two new permanent oversight committees, increasing the number of congressional overseers of intelligence from six committees to eight, albeit ones with more access to information. Yet the institutional legacy of permanent select committees in each house of Congress has turned out to be an important one. The committees established the principle of rotating memberships, limiting tenures to six years in the House and eight in the Senate, to broaden their representation within Congress, thus guarding against a recurrence of the buddy system in image or in fact.

Reflecting their different lineages, the Senate committee was initially more self-confident in its approach to oversight. A cadre of members and staff from the Church committee moved to the new permanent committee, while the House started afresh, staffed mostly by ex-intelligence officials. Over time, however, the House staff, though smaller and divided along partisan lines, acquired the reputation of being more professional, especially in those aspects of oversight that seldom find their way into headlines—budgets, collection systems, and intelligence products.

Over time, too, the committees were stamped by the styles and personalities of their chairmen as well as by the character of their parent bodies. The House committee was chaired in the 1980s by Edward Boland and Lee Hamilton, members of experience and stature in the legislature by comparison with their counterparts on the Senate side, Republican David Durenberger and Democrat Patrick Leahy. The Republican ascendance to control of the Senate in 1980 not only brought new young senators to control of the committee, but also shifted the focal point for congressional scrutiny of secret operations to the House. And it frayed cooperation between the two committees.

By the latter half of the 1980s, with the Democrats again in control of the Senate, the Senate committee reflected its parent body in being less partisan than the House. Its Democrats were mostly moderates, senators like David Boren, Sam Nunn, and Ernest Hollings, who had few counterparts on the House committee. Some of those moderate Democrats, especially southerners, were attracted to the Intelligence Committee as a way to become active in foreign affairs without acquiring the liberal taint of the Foreign Relations, Committee.

The Carter administration, disinclined from the start to resort to covert action, found its intelligence relations with Congress easy. It first pressed the House to establish a permanent intelligence committee, then cooperated with Congress in passing the Intelligence Oversight Act of 1980, the most important law in the realm of covert action. The act cut back the executive's reporting requirements for covert action to the two Intelligence committees; eight committees were too unwieldy for both executive and Congress, and virtually invited executive charges of being "too leaky." At the same time, however, the act charged the two committees with informing other relevant committees, especially Foreign Affairs, Foreign Relations, and the two Appropriations committees. It also made clear that Congress wanted to be notified of all covert actions, not just those carried out by the CIA; secret executive recourse to other agencies, in particular the military, was denied.

Congress also tiptoed toward prior notification of covert action; the "timely fashion" of the Hughes-Ryan act, which allowed notification after the fact (within twenty-four hours came to be the understanding), became "fully and currently informed," including "any significant anticipated intelligence activity," in the 1980 act. Yet notifying Congress still was not a "condition precedent to the initiation" of covert action. And the act gave the president another escape hatch, for in emergencies he was permitted to limit notice to eight members—the chairmen and ranking minority members of the Intelligence committees, the Speaker and minority leader of the House, and the majority and minority leaders of the Senate—the "gang of eight" or the "eight wise men," depending on the describer's inclinations.

The "Covert" War in Central America

The tussle between executive and Congress, which had been restrained when operators and overseers shared the view that the covert instrument should be used sparingly, grew more passionate with the surge of covert actions in the 1980s. The Reagan administration came into office determined to make covert assistance to "freedom fighters" around the world a key element of its global pressure on the Soviet Union. Strikingly, in light of what came later, Reagan's executive order 12333 gave the CIA full responsibility for covert actions except in time of war or by specific presidential instruction.[18]

With the new administration, however, attitudes changed more than directives or procedures. One congressional staffer referred to men like NSC staffer Lieutenant Colonel Oliver North as "field grades," people eager for action, long on energy, but short on political savvy. William Miller, the staff director of both the Church committee and the first permanent Senate Intelligence Committee, observed that the CIA and its sister agencies were led in the late 1970s by people who had been through the experience of investigation and reform. They were "so immersed in the constitutional questions that they could recite chapter and verse. Questions of law and balance occurred naturally to them." By contrast, the Reagan leadership was dominated by "advocates, people who were always trying to get around the roadblocks, who were looking for a way to get it done."[19]

In Central America, the long reign of the Somoza family in Nicaragua had come to an end in 1979, bringing to power the regime's armed opponents, the Sandinista National Liberation Front, in uneasy part-nership with a range of civilian opposition groups. Early in its tenure, the Reagan administration charged that the Sandinistas were becoming a base for Cuban and Soviet subversion in the region and, specifically, that they were shipping arms to guerrilla opponents of the U.S.-supported government of El Salvador. At first, the Sandinistas were confronted primarily by remnants of Somoza's hated National Guard who had found sanctuary in Honduras, but over time several of the Sandinistas' original allies fell out with the government. One of them opened a new anti-Sandinista front operating out of Costa Rica.

Congressional opposition to the administration's course in Nicaragua grew in direct proportion to the breakdown in congressional-executive relations. The administration sought to unite the Sandinistas' armed opponents—dubbed the contras—and to support them. Yet the purpose of that covert support seemed a moving target, which suggested to

18. The order was printed in *New York Times*, December 5, 1981, pp. 18–19.
19. Interview, January 16, 1986.

Congress either confusion or deception. In November 1981 President
Reagan signed National Security Council Decision Directive 17,
proposing to build a force of contras to interdict arms shipments from
Nicaragua to the rebels in El Salvador. However, the directive, when
turned into a finding, contained language—"engage in paramilitary
. . . operations in Nicaragua and elsewhere"—that seemed to permit
almost anything.[20] The congressional Intelligence committees first
made clear in their classified reports on the CIA budget that they
opposed covert efforts to overthrow the Sandinista government of
Nicaragua. Then, at the end of 1982, they put that language, as the
Boland amendment, publicly into the appropriations bill. Named for
Edward P. Boland, then chairman of the House Intelligence Committee,
it stipulated that no money could be used "for the purpose of
overthrowing the Government of Nicaragua or provoking a military
exchange between Nicaragua and Honduras."[21]

The aims of America's covert intervention remained in dispute while
the war intensified, especially as the CIA opened a second front in
Costa Rica. In response, Boland and the House Intelligence committee
shifted their focus from appropriations to authorization, proposing not
to limit covert action in Nicaragua but to end it. The House voted to
do so in July 1983. However, the Senate Intelligence committee, with
the Republicans in the majority, was prepared to approve more money
if the administration would be precise about its objectives. The
administration "thoroughly scrubbed" a new finding, which was signed
in September 1983.[22]

In October the House again voted to end the contra program, but
at year's end the House-Senate conference compromised, accepting
the revised presidential finding, which expanded the American aim
from halting arms flows from Nicaragua to pressuring the Sandinistas
to negotiate with their neighbors. However, Congress capped funding
at $24 million, enough for one year's operations, thus requiring the

---

20. This account is drawn primarily from the subsequent congressional investigation,
*Report of the Congressional Committees Investigating the Iran-Contra Affair with Supplemental,
Minority, and Additional Views,* H. Rept. 100-433, S. Rept. 100-216, 100 Cong. 1 sess.
(GPO, 1987) (hereafter cited as *Iran-Contra Affair*); and from the earlier *Report of the
President's Special Review Board* (known as the Tower commission after its chairman,
former Senator John Tower) (GPO, 1987). (Hereafter cited as *Tower Commission.*) The
NSC documents are quoted in *Washington Post,* March 10, 1982.

21. *Report of the Select Committee on Intelligence, U.S. Senate, Jan. 1, 1983 to Dec. 31, 1984,*
S. Rept. 98-665, 98 Cong. 2 sess. (GPO, 1984), pp. 4–5. (Hereafter *Intelligence Report.*)

22. The phrase is Oliver North's, quoted in *Iran-Contra Affair,* p. 35.

administration to return to Congress before the end of the fiscal year if it wanted the program to continue.[23]

Any limited American objective seemed less plausible after revelations early the next year that the CIA itself had mined Nicaraguan harbors. The mining, a new phase in the covert war, was itself an act of war and one that threatened the shipping of both American allies and the Soviet Union. The operation was approved by the president in the winter, probably in December 1983.[24] The Sandinistas protested on January 3, 1984, that the contras were laying mines in Nicaraguan harbors, and the rebel leaders, who plainly had no capacity to lay mines on their own, finally learned their lines and announced on January 8 that they would do so.

On January 31, 1984, DCI William Casey met with the House Intelligence committee and mentioned the mining, though the meeting was primarily about releasing further funds for the overall contra project. The House committee apparently did not share its information with its Senate colleagues, although the CIA may have briefed several members of the Senate committee and its staff. The Senate, however, was pushing toward its February recess, and the administration twice asked for a delay so that Secretary of State George Shultz could also attend. As a result, a full briefing of the Senate committee was delayed, and many, perhaps most, members remained unaware of the operation, especially of the direct CIA role in it.

Casey first met with the full Senate Intelligence committee on March 8, for over an hour, but this meeting too dealt primarily with authorizing the release of funds, over which the Intelligence committee was fighting a jurisdictional battle with Appropriations. Only one sentence dealt with the mining, and it, like the rest of the briefing, was delivered in Casey's inimitable mumble.[25] Many on the committee did not learn of the mining until a month later, and then almost by accident.

23. The House-Senate conference report spoke of Nicaragua "providing military support (including arms, training, and logistical, command and control, and communications facilities) to groups seeking to overthrow the Government of El Salvador." See *Intelligence Report*, pp. 6–7.

24. See Stephen Kinzer, "Nicaraguan Says No Mines Are Left in Nation's Ports," *New York Times*, April 13, 1984, p. A1; Philip Taubman, "How Congress Was Informed of Mining of Nicaragua Ports," *New York Times*, April 16, 1984, p. A1; and Bernard Gwertzman, "C.I.A. Now Asserts It Put Off Session with Senate Unit," *New York Times*, April 17, 1984, p. A1. See also the account in *Intelligence Report*, p. 4ff.

25. Interviews with Intelligence Committee staff members, January 1987.

Casey nodded toward the letter of the law with his brief reference, but the episode angered even Senator Barry Goldwater, the Republican committee chairman and a man not known for his opposition to covert action. He had not understood the reference. When he learned about the mining operation, once the committee staff received a full briefing on April 2, he was furious. His letter to Casey, which leaked into the press, was notable for its unsenatorial prose as well as for its displeasure: "It gets down to one, little, simple phrase: I am pissed off!"[26] In the wake of this episode, the Senate committee moved toward the House's position, and Congress cut off further covert assistance with a second Boland amendment enacted into law in October 1984, thus rejecting the president's request for $21 million more.

By the end of 1984 the House of Representatives had voted three times against paramilitary aid, only to have the operation rescued by House-Senate conferences. Yet despite these losses, the Reagan administration was succeeding in framing the debate on its own ground. Americans' deep ambivalence—their fears of U.S. involvement competed with their distaste for the Sandinistas—left covert support standing as a "middle option," cheap in money and American blood, and hard for members of Congress, even Democrats, to vote against lest they be branded "soft on communism" by a popular president.

In early 1985 President Reagan again asked for aid to the contras, this time for $14 million. The House again voted down the aid after a sharp debate. However, when Sandinista leader Daniel Ortega unwisely journeyed to Moscow just after the vote, those Democrats who had voted against covert aid looked soft and foolish. They responded by enacting economic sanctions, largely symbolic, against Nicaragua. In August 1985 Congress compromised on $27 million in "nonmilitary" aid to the contras; this was not to be administered by the CIA, and the agency was barred from direct contact with the contras or assistance in their training. Congress did not restore CIA funding for this purpose until October 1986.

This off-again, on-again funding, deeply frustrating to those in the Reagan administration most committed to the contras, bred circumventions of the congressional restrictions—efforts suspected in press accounts as early as the spring of 1985. The second Boland amendment

26. The letter was dated April 9; see Joanne Omang and Don Oberdorfer, "Senate Votes, 84–12, to Condemn Mining of Nicaraguan Ports," *Washington Post*, April 11, 1984, p. A16.

applied to the CIA, the Defense Department, and "any other agency or entity involved in intelligence."[27] Some in the administration felt it did not prevent the NSC staff or other officials from seeking aid from other sources. By early 1984, as the $24 million ran out, the president directed the NSC staff, in the words of national security adviser Robert McFarlane, "to keep the contras together 'body and soul.' " Casey and other officials began to approach governments ranging from Israel to Brunei to Saudia Arabia and quietly canvassed private sources in the United States, South Korea, Taiwan, and Latin America. That private support totaled some $34 million during the period of the aid cutoff.[28]

By May 1984, when the congressional appropriation ran out, Oliver North, the NSC staff's deputy director for political-military affairs, had become coordinator of the private support, dubbed "the Enterprise" by those involved. In October when Congress barred any CIA involvement, the agency issued a "cease and desist" order to its stations. Nevertheless, about a dozen CIA officers remained involved in North's operation, apparently construing his role to signify White House authorization. By the fall of 1985, North was overseeing the shipping of privately purchased arms to the contras and the construction of a secret airfield in Costa Rica. North, who also called his operation "Project Democracy," relied on a network of conservative organizations and ex-military men, one of whom, retired general Richard V. Secord, was also a key conduit for arms sales to Iran.

In the fall of 1986 a Beirut newspaper published a bizarre account of a secret mission to Iran the previous May by former national security adviser McFarlane. The account, which first seemed another piece of partisan Middle East nonsense, turned out to be true. McFarlane's delivery of U.S. weapons to Iran was part of a sequence running back to August 1985. The first two shipments had been made by Israel, through middlemen, with U.S. approval and assurance that depleted Israeli stocks would be replenished. The operation, also managed day to day by North, was so closely held that even the CIA was at first cut out, though Casey himself was central. Critical meetings were held with no analytic papers prepared beforehand and no record of decisions kept afterward.

North sought and received CIA help in November 1985 when, in

27. *Iran-Contra Affair*, p. 41.

28. The quote and the estimate are both from *Iran-Contra Affair*, pp. 37 and 4, respectively.

a comedy of errors, Secord could not get one shipment through Portugal to Israel. When he heard of the CIA involvement, John McMahon, the agency's deputy director, angrily barred any further CIA involvement without a presidential finding. The next month the president signed one finding to provide retroactive approval for the shipments; the new national security adviser, Admiral John Poindexter, destroyed that finding a year later because, he later testified, it would have been embarassing to the president.[29]

The president approved another finding on January 17, 1986, "to establish contact with moderate elements within and outside the Government of Iran by providing these elements with arms, equipment and related materiel." However, the accompanying background paper, prepared by North, was explicit about the link to getting U.S. hostages out of Lebanon: "This approach . . . may well be our *only* way to achieve the release of the Americans held in Beirut. . . . If all of the hostages are not released after the first shipment of 1,000 weapons, further transfers would cease."[30]

In February, American arms were first shipped directly from the United States by the CIA to Israel for transfer to Iran. Three other shipments were made, the last in late October. In all, some 2,000 TOW antitank weapons, as well as other weapons and spare parts, were sold to Iran. Three U.S. hostages were released, but three more were taken during the course of the operation.

The strange tale became more bizarre when it was revealed that the profits of the Iranian arms sales had been diverted to support the Nicaraguan contras. The arms had been sold to Iran for nearly $16 million more than the CIA had paid the Pentagon for them. In a scheme masterminded by North, the profits were then laundered through Swiss bank accounts, to be drawn on by the contras. When the scheme was revealed, North was fired, and his boss, Poindexter, resigned.

The story unfolded first through an executive investigating panel, named by the president in December 1986 and chaired by former Senator John Tower. Then Congress began a joint Senate-House investigation in January 1987, which treated the nation to the spectacle of public testimony by the central figures, most notably Oliver North,

29. *Iran-Contra Affair*, p. 7.
30. The finding is printed in *Tower Commission*, pp. B60, B66 (emphasis in the original).

through the hot summer of 1987. The focus of both investigations was narrowly the diversion of profits from the Iran arms sales to the contras: had the president authorized or known of it? This charge remained unproven. The investigations, however, did what Congress had been unable, in part unwilling, to do before—unravel the trail of private support for the contras.

The narrow initial focus broadened further through the criminal trials of McFarlane, North, and Poindexter. McFarlane, distraught to the point of breakdown by what had been done, pleaded guilty to lying to Congress. North, the loyal soldier to the end, asserted his innocence; he was found guilty of destroying documents and other charges but not of deceiving Congress. North's light sentence reflected the discrediting of what had been the administration's primary defense, one accepted by the Tower panel: that the wrongdoing was the result of a small cabal centered on North. North plainly was central, but just as plainly the circle of those involved was wider than the administration wanted to acknowledge.

Sources of Tension: External and Internal

The sources of tension in the intelligence role of Congress are displayed in this history. They are both external and internal to Congress. The houses of Congress not only share a distrust of the executive, no matter which party is in power, but they are also jealous of each other. The two Intelligence committees do not automatically share information, as is apparent in the case of the mining of Nicaragua's harbors. Working together is all the harder if, as in this case, there is both disagreement on the merits and partisan division: Democrats controlled the House, Republicans the Senate from 1980 until 1986. In December 1985, during the time CIA assistance was cut off, the Intelligence committees did approve some money for "communications" and "advice" to the contras, subject to conditions negotiated with the committees. There then ensued an exchange of letters suggesting that the two chairmen were uncertain—or disagreed—over what was permitted and what was proscribed.[31]

Moreover, despite their authority, the Intelligence committees do not monopolize oversight of covert operations. Because covert actions are foreign policy, the Foreign Affairs and Foreign Relations committees

---

31. *Tower Commission*, p. III-22.

have an interest in their authorization; because they cost money, the Appropriations committees have their stakes. The tracks of both sets of jurisdictional battles are visible in the Nicaraguan episode.

However, the sharper tensions arise between Congress and the executive. Even with good will in both branches, congressional overseers have to get deeply into the details of ongoing operations, which is hard for them and uncomfortable for covert operators in the executive branch. Critical details can fall between the cracks: it may be that Senate committee members, like Goldwater, simply were not paying attention when Casey mumbled about the mining. Even their staffs are hard-pressed to keep up with the details of forty-odd covert actions. As one staffer close to the process put it: "How can you know which detail will jump up and bite you? Things move fast. How long did the mining take from beginning to end? A few weeks."[32]

For members, oversight remains something of an unnatural act. They are not hard to interest in intelligence; the lure of secrecy and the mystique of covert operations are a powerful tug on their attentions. At the beginning of the One-hundredth Congress in 1987, sixty members of the House signed up for four openings on the Intelligence Committee. Given rotating memberships, chairs can come quickly; Republican Senator Dave Durenberger became chairman of the Senate committee after only six years. Still, the assignment is one among many, whatever its fascination. Members have little political reason to become involved, still less to take responsibility for particular operations. Politicians' temptation to use their special access to information on morning talk shows competes uneasily with the disciplines of committee membership. Sometimes the special access is, in political terms, more a burden than an asset; as Senator Daniel K. Inouye, the first chairman of the permanent Senate Intelligence Committee, observed, in words not much different from Saltonstall's thirty years before: "How would you like to know a very, very high official of a certain government was on our payroll?"[33]

On balance, members have resolved the contest between responsibility and self-promotion or credit taking in favor of the former. The temptations of the latter are always there, and the dividing line is fine,

32. Interview, January 9, 1986.
33. As quoted in "Overseeing of C.I.A. by Congress Has Produced Decade of Support," *New York Times*, July 7, 1986, p. A10.

but the penalties for being seen to traverse it are high: recent incidents demonstrate both these points. In early 1987 Senator Patrick Leahy, the chairman of the Senate Intelligence Committee, was forced to resign his chairmanship after leaking an unclassified but not yet released version of the committee's Iran-contra report. His action was unwise, but by the standard applied to Leahy, the executive branch would be depopulated. In 1988 House Speaker Jim Wright told a reporter that he had "received clear testimony from CIA people that they have deliberately done things to provoke an overreaction on the part of the Government in Nicaragua."[34] He was not the first to characterize American policy in that way, he later denied he had leaked secret testimony, and the incident was later overshadowed by his other ethical problems. But at the time, invoking the CIA as the source was enough to earn him a storm of criticism.

Iran-contra provides most graphic testimony to the tensions in the congressional role when the committees confront a determined president, especially if they themselves are of divided mind. Administrations, especially one as committed to covert operations as the Reagan administration, are bound to want the flexibility of broad, general findings that give the CIA room to adapt to changing circumstances. Congress is almost equally bound to be wary of signing a blank check, particularly when the administration is committed. McGeorge Bundy, who ran the NSC review committee for the Kennedy and Johnson administrations, emphasized by understatement in 1975 the difficulty reviewers outside the CIA confront: "I think it has happened that an operation is presented in one way to a committee . . . and executed in a way that is different from what the committee thought it had authorized."[35] Norman Mineta, a charter member of the House Intelligence Committee, put his frustration more colorfully in speaking of the executive: "They treat us like mushrooms. Keep us in the dark and feed us a lot of manure."[36]

At more than one point in the Iran-contra affair, administration officials deceived Congress. The January 1986 arms sales finding was explicit: do not tell Congress. The congressional overseers did not find

34. Quoted in Susan F. Rasky, "Walking a Tightrope," *New York Times*, October 11, 1988, p. A26.

35. Quoted in Johnson, *America's Secret Power*, p. 125.

36. Quoted in Martin Tolchin, "Of C.I.A. Games and Disputed Rules," *New York Times*, May 14, 1984, p. A12.

out about the operation until the following autumn—not "fully and currently informed" by anyone's definition. Earlier, the Intelligence committees responded to press accounts that the ban on aid to the contras was being circumvented. In August 1985, for instance, the House asked the administration about North's activities. The response, drafted by McFarlane and North and signed by the former, said that "at no time did I or any member of the National Security Council staff violate the letter or spirit" of the restrictions.[37]

That is outright deception, even granting some ambiguity in the wording of the ban. Did the wording mean no administration official could seek other sources of aid? If so, how could Congress enforce the ban? Its means were limited, as they are in more normal cases. Even if the committees are united in their opposition to an operation, they cannot easily stop it, for if the administration is determined to proceed, it can fund the operation for a year from the CIA Contingency Reserve.[38] Congress has in two cases resorted to public legislation banning covert action—the Boland amendments and the 1976 Clark-Tunney amendment on Angola. These were signs that it did not trust the administration, or its designated overseers of covert action, or both.

In the instance of aid to the contras, however, Congress's will was also limited. In part, it was reluctant to take on a popular president even on a controversial issue. The reluctance is customary in relations between the executive and Congress, even if the president is less popular than Reagan; unless the president is plainly out of step with the American people, members of Congress do not like to confront the presidency. The House Intelligence Committee, like its parent body, was sharply divided over aid to the contras; in later votes, whichever side captured a group of thirty-odd swing votes, mostly Democratic and mostly conservative southerners, carried the day. The Senate, although wavering, probably had a consistent majority favoring aid in principle.

In those circumstances, it is perhaps less surprising that the committees were halfhearted in inquiring into violations of the ban; that their later, retrospective investigations framed the issues narrowly; or that Congress breathed an audible sigh of relief that Reagan had left the presidency by the time new revelations during the trials of his former aides might have raised questions of impeachment.

---

37. *Iran-Contra Affair*, p. 123.
38. Interview with CIA officials, August 1986 and January 1987.

Limits to the System

Aid to the contras was as divisive within the Intelligence committees as it was in the nation, but almost every other covert action has elicited a near consensus, even within the House committee. The congressional overseers have been informed of the covert action and recorded their views; presidents cannot lightly ignore those views, especially if they are held by senior committee members in both parties. Lest the president miss the point, the committees can take a formal vote to underscore their view. More than once, apparently, such votes have induced a president to rescind approval of an operation.[39]

In other cases the committees have said, in the words of one staff member, "Hey, do you know how risky that is?"[40] Hearing an affirmative response, they have let the program go ahead despite their doubts. They did so in the case of Angola, letting the administration resume covert aid to Jonas Savimbi's UNITA (Union for the Total Independence of Angola, in its Portuguese acronym) in 1986 to the tune of some $15 million a year; they did so in that case despite the fact that Lee Hamilton, the House Intelligence committee chairman, took his personal opposition to the House floor.

The Reagan administration wanted to make use of covert action much more frequently than did its predecessor, and the oversight committees, reflecting the mood of Congress and probably of the American people as well, assented to that expansion of covert action. The centerpiece of the Reagan program was aid to the resistance in Afghanistan, begun under the Carter administration, which came to total more than a half billion dollars a year by 1986. Indeed, Congress was if anything ahead of the executive, appropriating unrequested additional money for the resistance in 1983 and pressing the administration to deliver more sophisticated weaponry.

In a sense the system "worked" even in the instance of arms sales to Iran. In deciding to sell, the president pursued a policy that was opposed by his secretaries of state and defense and about which he was afraid to inform the congressional oversight committees. Those should have been warning signals aplenty that the policy was unwise.

---

39. One reported instance was an operation in Suriname in early 1983. See Philip Taubman, "Are U.S. Covert Activities Best Policy on Nicaragua?" *New York Times*, June 15, 1983, p. A1.

40. Interview, January 9, 1987.

If presidents are determined to do something stupid, they will find someone, somewhere, to do it.

In seeking to circumvent the requirements of process, the president, it appears, also set himself up for deception. It was he who was not told when the Iran and contra operations crossed. Keeping Congress in the dark also encouraged looseness within the executive, just as it did a quarter century earlier in the CIA's attempted assassinations of Fidel Castro. North and Poindexter mistakenly construed plausible denial after their own fashion, much the same as Helms and his colleagues had, keeping their president ignorant in order to protect him. Although convinced the president would approve the use of proceeds from the Iranian arms sales for the contras as an "implementation" of his policy, Poindexter "made a very deliberate decision not to ask the President" so that he could "insulate [him] from the decision and provide some future deniability."[41]

When the president's closest advisers become the operators, the president loses them as a source of detached judgment on the operations. They become advocates, not protectors of the president (even if he does not quite realize his need for protection). So it was with McFarlane and Poindexter; once committed, they had reason to overlook the warning signals thrown up by the process. Excluding Congress also excluded one more "political scrub," one more source of advice about what most Americans would find acceptable.

In circumventing the ban on aid to the contras, the Reagan administration's approach to Congress was more one of contempt than of exclusion. An isolated act or two of aiding the contras would have been a close call, given the ambiguity of the ban. But close congressional votes do not excuse establishing "the Enterprise." Poindexter and North were explicit in their later testimony before Congress: "I simply did not want any outside interference," and "I didn't want to tell Congress anything," they said, respectively.[42]

"The Enterprise" is the most troubling piece of the entire story, one the congressional investigations paused over far too briefly. It was an attempt to escape congressional oversight entirely, to construct a CIA outside the American government. As North put it: "Director Casey had in mind . . . an overseas entity that was . . . self-financing,

---

41. Testimony before the Iran-Congress investigation, quoted in *Iran-Contra Affair*, p. 271.

42. *Iran-Contra Affair*, p. 19.

independent of appropriated monies."[43] The idea was dangerous, but the price the administration eventually paid for it was high. If covert actions are to be undertaken, they should be done by the agency of government constructed to do them—the Central Intelligence Agency. It has both the expertise and the accountability.

Information and the Balance of Power

Disputes over secret operations between Congress and the executive have grabbed the headlines, yet the day-to-day balance of power between the two branches has been more affected by the sharply increased availability of intelligence analysis to Congress. This latter change has coincided with the tug-of-war over operations and so has been obscured by it. However, Congress now receives nearly every intelligence item the executive does. In this way, too, the intelligence agencies are coming to have a more customary relationship with Congress, but one that is more awkward for them than for the Agriculture or Commerce departments.

Intelligence agencies, the CIA in particular, were conceived as servants of their executive masters. It bears remembering that *the* intelligence issue in the early postwar period was not operations; rather it was avoiding another Pearl Harbor. That problem was what to do about fragmented intelligence that could neither sort out signals of warning from surrounding "noise" nor make the warning persuasive to senior officials of government. This problem, along with the balkanized way the separate armed services had fought World War II, begat the National Security Council. It also begat the sequence of efforts to coordinate American intelligence, beginning with the Central Intelligence Group in 1946.

Congress was a promoter of these changes but essentially a bystander to them. As in other areas of government, it used laws to shape processes in the executive branch. Long after it had tried to centralize and formalize the intelligence process in the executive, it left its own oversight of intelligence and its role in receiving intelligence information informal and fragmented. Changing congressional attitudes toward operations both coincided with and produced an altered view of intelligence products. If Congress was to know about and judge covert

43. *Iran-Contra Affair*, p. 333.

operations, it was logical to assess them in light of the intelligence premises on which they were based.

Some numbers suggest the extent of the change over the past decade. Virtually everything the CIA produces goes to the two Intelligence committees, and most also goes to the Foreign Affairs, Foreign Relations, Armed Services, and Appropriations committees. All eight committees receive the CIA "newspaper," the National Intelligence Daily (NID). The CIA alone sends some 5,000 reports to Congress each year and conducts over a thousand oral briefings.[44] By contrast, CIA records show only twenty-two briefings to Congress (on topics other than covert action) about Chile in the decade 1964–74.[45] Overall, the CIA gave perhaps a hundred briefings a year to Congress in the mid-1970s.[46]

What is true of CIA analyses is also the case in varying degrees for the products of other intelligence agencies. Just as the Intelligence committees get a biweekly list of new CIA publications. they receive indexes from the Defense Intelligence Agency (DIA), along with the DIA daily summary.[47] The National Security Agency provides weekly summaries of signals intelligence. Committee staffers can get access to "raw" intelligence, like defense attaché or CIA agent reports, by special request, although in the most sensitive cases these must be made by the committee chairman to the DCI. People move in both directions from committee staffs to intelligence community analyst jobs, and occasionally committee staffers get friendly calls from intelligence community analysts suggesting that they ask for a particular item.

The change is marked enough without overstating it. Because intelligence is available on Capitol Hill does not mean it is read. Congress is an oral culture, while written products are the intelligence analyst's predilection. If they read, members of Congress, like their counterparts in the executive, will turn to the *New York Times* and *Washington Post* before they pick up the NID. The committees, especially the Intelligence committees, are tightly compartmented in their handling of classified material, which means that getting access to some intelligence is at least a bother. And since knowledge is power

44. Robert M. Gates, "The CIA and American Foreign Policy," *Foreign Affairs*, vol. 66 (Winter 1987–88), p. 224; and Gries, "The CIA and Congress," p. 78.

45. *Covert Action in Chile*, p. 49.

46. "Taking Toshiba Public," p. 5.

47. The information in this paragraph derives from interviews with congressional staffers conducted principally in September 1988.

and access prestige, Hill staffers who receive intelligence may hold it, not share it.

The people within the intelligence community who conduct the briefings or write the reports are analysts, not operators. They are more professorial than conspiratorial in temperament. They work for the CIA's Directorate of Intelligence, not its Directorate of Operations, and they tell their neighbors openly that they work for the CIA or for the State Department's Bureau of Intelligence and Research or the Pentagon's DIA.

They get much of their information about foreign governments the same way academics do, through reading periodicals or transcripts of media monitored openly by the Foreign Broadcast Information Service. In addition they have access to two sets of secret sources—diplomatic cables sent by State Department officers abroad and raw intelligence, such as agent reports produced by the CIA's Directorate of Operations or foreign communications monitored secretly by the National Security Agency.

The change is dramatic for these analysts, many of whom had never dealt with Congress before a decade ago and all of whom have been steeped in a professional culture that separates intelligence from policy lest the former be biased or politicized through contact with the latter. When the subject is technical and, preferably, out of the limelight, briefing Congress is a welcome chance to educate another set of consumers. Yet the analysts recognize that members of Congress, like executive officials, seldom are disinterested consumers of information. They seek it as leverage, often to be used against the executive that is the analysts' ostensible master. If the subject is politically hot, like Central America in the 1980s, the experience is painful, the sense of being manipulated keen.

Congress as Lever or Ally?

Sometimes, Congress listens to intelligence analysis when the executive will not. In such cases, benefits and risks are two sides of the same coin. In June 1987, Representative Duncan Hunter smashed a Toshiba radio-cassette player on the steps of the Capitol. The purpose of his stunt was attention: Toshiba and a Norwegian firm had deliberately sold the Soviet Union milling equipment that would make Soviet submarines quieter, hence harder to track. Hunter charged that the $17 million sale might "cost the West $30 billion to regain the

superiority we lost."[48] The Toshiba bashing was the culmination of a
series of events in which the CIA's Technology Transfer Assessment
Center (TTAC) had, in effect, hawked its analyses around Washington.

The story began not with TTAC but with a disaffected Japanese
employee who took the story of the Toshiba sale to COCOM, the
Paris-based export control organization comprising the NATO allies
and Japan. Staffers at COCOM, however, accepted Toshiba's word
that it had sold only permitted technology. The employee then took
his story to the U.S. embassy in Tokyo, which put him in touch with
TTAC. The first stop for TTAC was the State Department, which
made a diplomatic "demarche" to Japan. Like most such demarches,
it was, however, brushed off for want of hard information. Moreover,
the State Department looked askance at TTAC: TTAC's desire to
control the issue left its colleagues at State's Bureau of Intelligence and
Research feeling cut out, and policy officials at State were nervous
about the repercussions of the issue on relations with two allies. Yet
the tradition of CIA independence, plus TTAC's control of the issue,
made it difficult for State to influence what TTAC said.

The next stop was the Defense Department, where Undersecretary
Fred Iklé, a willing listener, agreed to take the issue up in his
forthcoming trip to Japan. For Iklé the issue was one among several,
not primary, and his trip produced little more than the demarche. But
Iklé's office, briefed by TTAC and now with a better case in hand,
in turn briefed Senator Jake Garn, a kindred hard-liner on technology
transfer. At about the same time, December 1986, mention of this
"major technology transfer" appeared in classified written briefings to
the two Intelligence committees. Word was spreading.

Within two months the issue was public. First it went again to
COCOM, where this time TTAC briefed representatives of the fifteen
member nations. As Japan and Norway responded, Washington buzzed
with rumors of a big new case. In late February the House Armed
Services seapower subcommittee was briefed on the issue, and the
next month, at hearings on the omnibus trade bill, Iklé's deputy,
Richard Perle, referred obliquely to an export control violation he
"could go into in a classified hearing." A week later the conservative
Washington Times broke the story, quoting unnamed officials "outside
the government."

From then on, TTAC did not lack audiences; it had more than it

48. "Taking Toshiba Public," p. 1.

wanted. Members of Congress outbid each other in proposals for retaliating against the wrongdoers, especially Toshiba, for Norway had acted to defuse the issue by admitting guilt and working with the United States. In the end, the weight of other interests at play in U.S.-Japanese relations began to be felt, and congressional leaders cooperated with the executive in enacting sanctions against Toshiba that, while sounding tough, were relatively mild.

The kind of interaction with Congress reflected in the Toshiba affair was uncharted water. On one hand, Guy DuBois, the principal TTAC analyst, sought to hold to the traditional line between intelligence and policy: "Once you state a position, how that position affects policy . . . is not your business."[49] On the other hand, DCI Casey had given TTAC a mandate that was more than providing information; it was to be a player in a quasi-prosecutorial process. In that sense, its information was to be nearly self-implementing: if it could prove guilt, then that would frame the response. Congress was not the principal prosecutor, but telling it was a way to make sure someone paid attention.

The Toshiba case coincided with William Webster's arrival as DCI, replacing the late William Casey; plainly, Webster's main mission was repairing relations with Congress after Iran-contra. "To Webster," the TTAC analyst recalled, "Congress has an insatiable appetite and to the extent we can, we satisfy it." Moreover, "if a Congressman finds out that you decided not to be completely forthcoming," the credibility of the CIA could be damaged. The CIA's role, however, was not simply responding to congressional requests: "If they ask a stupid question, tell them it's stupid, then tell them what the smart question is and answer it."

It is still rare for Congress to be the lead consumer of intelligence. Most of the time Congress's effect is indirect. Since Congress will also know what the executive knows, executive officials are prudent to pay attention to intelligence lest they be skewered by Congress for the failure. Consider the contrast between the fall of the shah of Iran in 1978 and the departure from the Philippines of President Ferdinand Marcos in 1986.[50] The experience with the shah had taught policy officials in both the executive and Congress not to dismiss unwelcome

49. This and subsequent quotes from DuBois are from "Taking Toshiba Public," pp. 14–15.
50. The source for this account is W. E. Kline, "The Fall of Marcos," Case C16-88-868.0, Harvard University, Kennedy School of Government, 1988.

news about Marcos, nor to assume, as they had about the shah, that
Marcos knew his politics better than Washington did. That the
Philippine opposition—moderate, Catholic, and U.S.-educated—was
both much more accessible to intelligence collection and much more
acceptable than Iran's mullahs made the lesson easier to learn.

The Philippine crisis moved more slowly than the Iranian, beginning
in earnest with the assassination of opposition leader Benigno Aquino
on the airport tarmac in Manila as he returned from the United States
in August 1983. The intelligence community concluded that if Marcos
had not ordered the assassination, it almost certainly had been done
on his behalf. From then on the Philippines was on the congressional
agenda almost as much as it was on that of the executive. The contrast
with Iran could hardly be sharper; a 1979 House Intelligence committee
postmortem on the Iran case contains not a single reference to
Congress.[51]

The State Department worried about Congress in the instance of
Toshiba, but in the instance of the Philippines the East Asia "mafia"
in the executive—including State, Defense, and the NSC—welcomed
congressional pressure as a way to persuade *their* bosses, not least the
president, that Marcos might have to go. An August 1985 Senate
Intelligence Committee report concluded that "the Marcos government
is unlikely to pursue the changes necessary to stop the economic
hemorrhaging, to slow or halt the insurgency or to heal the major
lesions that are infecting the political process."[52] Later in the year, the
links between Congress and the executive were tightened when one
Senate Foreign Relations Committee staffer moved to the intelligence
community to be national intelligence officer for East Asia and the
Pacific.

Another Senate Foreign Relations Committee staff member described the interaction:

The people in the State Department were using us, the Foreign
Relations Committee, to get their point across in the White
House. They were delighted when [Chairman Richard] Lugar
decided to write a letter, not to Marcos but to the President of
the United States. In other words, we laid it right on the

51. See *Iran: Evaluation of U.S. Intelligence Performance Prior to November 1978*,
Committee Print, Subcommittee on Evaluation of the House Permanent Select Committee
on Intelligence, 96 Cong. 1 sess. (GPO, 1979).
52. This and the following quote are from "The Fall of Marcos," pp. 18–19.

President. We shifted our focus from the President of the Philippines to the President of the United States.

In November 1985, Marcos called a snap election for February 1986. The opposition managed to unite to name Aquino's widow, Corazon, as its presidential candidate. In December 1985 the intelligence community was still predicting a narrow Marcos victory, but by January 1986 it labeled the election too close to call, and on the eve of the vote it actually predicted an Aquino victory while also betting that Marcos would fix the results if need be. On January 30 President Reagan announced a bipartisan mission of U.S. election observers, cochaired by Lugar.

The effect of Congress's access to intelligence was most evident in the crunch. Most of the U.S. observers witnessed fraud by the ruling party, but as late as February 11, as votes trickled in, Reagan commented that the United States was concerned about both violence and "the possibility of fraud, although it could have been that all of that was occurring on both sides," a quote that so pleased Marcos that he had it shown over and over on Philippine television.[53]

At this point, the intelligence community was told, in effect, to put up or shut up. It responded with convincing proof of massive fraud by Marcos's party. Thus the administration had to act in the knowledge that Congress would soon have the same proof. Its options—to ride out the storm with Marcos, for instance—were correspondingly constrained. By February 15 the White House had dropped the "fraud on both sides" line, and on the 17th Lugar called for Marcos to resign.

Judgments about whether the sharing of intelligence with Congress creates more consensus or less, let alone whether it produces wiser policy or more foolish, are hard to make and inevitably subjective. In retrospect, if the departure of Marcos is regarded as a success, the fact that Congress knew what the executive did seems to have contributed to that success. Unwise options were foreclosed, and senior officials, especially the president, had to see the election as it was, not as they might wish it to be: Congress was watching. At the end, sharing intelligence about what Marcos had done in stealing votes made a compelling case and was enough to produce consensus.

In the case of Nicaragua, however, if shared intelligence produced a more enlightened debate, it surely did not produce consensus. This

53. "The Fall of Marcos," p. 20.

issue, like so many others, turned not on what the Sandinistas did, but what their actions meant, implied, or portended. On those latter questions, even good intelligence assessments are seldom convincing. Officials in the executive and Congress disagreed, unsurprisingly, despite looking at the same data and reading the same analyses of it.

So far, there is little evidence of analysts cutting their cloth to suit congressional consumers. However, it may simply be that the congressional role is new. A cynic would say that analysts always hedged their bets, and critics would argue that analysts feel the most formidable pressures to change assessments from their bosses in the executive branch. Analysts did not soften the news in the Philippines even though it was unwelcome to some in the administration; nor did TTAC hold back in the Toshiba case because the State Department did not much like its assessment (and Congress liked it too much). In the heat of the debate over Nicaragua, the House Intelligence Committee, while generally praising intelligence community performance, certainly did not feel it had been pandered to—quite the contrary.[54]

The Special Case of Verification

The more direct role of intelligence agencies in the political process is especially apparent in battles over arms control verification. Since the Senate must ratify treaties, verification is plainly an issue for Congress. Treaty supporters and opponents, as well as those who seek a way out by voting against the treaty without being labeled against arms control, all use verification as an argument. In the process they seek, understandably, to push decisions about what is finally a political issue—whether existing monitoring arrangements provide for adequate verification—onto the technical intelligence agencies, which in turn want, again understandably, to confine their role to describing those monitoring arrangements.

Verification was not an issue during the debate over SALT I in 1972, but charges of Soviet violations of that treaty, as well as the much more ambitious aims of SALT II, raised the issue five years later. Accordingly, in 1977 the Senate Foreign Relations Committee asked the Intelligence Committee for a thorough review of monitoring

---

54. See *U.S. Intelligence Performance on Central America: Achievements and Selected Instances of Concern*, Committee Print, Subcommittee on Oversight and Evaluation of the House Permanent Select Committee on Intelligence, 97 Cong. 2 sess. (GPO, 1982).

capabilities. The report was relatively sanguine. It appeared verification would not, after all, be a stumbling block in the ratification debate.[55]

Then, in March 1979 the United States lost access to monitoring facilities in Iran. Verification returned to the agenda, especially for the fence sitters, prominent among whom was Senator John Glenn, who said he could not support the treaty until the lost capabilities were replaced. The Intelligence Committee's final report, released on the eve of the floor debate, distinguished between the treaty's numerical limits and many of its qualitative constraints that could be monitored with high confidence, and several qualitative limits for which confidence was relatively low.[56]

Opponents zeroed in on the low-confidence provisions, while supporters pointed to the committee judgment that the treaty itself would enhance America's ability to monitor the treaty limits. The ratification vote boded to be a close-run thing, due largely to verification issues, but the whole debate was rendered moot by the Soviet invasion of Afghanistan. President Carter withdrew the treaty from Senate consideration.

In 1988 the Senate Intelligence Committee's unanimous judgment was decisive in removing verification as an issue in the discussion over the Intermediate Nuclear Forces (INF) treaty.[57] The treaty itself both embodied the most elaborate verification arrangements ever negotiated and simplified verification by eliminating weapons systems entirely, not merely reducing them in number. In its report approving the INF treaty, the commitee explicitly opened the debate on a future strategic arms treaty by observing that strategic reductions would be far more demanding to monitor than those in the INF treaty.

The committee report also sought to protect the intelligence community by noting that verification is not simple, nor does it alone settle whether a treaty is desirable; a bad treaty that can be verified is still a bad treaty. It also distinguished carefully between monitoring and verification—the former an intelligence community responsibility, the

---

55. See Stephen J. Flanagan, "The Domestic Politics of SALT II: Implications for the Foreign Policy Process," in John Spanier and Joseph Nogee, eds., *Congress, the Presidency and American Foreign Policy* (Pergamon Press, 1981), pp. 63–64.

56. *Principal Findings on the Capabilities of the U.S. to Monitor the SALT II Treaty*, Committee Print, Senate Select Committee on Intelligence, 96 Cong. 1 sess. (GPO, 1979).

57. *The INF Treaty Monitoring and Verification Capabilities*, S. Rept. 100-318, Senate Select Committee on Intelligence, 100 Cong. 2 sess. (GPO, 1988).

latter a judgment by the executive of whether Soviet behavior as reported by the community is compatible with the treaty.[58]

Clients and Patrons

Yet another sign that the intelligence community has joined the American government is that the institutional relations that have grown up between intelligence agencies and their congressional overseers have come to resemble those between domestic agencies and their congressional committees. Although the committees can be sharply critical of their agencies—witness covert actions or particular "intelligence failures"—in general the interests of the overseers and those overseen run parallel. The creation of the two intelligence oversight committees was thus the best thing that ever happened to the intelligence community, even if the heat of specific disputes sometimes has obscured that fact for intelligence officials.

The committees and their staffs have created a pool of people knowledgeable about intelligence and able to serve as advocates throughout the two chambers. By the time both new committees had been formed, in 1977, only 3 percent of House and 20 percent of Senate incumbents had served on the then-existing oversight subcommittees of Appropriations and Armed Services. Ten years later the percentages were 8 and 43. Over the period between 1980, when the Intelligence committees became the budget authorizers for intelligence, and 1986, the CIA budget more than doubled, growing faster than the defense budget. The total budget for the intelligence community nearly tripled, reaching close to $20 billion.[59]

Indeed, the committees have been accused of becoming as much protectors of the intelligence community as overseers—a risk that runs through all relations between Congress and executive agencies. It is true that the base of knowledge among members and staff does build understanding. The difference between the congressional investigations of intelligence in the mid-1970s and the Iran-contra panel was, for better or worse, striking: the latter was narrow, disciplined, and,

58. *INF Treaty*, S. Rept. 100-318, p. 5.

59. Numbers of members and the CIA budget are from Gries, "The CIA and Congress," p. 78. The total intelligence community budget is an estimate, compiled from interviews and published sources.

Oliver North excepted, boring, with no visible sentiment for ending covert operations, much less for dismantling the CIA.

The bulk of the increase in the intelligence budget has gone for expensive satellites and other technical collection systems, where the role of Congress and the link to arms control have been central. The fall of the shah underscored the need for better human intelligence and analysis, and the closing of the Iranian monitoring sites showed just how fragile U.S. technical collection could be. As members of the Intelligence committees came to know what U.S. intelligence can do, they naturally became sympathetic to what more it could do with more money. That was particularly the case in monitoring arms control, for if judgments about verification are subjective, those about monitoring are less so: if existing systems provide 50 percent confidence in monitoring some aspect of Soviet weaponry, the argument that an additional system would increase the confidence to 80 percent can be relatively straightforward.

For example, in its report on the INF treaty, the Senate Intelligence Committee prefaced its positive judgment about verification with this statement on behalf of new technical collection systems needed to verify a future strategic arms treaty: "The Committee feels that this potential gap between intelligence capabilities and intelligence requirements must be appreciated by Members of the Senate."[60] As is typical of the multifaceted relations between committees and agencies, the committee apparently had in mind not only systems the intelligence community eagerly sought, but also ones about which it had doubts.

Other cases of congressional involvment, departures in the realm of intelligence, also look more familiar in the domestic sweep of executive-congressional relations. A good example is counterintelligence. Early in the Reagan administration the breaking wave of spy scandals elicited a number of dramatic proposals from political officials in and around the White House. Most of these ideas were judged excessive or unwise by career counterintelligence professionals; the Senate Intelligence Committee came to share that judgment, and careerists and Congress cooperated in beating back the proposals.

Later in the administration, concern remained high, fed by evidence that the new U.S. embassy in Moscow was riddled with eavesdropping devices. By then, cooler heads had come to the fore in the White

60. *INF Treaty*, S. Rept. 100-318, p. 3.

House, and the Senate committee now sided with them about counterintelligence even as Congress and the White House were at loggerheads over aid to the contras.[61] The committee became a player in the administration debate, siding with those who proposed to take strong measures (the FBI and part of the CIA) against those who worried that Soviet retaliation could hinder America's ability to run foreign policy (State and the CIA's espionage managers). Liberals on the committee were persuaded to the FBI view both because they came to believe the administration was not doing enough and because they wanted to demonstrate that their attitude toward the intelligence agencies was not purely negative, that they could say "yes" as well as "no."

Joining the government means pluses and minuses for the intelligence community that are familiar from the experience of domestic agencies. For instance, for most of its history the CIA was better at understanding foreign governments than its own. One congressional staffer described Clair George, the CIA director of congressional affairs during the contra affair and a career clandestine service officer, as a man convinced that "Washington was a foreign country and he was the station chief in hostile terrain, mounting operations against the Congress."[62] Joining the American government provides both sympathetic guides to and experience in reconnoitering that terrain.

The negative side is also familiar: the more "your" congressional committees know, the more able they are to help you, but also the more they are tempted to tell you how to do your business. The Intelligence committees have been voracious requirers of reports even if, like other committees, they receive more than they can digest. Like other committees, they have also been tempted to "micromanage"; the line between oversight and management can blur, especially perhaps if the subject to be managed is exciting.

To be sure, micromanagement is relative, and the intelligence budget is not subject to anything like the intrusions of, say, the Armed Services committees into the defense budget. The CIA, for instance, has all training lumped under a single budget line item. Still, the CIA is coming to look like other agencies of government, for good and ill. Simple aging has made it more bureaucratic in any case, but congres-

61. See, for instance, *Meeting the Espionage Challenge: A Review of United States Counterintelligence and Security Programs*, S. Rept. 99-522, Senate Select Committee on Intelligence, 99 Cong. 2 sess. (GPO, 1986).

62. Interview, January 18, 1987.

sional oversight has abetted that tendency. Projects conceived one year do not get approved until the next. Even minor operations require major paperwork. And despite renewed fondness for covert action on the part of American administrations, CIA officers retain an anxious eye on their political masters outside the executive; no one wants to be a subject of the next congressional investigation. The CIA is becoming more cautious; its officers want authorization in writing. On balance, the caution is a benefit, but it has come at some cost to the entrepreneurial spirit of the CIA.

Open Questions

The process of intelligence becoming a more ordinary part of the government is an uncompleted experiment. It is not, however, reversible. It was inevitable that the intelligence community would come to resemble the rest of the government as the conditions that spawned it as an exception changed: the waning of the deepest fears of the cold war, the loss after the Bay of Pigs of the CIA's image of mastery, the tarnishing of the presidency by Watergate, and the rise of investigative journalism. Perhaps the most important changes are internal to Congress, for intelligence oversight had been the quintessential working of the congressional club. When age removed those few committee chairmen from Congress, and reform meant that they would not be replaced, intelligence's relation to Congress was bound to change.

In 1954 when news of the covert operation to overthrow Guatemala's President Jacobo Arbenz leaked out, it was the leak that was discredited, not the operation. In *Time*'s overheated prose, the revelations were "masterminded in Moscow and designed to divert the attention . . . from Guatemala as the Western Hemisphere's Red problem child."[63] Not so three decades later, not even if the initial leak was in Beirut in Arabic.

The government that intelligence has joined is a divided one, its divisions institutionalized. The executive-legislative division is the most obvious but not always the most important. In areas like agriculture or commerce, for instance, it is taken for granted that, whether particular observers like it or not, executive agencies and congressional committees serve essentially the same domestic constituencies. Those

63. *Time*, February 8, 1954, p. 36.

agencies and committees then contend within their respective arenas against representatives of other constituencies.

Intelligence analysis, by contrast, represents no conventional domestic interest groups. It is a source of advice about foreign countries. Offering advice within a single branch is political enough. Whether the intelligence community can sustain its credibility in offering advice across two branches, often in sharp contention, remains to be seen. Congress may come to feel it wants its own intelligence analysts, as it came in another area of advice, the budget, to feel it required its own budgeteers, the Congressional Budget Office. A Congressional Intelligence Office does not seem imminent, however. It would ensue, if it did, only from a bitter conflict between the executive and Congress. Nor is there is a stream of congressional action whose shape and deadlines would argue for an in-house intelligence service comparable to the one that exists for the budget.

Yet it is instructive, and perhaps a little fearsome, to contemplate, now that Congress and intelligence analysts are acquainted, just how perfect they are for each other. The lives of foreign policy officials in the executive are dominated by their in-boxes; for them, analysis is a nuisance unless they can be sure it will support their predilections. Moreover, when assistant secretaries average not much more than a year in tenure, neither they nor intelligence analysts have much incentive, or much opportunity, to take the measure of each other.

By contrast, members of Congress, and still more their staffs, are not so driven by their in-boxes. Their quest to signify means a hunt for information and for issues, just what intelligence analysts have to offer. And career paths in Congress and intelligence fit together neatly; most members are, in effect, elected for life if they choose, and the tenures of their senior staffers are much longer than those of assistant secretaries.

Arrangements linking Congress to intelligence analysis are portentous but will change only gradually, for the most part out of the spotlight and out of the headlines. The focal point of conflict between the two branches will remain covert operations. There, in the nature of both constitutional and political reality, the conflict cannot be resolved, for it runs to the heart of foreign policy: balancing the responsibility of Congress with the primacy of the president.

The 1988 debate over when Congress would be notified of covert actions is illustrative of that fact. On its face the debate seemed almost trivial: both sides agreed that normally the president should inform the committees of a covert action in advance if possible, within a day or so of its start; and so the debate was over whether the forty-eight-hour requirement would be binding or not. Both sides cited examples to suit their preferences: proponents of a mandatory requirement cited arms sales to Iran; opponents, an offer by Canada during the Carter administration to help in smuggling U.S. hostages out of Iran but only if the U.S. Congress were not notified.[64]

Like most debates about intelligence, the argument was about not only the powers of the president but also about where to strike the balance between expediency and accountability. Over the past two decades the balance has moved toward accountability, and, in one sense, the Iran-contra affair can be seen as confirmation that the evolution has worked tolerably well. Yet there can be no full resolution to the dilemma, for secret operations inescapably raise the trade-off between democratic, thus open, process and effective, hence secret, foreign policy.

Observers fearful that increased congressional involvement poses a risk to secrecy have proposed combining the two separate House and Senate committees into one joint intelligence committee. The idea of a joint committee, however, is misdirected. While a single committee might give the president less justification for excluding Congress as "too leaky," Congress has not been leaky, certainly not by comparison with the executive.

The disadvantage of having two committees is the risk of miscommunication: witness the mining of the Nicaraguan harbors. Yet given the institutional jealousies of the two houses, the advantages of two committees—their different personalities, different priorities, and a greater claim to credibility in their respective houses—outweigh that risk. Moreover, the greater risk to oversight is that the overseers will become co-opted. So it was by all accounts with an earlier joint committee, the Joint Atomic Energy Committee. Having two points of oversight, and even a certain amount of competition between them, reduces the chance that the overseers will become only the patrons of those they oversee.

Congress neither desires nor is able to approve every covert action in advance. Apart from constitutional questions, the process is simply

64. *Intelligence Oversight Act of 1988*, H. Rept. 100-705, 100 Cong. 2 sess. (GPO, 1988), pt. 1, pp. 56–57. See also Dick Cheney, "Covert Operations: Who's in Charge," *Wall Street Journal*, May 3, 1988. However, a subsequent investigation by the Senate Intelligence Committee left doubt that the Canadian example actually happened.

too slow: Congress's instruments are blunt. One way to increase congressional control over controversial operations would be to require the Intelligence committees to approve any withdrawal from the CIA Contingency Reserve. That would be uncomfortable for the committees in that it would put them more directly on the line in the eyes of their congressional colleagues, but it would at least spare them the discomfort of having to choose between silent opposition to an operation and public exposure of it.

When administrations feel secrecy is at a premium, they can resort to informing only the "gang of eight," a procedure that had been used only once by mid-1988.[65] Had relations between Casey and the committees been better, the Reagan administration might have done so in the instance of Iranian arms sales. That would not necessarily have resulted in wiser policy, for it is conceivable that the gang of eight would have been seduced down the path from geostrategic interests to releasing hostages just as the president was. But the subsequent debate would then have been about the wisdom of the policy, not about whether Congress was deceived.

In the future, major covert actions will be overt, as was aid to the contras or to the resistance in Afghanistan. The controversy over them will spill into public, even if they are not propelled there by the executive. If some options are thereby foreclosed, at least the choices will be openly debated. Administrations will have to make evident how those covert programs support coherent public policies. And because major covert actions will not remain secret, presidents will be well advised, before the fact, to ask themselves whether the covert action could bear the test of disclosure: would it still seem sensible once it were public?

The views of congressional overseers will give the president a good indication of what the public would think if it knew of the operation. If the administration is out of step with what the public will accept, as in the case of arms sales to Iran, it may learn that in advance, rather than being punished by Congress after the fact. If the public is divided or confused, as with aid to the contras, the administration probably can have its way. This process is about the best we can do. It is, as Iran-contra testifies, no guarantee against stupid presidential decisions or the resulting public scandals.

65. *Intelligence Oversight Act of 1988*, H. Rept. 100-705, p. 11.

The New Congressional Role in Arms Control

BARRY M. BLECHMAN

IN THE PAST twenty years Congress's role in the making and implementation of foreign and defense policies has undergone a revolution. The congressional role has grown from that of a relatively minor actor, frequently outspoken but only sporadically consulted, rarely involved in actual decisionmaking and never in policy execution, to that of a player with star billing in the making of U.S. national security policy and sometimes the lead role in U.S. government decisions. Spawned, of course, in the turmoil of political unrest associated with the Vietnam War, this shift in relative executive-legislative power has not only survived the conservative tide that brought Ronald Reagan and a Republican Senate to power in 1980, but has also gathered new momentum and scope during the past decade.

There are many reasons for the trend toward a greater congressional role in defense policy. The American political system has been transformed during this same period by the effect of television and other electronic media, by the rising cost of running for office and the emergence of interest-based, nationwide fundraising techniques, and by the democratization of Congress itself—that is, such developments as the diminution of the power of committee chairmen and other senior figures and the rise of party caucuses. In a variety of ways, each of these changes has made it more rewarding, both electorally and personally, for congressional candidates and officeholders to take

This chapter, derived in part from a more comprehensive study of Congress and U.S. defense policy, is based primarily on interviews with about fifteen members of Congress and twenty-five congressional staff members conducted during 1987 and 1988. That research was funded in part by the Twentieth Century Fund. The author is grateful to the fund for its support but wishes to make clear that the opinions expressed in this study are entirely his own and not necessarily endorsed by that organization. The complete study will be published as Barry M. Blechman, *The Politics of National Defense: Congress and U.S. Defense Policy from Vietnam to the Persian Gulf* (Oxford University Press, 1990). The author also wishes to thank Wayne Philip Ellis and Margaret Sullivan for their research assistance.

publicly visible positions on defense issues and to demonstrate an
ability to help shape defense policy. Furthermore, successive administrations colluded with Congress—inadvertently, of course—to facilitate expansion of the congressional role. Congressional participation
in defense issues today would be far different had not both Republican
and Democratic administrations proven unwilling or unable to modify
specific policies long after they had generated powerful opposition. It
was the potential rewards of playing to political forces opposed to
administration policies that provided the primary impetus for Congress
to revise its role in the formulation and implementation of defense
policy.

   The reasons for the new congressional role in defense policy, and
its scope, are demonstrated clearly in the recent history of arms control
issues. Until the mid-1970s, Congress had only a cursory role in these
issues, based primarily on the Senate's treaty ratification powers. The
political context in which arms control negotiations were carried out
began to change significantly at that point, however, and the congressional role grew dramatically in response. Congressional concerns about
an alleged negative effect of negotiated arms control arrangements on
U.S. security interests contributed to delays by both the Ford and
Carter administrations in turning the informal 1974 Vladivostok accord
on strategic weapons into a formal treaty. These delays spelled the
treaty's death knell when it was finally completed, as the once supportive
international and domestic political environment had crumbled around
the negotiation and ratification process.[1]

   In the early 1980s public attitudes toward arms control became
more positive than those expressed initially by the Reagan administration, and Congress followed closely behind. Congressional initiatives
not only helped persuade the administration to reopen negotiations for
reductions in both intermediate-range nuclear forces (INF) and long-
range strategic forces, but also helped to shape the U.S. negotiating
posture in both sets of talks and clarified several aspects of the treaty
that eventually emerged from the INF negotiations. Congressional
actions also caused the administration, against its wishes, to continue
to adhere to the terms of the unratified 1979 Strategic Arms Limitation
Treaty (SALT II) and to maintain the narrow, traditional interpretation

   1. Alan Platt, *The U.S. Senate and Strategic Arms Policy, 1969–1977* (Westview, 1978),
pp. 61–65, 110.

of the 1972 treaty limiting antiballistic missiles (ABMs). Congress also has caused the United States to take unilateral actions intended to facilitate progress in various negotiations, including the imposition of a moratorium on tests of antisatellite (ASAT) weapons, and the near imposition of a moratorium on all nuclear weapon tests above a minimal explosive yield. Moreover, Congress conceived a whole new approach to reducing the threat of nuclear catastrophe—nuclear risk reduction centers—and, over the course of five years, persuaded the administration to endorse the concept and negotiate an agreement with the Soviet Union that created such centers in 1987.[2]

The stark change in relative congressional-executive influence in arms control can be symbolized by the difference between 1969, when the Nixon administration abruptly canceled the planned first congressional appearance of the chief U.S. negotiator in the strategic arms limitation talks one week before the opening of the negotiations, and 1983, when Congress compelled the Reagan administration to incorporate the so-called build-down proposal, a congressional invention, as part of the U.S. negotiating position in the strategic arms reduction talks (START). The Nixon administration continued to refuse to inform Congress about its SALT negotiating position until just before the second round of talks in the spring of 1970, and even then consented to brief only a selected group of members in secret in the Old Executive Office Building on Pennsylvania Avenue.[3] The fact that the lawmakers had to go to the White House complex to be informed about the central arms control issue of the day, rather than receiving executive branch officials in their own committee rooms for testimony and discussion, made clear the relative distribution of power. In 1983, however, not only did Congress establish the U.S. negotiating position, but it even forced the administration to add an individual to the negotiating team whose sole function was to ascertain that the congressional build-down proposal had been put on the table accurately and was being pursued with diligence.[4]

2. *Congressional Quarterly Almanac, 1984*, vol. 40 (1985), p. 54; and Barry M. Blechman, "A Minimal Reduction of a Major Risk," *Bulletin of the Atomic Scientists*, vol. 44 (April 1988), pp. 44–46.

3. See Donald May, "Nuclear Criteria Remain Secret as Arms Negotiations Resume," *National Journal*, April 18, 1970, pp. 810–12; and John Newhouse, *Cold Dawn: The Story of SALT* (Holt, Rinehart and Winston, 1973), p. 182.

4. *Congressional Quarterly Almanac, 1983*, vol. 39 (1984), pp. 201, 204.

Not unexpectedly, this expanded congressional role in arms control has drawn sharp criticism from executive branch officials. In 1988, for example, a congressionally imposed prohibition on tests of strategic missiles in depressed trajectories was cited by President Reagan as one reason for his veto of the Defense Authorization Act, an extremely unusual step.[5] A second reason was the act's limitations on "star wars" research. By delaying development of certain types of systems, Congress had intended to make early deployments of space-based defenses even less likely and thus to reduce pressures against the ABM treaty. Although they had never prompted a veto previously, similar executive-legislative jurisdictional disputes attended defense legislation throughout the mid- and late 1980s.

To achieve its expanded role in arms control, Congress turned to unorthodox means of influencing the executive branch. Traditional instruments of influence—the requirement that the Senate consent to treaties, the consultative powers derived from that authority, and Congress's general powers to compel explanations of executive policies in hearings, to require reports on specific aspects of policy, and to pass on nominees for diplomatic and executive positions—were all found wanting in the 1970s and 1980s. As a result, in arms control as in many other aspects of national security policy, Congress turned increasingly to the power of the purse, its appropriating authority, to impose its preferences on the executive branch. This redirection in the legislature's means of influence resulted in turn in a redistribution of power within Congress. The House of Representatives, which traditionally played almost no role in the formulation of arms control policy, became in many respects the leading chamber on these issues. Within both chambers, moreover, de facto jurisdiction over arms control matters, traditionally vested in the Foreign Relations and Foreign Affairs committees, shifted to other committees, particularly Armed Services and Intelligence, which became central crucibles for working out congressional positions. Within the House, finally, the Democratic Caucus, particularly its leaders, became the dominant players, compelling the chairmen of all three committees to pay greater attention to the preferences of the caucus majority.

The question of how far Congress should go in attempting to influence arms control policy is the heart of the controversy. Certainly,

5. "Reagan Vetoes Fiscal 1989 Defense Authorization Bill," *Congressional Quarterly Weekly Report*, August 6, 1988, p. 2223.

the build-down proposal goes well beyond usual judgments about the appropriate level of congressional involvement in the formulation and execution of U.S. negotiating positions. And it is undeniable that a requirement to negotiate with Congress before negotiating with foreign nations, to say the least, would be a serious complication in the conduct of U.S. arms control policy. Yet it is equally obvious that until Congress shouldered its way into the process, the Reagan administration not only had completely shut out the legislature from any role in arms control policy, but also had pursued policies that deviated widely from the popular will. The first effect of Congress's achievement of a new role in arms control was simply to enable the legislature to carry out its constitutional responsibility to represent popular opinion. That a correction in the respective roles of the branches was necessary should not be in question, and that the correction went too far also should not be in serious dispute; the relevant question is where the future balance should lie.

The Politics of Arms Control

The control of nuclear arms, as opposed to their elimination, first became the official policy of the United States in 1955. President Dwight D. Eisenhower's special assistant on disarmament, Harold Stassen, articulated the new policy in his first annual report in the spring of that year.[6]

From its inception, the new policy had both international and domestic political dimensions. Insofar as the United States increasingly was coming to rely on nuclear weapons—or at least on the threat of their use—to underpin its security commitments and alliances abroad, nuclear disarmament had distinct liabilities. Even though it was obvious at the time that there was no possibility of achieving "general and complete disarmament," as allegedly was being pursued, the simple recitation of the goal seemed to undermine the increasingly central place of nuclear threats in Western security policies. The difficulty of verifying any disarmament proposal, moreover, particularly in view of the USSR's obsession with secrecy, suggested that disarmament negotiations were an impractical and probably counterproductive enterprise. Yet direct opposition to disarmament had negative conse-

6. Cited in Stephen E. Ambrose, *Eisenhower: The President*, vol. 2 (Simon and Schuster, 1984), p. 246.

quences as well—casting the United States as a bloodthirsty villain, particularly in Europe where the antinuclear movement was already gaining currency. The idea of seeking constraints on nuclear weapons, rather than trying to dispose of them altogether, was seen as a way of reducing the risk of war, improving relations with the Soviet Union, and associating the United States with popular "pro-peace" positions. It was hoped that such a stance would improve relations with allied governments and their people, without undermining the increasingly crucial role being played by nuclear weapons in U.S. security commitments and alliances.

Domestically, the pursuit of nuclear arms control served similar political purposes. The threat of nuclear war was far more tangible in the 1950s than it is today, brought home to millions by nuclear tests in the atmosphere and accompanying radioactive fallout, air raid drills that emptied cities at noon, and a civil defense program that intruded daily into ordinary life. While President Eisenhower was clearly sincere in seeking movement toward the control of nuclear arms to reduce the risk of a terrible calamity and to ease the burden of military expenditures, the positive political effects of an emphasis on arms control were not lost on him either. Democrats had made hay with Secretary of State John Foster Dulles's policy of "massive retaliation" and its associated stress on nuclear preparedness and nuclear threats. The appointment of Harold Stassen, a prominent moderate Republican politician, as the president's disarmament adviser was intended to offset somewhat the political liabilities associated with the dominance of nuclear hard-liners within the Eisenhower administration. Progress toward an "open skies" agreement or other measures to reduce the risk of surprise attack, the key arms control initiative at the time, was seen as further strengthening the Republican party's image, possibly preempting what was shaping up as one of the Democrats' key issues in the 1956 election.[7]

THE POLITICS OF ARMS CONTROL IN THE 1970S

Twenty years later, much had changed, but political objectives still remained central, if unstated, incentives for both the Nixon and Ford administrations to seek progress in arms control talks. At this time,

---

7. Robert J. Donovan, *Eisenhower: The Inside Story* (Harper, 1956), chap. 26, esp. p. 344.

the talks were concentrating on controlling the numbers of long-range offensive weapons deployed by each side and slowing the rates at which they were being modernized. President Richard Nixon, especially, perceived progress in arms negotiations as a means of offsetting public opinion about the difficulties of U.S. policy in Vietnam. He and National Security Adviser Henry Kissinger maintained that the arms talks were building a "structure of peace" that would last for generations—by implication a far more important goal than the transitory problems of Southeast Asia.[8]

But the political context for arms control changed markedly during the 1970s. In part because of the continuing growth of Soviet military power and rising Soviet military activism in the third world and in part because of a backlash from the loss of U.S. allies in Southeast Asia, the political forces influencing arms negotiations shifted measurably between the early and the late 1970s.

Pluralities in most public opinion polls continued to support the objective of controlling nuclear arms and to support the SALT II treaty when asked their general view.[9] However, critics of the agreement were able to exploit popular fears of Soviet military power to raise concerns about specific aspects of the agreement. The basic context of uneasiness over the rise of Soviet military power, and the specific weaknesses in the prospective treaty, which played into popular concerns, were used cleverly by groups opposed to the agreement, such as the Committee on the Present Danger.[10] Such groups were able to nudge senators and other politicians away from their previous

8. See "United States Foreign Policy for the 1970's: The Emerging Structure of Peace," *Weekly Compilation of Presidential Documents*, vol. 8 (February 14, 1972), pp. 232–34.

9. Polling data suggest that most of the public was ambivalent about arms control—torn between their desire to eliminate nuclear risks and their deep suspicion of the Soviet Union. SALT II and other arms control agreements could gain wide public support, however, when they were coupled with unilateral measures to allay security concerns regarding the USSR. Indeed, the strategic modernization program begun during the Carter administration probably would have satisfied these concerns and cemented public support for the SALT agreement if the Soviet invasion of Afghanistan had not suddenly shifted the entire political debate to the right. For examples of these attitudes, see Hedrick Smith, "Poll Shows Belief Soviet Leads in Arms," *New York Times*, June 13, 1979, p. A15; and "Public Attitudes on SALT II," in Charles Tyroler, II, ed., *Alerting America: The Papers of the Committee on the Present Danger* (Washington: Pergamon-Brassey's, 1984), pp. 119–23.

10. Tyroler, *Alerting America*.

uncritical support into positions that, if not hostile, conditioned their support upon concomitant "improvements" in the U.S. military posture.

As a result, while early in the decade it had been a decided advantage to speak favorably of arms talks, by mid-decade many politicians were more cautious. Among the Democrats, Senator Henry Jackson attempted to exploit this more skeptical attitude toward the Soviet Union and military issues in pursuing his party's presidential nomination in 1976, but he was slightly premature.[11] This is not to say that Jackson's criticisms of the 1972 ABM treaty and agreement on strategic offensive forces, and, even more pointedly, the 1974 Vladivostok accord, were insincere; it is simply that in articulating these positions, he was pursuing political as well as substantive goals. On the Republican side, Ronald Reagan came close to defeating President Gerald Ford for the 1976 nomination, using charges of Soviet cheating on already-concluded agreements as one arrow in a quiver of positions against arms control.

Political incentives to oppose the SALT II treaty grew sharply during the ensuing four years. A virtual anti-Soviet fervor had seized the nation (or at least its capital) by 1979, aided by further evidence of Soviet military gains and activities in third world nations, charges of Soviet cheating, and—most important—continued defeats of American clients, notably the shah of Iran. When the USSR invaded Afghanistan at the end of that year, the Carter administration was forced to withdraw the recently concluded SALT II treaty from congressional consideration,[12] even though before the invasion several deals between the administration and leading congressional figures had apparently secured the necessary two-thirds of the Senate in favor of passage.

American politicians both responded to the changing public mood in the late 1970s and contributed to the emergence of the new consensus. Senator Jackson, among other Democrats, remained a critic, using the hearings on Paul Warnke's nomination to be director of the Arms Control and Disarmament Agency and chief SALT negotiator to publicize his increasingly negative view of the new administration's arms control stance. Repeated efforts by the Carter administration to placate Jackson through modifications to arms control positions failed. Some observers maintained that Jackson's disappointment at losing the

11. Platt, *U.S. Senate and Strategic Arms Policy*, pp. 56–59, 61–62.
12. *Congressional Quarterly Almanac, 1979*, vol. 35 (1980), p. 411.

presidential nomination, reinforced by the bitterness of individuals long associated with him who had been shut out of policymaking positions, added a special fervor to his opposition. One key adviser, Paul Nitze, later special assistant for arms control to Secretary of State George Shultz, was especially vitriolic during the Warnke hearings,[13] and organized soon thereafter the anti-SALT lobby called the Committee on the Present Danger.

It was the Republicans, however, who garnered the political benefits of the growing dissonance between the Carter administration's policies and public opinion about arms control. Allegations of Soviet cheating on existing agreements became a staple of speeches by Republicans, from moderates like Melvin Laird to more conservative figures like Senator Jake Garn. The 1980 Republican party platform included these charges, along with a plank rejecting the SALT II treaty.[14] Although certainly not as important as the nation's disastrous economic situation, this image of the Carter administration and the Democratic party as weak on defense is believed to have contributed significantly to Carter's failure to win reelection in 1980 and the Republicans' achievement of a majority in the Senate.

THE POLITICS OF ARMS CONTROL IN THE 1980S

With the fickleness of a summer storm, the nation's mood shifted abruptly again in less than two years. In the early 1980s, American political leaders were confronted by a constellation of local organizations seeking to promote the "nuclear freeze," a halt to the development and procurement of all nuclear weapon systems. The withdrawal of the SALT II treaty from the Senate before ratification, the virtual termination of arms control negotiations, and the intemperate rhetoric of the new Reagan administration about the feasibility of fighting and winning nuclear wars had stimulated widespread concerns about nuclear dangers.[15]

Milestones in the ascension and decline of the antinuclear movement in the 1980s are clear. In March 1981 the first National Strategy

13. *Congressional Quarterly Almanac, 1977,* vol. 33 (1977), pp. 324–27.

14. "1980 Republican Platform Text," *Congressional Quarterly Almanac, 1980,* vol. 36 (1981), pp. 79-B–81-B.

15. The following account of the political history of the freeze movement is based largely on Fox Butterfield, "Anatomy of the Nuclear Protest," *New York Times Magazine,* July 11, 1982, pp. 14–17; and Douglas C. Waller, *Congress and the Nuclear Freeze: An Inside Look at the Politics of a Mass Movement* (University of Massachusetts Press, 1987).

Conference of the Nuclear Weapons Freeze Campaign set out the movement's overall approach and organizational structure. By November, as mass protests in Europe against the deployment of new nuclear-armed missiles played on American television against facile statements by administration officials about the feasibility of surviving nuclear war, increasing numbers of Americans began to worry that the new administration might not have its bearings on this essential issue. A profusion of grass-roots organizations emerged, some professionally based—such as doctors, lawyers, and clergymen—but most centered on specific geographic constituencies. On Veterans Day 1981, teach-ins and marches were held in numerous locations, some involving thousands of participants, drawing the attention of mainstream politicians and commentators for the first time.

Drafts of congressional resolutions calling for a freeze on nuclear weapons began to circulate in the House of Representatives in early 1982. Congressional interest grew sharply, however, when Democrat Edward Kennedy and Republican Mark Hatfield introduced a freeze resolution in the Senate in March. Kennedy's support was particularly important to the freeze movement, giving the proposal greater legitimacy with large and powerful political constituencies and adding the senator's impressive political and media operations to the meager resources of the freeze movement itself. Because he was running hard for the presidency at the time, Kennedy's political motives were evident. However sincere his personal evaluation of the freeze, there was clear political advantage in being identified with this popular movement in its early stages.

Combined with continued grass-roots activities throughout the nation, the attention brought to the freeze proposal by the introduction of resolutions in both houses leapfrogged the idea to the top of the popular foreign policy agenda. In June 1982, more than 700,000 people demonstrated in New York City for the nuclear freeze, the single most impressive expression of its popular appeal.

The freeze was an issue in several parts of the country in the 1982 election; there were freeze resolutions on many municipal and state ballots, and many local candidates, as well as congressional candidates, were hard-pressed to avoid taking a position. The administration opposed the proposal in every manifestation, arguing that a freeze was not really arms control or limitation, that it was unverifiable, and that it would freeze the status quo and therefore favored the Soviet Union.

Some even suggested that the entire movement was inspired and guided by Moscow as means of disrupting the American military buildup.

Despite these arguments, the antinuclear movement did very well in the 1982 elections. Even though the the freeze resolution itself had been defeated narrowly on the floor of the House in August, local initiatives passed handily in seven of the eight states and thirty-six of the thirty-eight municipalities and counties in which they appeared on the ballot; polls showed that upwards of two-thirds of Americans said they supported the concept. Supporters claimed that the freeze had become an important issue in forty-seven House races, of which thirty-eight were won by freeze supporters.

While the economic recession that gripped the country at the time was clearly more important, it is clear that the freeze influenced a substantial number of races. The freeze had become the effective symbol of popular concerns about nuclear dangers, and in many districts candidates' support of the freeze gained votes, volunteers, and financial contributions. While there were important exceptions in both parties, the freeze was very much a partisan issue. Democrats found it an effective instrument to attack Republicans for the president's unresponsiveness to the popular impulse for nuclear arms control.

Some Republicans, particularly those from conservative districts, found "freeze-bashing"—talk of its alleged Soviet origins—to be equally rewarding in electoral terms. The political dynamic, however, favored the Democrats on this issue. For the most part, Republicans running for office in 1982 attempted to distance themselves from the administration on arms control. If they did not support the freeze, they at least declared a firm commitment to the objective of controlling nuclear weapons and seeking alternative proposals for achieving that purpose.

The freeze resolution, a nonbinding expression of congressional support for a nuclear freeze under carefully specified conditions, was passed by the House of Representatives in the spring of 1983 after a long and bitter struggle. The resolution never had a chance in the Senate, which was still controlled by the Republicans and is usually less responsive to popular movements. Passage of the resolution in the House, moreover, seems to have marked the political apogee of the movement. The compromises necessary to squeeze the resolution through even the overwhelmingly Democratic House antagonized the organizations that had originated and disseminated the freeze concept, thus fracturing their alliances with more centrist political organizations that had been forged in 1981 and 1982 when mainstream politicians had come to recognize the political strength of the movement. In the eyes of the true believers, the House's approval of funding for procurement of the MX missile within a month of passage of the freeze resolution demonstrated conclusively the cynical way in which their idea and their political strength had been expropriated.

The freeze movement never recovered; its influence on the 1984 presidential and congressional elections was far less than had been expected, serving mainly to lead Democratic presidential candidates to take extreme positions in the early primaries, from which they never recovered. The U.S.-Soviet agreement in the fall of 1984 to reopen arms control negotiations in January 1985 terminated whatever centrist support the movement had gained earlier in the decade and demonstrated just how easily a president can dissipate a public protest by seizing the initiative.

The freeze movement can hardly be termed a failure, however. The popular response in the early 1980s to the cessation of nuclear arms control talks and the Reagan administration's attitudes toward nuclear war, channeled through the freeze movement into politically relevant activities, radically altered the political calculus of arms control. Politicians who preferred to forget in 1980 that they had ever said a positive word about arms control could not work hard enough two years later to make clear their commitment and support. Senator John Glenn, one of the leading Democratic opponents of the SALT II treaty in 1979, is a good illustration of the trend. By December 1981, Glenn, already seeking financial support for the Democratic presidential nomination, had become a fervent supporter of the treaty, introducing the first pro–SALT II resolution in Congress.[16]

The administration itself recognized the change. From a position during Reagan's 1980 campaign and in his administration's first nine months that eschewed all arms negotiations in favor of an unprecedented nuclear buildup, Reagan moved in the fall of 1981 into a wide range of talks on arms control topics, several of which have been concluded successfully. It was not any personal epiphany that led to the president's reversal of his 1980 campaign stance; it was politics—cold and simple.

What was Congress's role in all this? It did not originate the freeze

---

16. *Congressional Quarterly Almanac, 1981,* vol. 37 (1982), pp. 145–46; and John Felton, "Congress Requests Non-Proliferation Policy," *Congressional Quarterly Weekly Report,* July 25, 1981, pp. 1348–49.

movement—far from it. It served instead as a conduit, responding to popular concerns about nuclear weapons. It conveyed to the administration, in tangible form, concerns that had sprung unexpectedly in constituencies throughout the country. Many representatives and senators sought to advance these demands and to be associated with them. Some did so because they shared the popular mood, others because they recognized a winning political trend, but most from a mixture of motives—some personal, others public-minded.

There was also a more lasting effect of the antinuclear movement of the early 1980s, however. It persuaded many in Congress that there could be considerable political benefit from visible involvement in arms control matters. It caused members of Congress—especially representatives, always concerned about the need to renew their mandate every two years and effectively shut out from decisions on arms control policy—to devise new means of influencing executive branch decisions. The effect was particularly strong on the Democratic side of the aisle; some members were looking for ways to advertise their support of the freeze, while others wished primarily to advance centrist alternatives to it as a way to avoid radicalizing their party. All Democrats, however, wanted to take advantage of this popular movement to isolate the president and other Republicans, thus setting the stage for future electoral victories. On the Republican side, some members wished to edge the administration toward a more popular stance on arms control issues in order to defuse the political consequences of the antinuclear movement. Other Republicans wished primarily to protect themselves, to declare an independent stance on this issue, and to demonstrate their commitment by working to compel positive actions by the executive branch.

Regardless of motive, members of Congress needed greater power to accomplish these goals. This power would have to surpass the indirect influence afforded by traditional instruments. Congress needed tangible means to force concessions in arms control policies from a recalcitrant executive. It found that power in the legislature's one unassailable constitutional authority—the power of the purse.

Arms Control and the Power of the Purse

Before the 1980s, Congress's involvement in arms control derived largely from the constitutional requirement that treaties be approved for ratification by two-thirds of the Senate. Some senators, of course, have attempted to use this requirement to alter significantly or simply defeat arms control agreements with which they disagreed. More frequently senators have used ratification debates as a means of seeking to influence an administration's approach to future negotiations. A prime example was Senator Jackson's amendment to the 1972 SALT agreement that called upon the president "to seek a future treaty that, *inter alia*, would not limit the United States to levels of intercontinental strategic forces inferior to the limits provided for the Soviet Union."[17]

Such opportunities are rare, however. In any event, legislators could be more effective, substantively as well as politically, if they were able to help shape an agreement during the course of negotiations, rather than being confined to seeking to alter the agreement—or to place markers for future treaties—during the ratification debate. Thus members of Congress have long argued that they should be involved more closely in arms control negotiations. They have proposed a variety of formal mechanisms to institutionalize the consultative process. During the SALT I negotiations, for example, Senator John Sherman Cooper tried repeatedly to persuade the Nixon administration to include a few senators in the U.S. delegation as observers, but Henry Kissinger's attitude toward congressional consultations—except for the brief period when his nomination as secretary of state was pending before the Senate—was caustic, and the requests were denied.[18]

A Senate SALT advisers group was established during the Carter administration. Members were permitted to attend plenary sessions of the negotiations as observers, to sit in on delegation meetings in Geneva, and even to read the joint draft text of the treaty. They were not permitted to attend the interagency meetings in Washington at which negotiating positions were debated, however, and most of the advisers remained dissatisfied with their ability to influence the talks.[19]

After a hiatus during the first Reagan administration, a Senate Arms Control Observer Group was reconstituted in 1985. In addition to the functions carried out by their predecessors, the new Senate observers were permitted to meet separately with Soviet negotiators, both to learn firsthand of Soviet positions and to express their own concerns.[20]

17. H.J.Res. 1227 (86 Stat. 747).
18. Platt, *U.S. Senate and Strategic Arms Policy*, pp. 19–20.
19. Platt, *U.S. Senate and Strategic Arms Policy*, pp. 116–17.
20. *Report of the Senate Arms Control Observer Group Delegation to the Opening of the*

By most accounts, this consultative process worked fairly well, creating a core of knowledgeable members who felt involved in the negotiations and producing a modicum of sympathy in the Senate for the negotiators' problems of concluding an agreement that satisfied all U.S. concerns without yielding anything of value to the Soviets.

Even so, the limitations of consultations remain evident. Insofar as the observer group cannot commit Congress in any sense, the administration perceives their views largely as a form of intelligence on congressional attitudes, to be heeded or ignored at the executive's option. The observers remain uninvolved in decisions on overall approaches to the talks, to say nothing of specific negotiating positions. Consultations cannot yield real power to Congress as long as the executive branch's interest in the consultative process is restricted to removing the unnecessary political frictions that result from denying Congress any access to the talks and obtaining intelligence on the broad issues that might prove disabling in the ratification debate—the two goals that had motivated both the Carter and second Reagan administrations. This is emphatically the case for the House of Representatives, which has no real role in either consultations or treaty ratification.

Congress's use of appropriations to influence arms control policy was initiated seriously in the early 1980s, when the administration seemed to have no real interest in arms talks and the political pressures on many members of Congress "to do something" about the threat of nuclear war were very great. The existence of political pressures, of course, also implies the existence of political opportunities. Many members of Congress shared their constituents' concerns about nuclear weapons, but the development of new instruments for influencing arms control policy reflected political ambitions, as well as substantive concerns.

The idea was not completely new. In 1971, for example, Senator Hubert H. Humphrey had introduced an amendment to the defense authorization bill that would have placed funds for the deployment of multiple independently targetable reentry vehicles (MIRVs) in escrow until the president and Congress jointly had determined that the USSR had tested and deployed such weapons. This was an attempt to preserve the option for the ongoing SALT negotiations to ban these new weapons. But the political forces favoring arms control were far less

Arms Control Negotiations with the Soviet Union in Geneva, Switzerland, S. Doc. 99-7, 99 Cong. 1 sess. (Government Printing Office, 1985); and interviews with staff of group.

powerful in the 1970s than in the 1980s, and prevailing congressional opinion considered such a direct intervention too radical an encroachment on executive privilege. Humphrey's motion was defeated soundly.[21] Repeated congressional efforts to deny funds for certain improvements in the accuracy of ballistic missiles—also intended to preserve options for arms negotiators—did meet with partial success a few years later. On the whole, however, the political foundations for the use of appropriations to influence arms control were not yet firm enough in the 1970s and, on the whole, the efforts failed.[22]

Political support for arms control had increased so dramatically by the mid-1980s, however, that not only was Congress willing and able to preserve negotiating options, as in its successful struggle to prevent testing of antisatellite weapons, but also in at least one instance it directly caused a change in the administration's negotiating posture. Leverage was provided by the administration's difficulty in securing congressional approval of a new intercontinental ballistic missile, the MX. The objections were based on the Defense Department's continuing inability to come up with a credible scheme to protect the missile from a Soviet first strike. There was also a perception by many members that the weapon was intended for an American first strike, or at least would be seen in this light by the USSR, and thus would be destabilizing.

After years of skirmishing, in 1983 a group of key Democratic representatives—most prominent, Les Aspin, Norman Dicks, and Albert Gore—had the idea that given the missile's obvious political vulnerability, the administration's pending request for funds to deploy the first fifty missiles might be held hostage to elicit concessions on related issues.[23] The strategy had the political advantage from a Democratic perspective of avoiding an action Republicans could point to as further evidence of Democrats' weakness on defense. By avoiding a direct vote to deny funds for the missile, the Democrats also would avoid providing the administration with an excuse for failing to negotiate new arms control arrangements. If Republicans could blame Congress's failure to fund the MX—thus diminishing the U.S. bargaining lever-

21. *Congressional Quarterly Almanac, 1971*, vol. 27 (1972), p. 318.

22. Alton Frye, *A Responsible Congress: The Politics of National Security* (McGraw-Hill, 1975), pp. 48–66.

23. *Congressional Quarterly Almanac, 1983*, p. 197.

age—for the failure of arms control talks, Democrats feared that the antinuclear vote would be divided in the 1984 elections.

The concession sought by the House members was a commitment by the administration to develop a smaller, mobile ICBM—the so-called Midgetman, which previously had been fiercely resisted by the Air Force. Centrist Democrats saw the Midgetman as the basis of both a more secure strategic posture and a less politically vulnerable Democratic approach to military issues. To ensure passage of the deal in the Senate, the representatives forged an alliance with two leading senators, Republican William Cohen and Democrat Sam Nunn. The senators had a special interest of their own, however—a commitment by the executive to include an idea originated by Cohen and Nunn, the build-down proposal, in the American negotiating position at the strategic arms talks.[24] The two senators viewed the build-down as a constructive alternative, substantively and politically, to the nuclear freeze. Unlike the freeze, the build-down would have permitted each side to modernize its nuclear weapons, but only so long as a number of warheads were retired for each new warhead deployed. The number required to be dismantled would vary with the type of weapon being modernized, with the purpose of penalizing either nation if it chose to deploy those types of weapons considered the most dangerous.

Senators Cohen and Nunn met in the White House with chief of staff James Baker to negotiate the build-down commitment. The agreement called for President Reagan to write a letter to the senators expressing the desired commitment, with the scheduled markup of the defense appropriations bill in the Senate as the deadline for receipt of the letter. When the letter arrived the day before the deadline, but seemed to fudge the specific terms of the agreement, the senators returned to the White House late at night to renegotiate. The next day, a new letter was brought to the committee room by courier during the course of the markup, and the MX missile was approved a few minutes later.[25]

24. *Congressional Quarterly Almanac, 1983*, pp. 197–98.

25. Pat Towell, "Letters Ask Reagan Assurances on MX Plan," *Congressional Quarterly Weekly Report*, May 7, 1983, pp. 889–90; Towell, "Reagan's Assurances on MX Persuasive on Hill," *Congressional Quarterly Weekly Report*, May 14, 1983, pp. 933–34; and "Text of Reagan Letter on Arms Control Policy," *Congressional Quarterly Almanac, 1983*, p. 32-E. Details of the negotiations between the senators and the administration obtained from interviews.

The deal was overtaken by events almost immediately, however, as the Soviets walked out of the talks in late 1983, protesting the first deployments of new nuclear missiles in Europe.[26] When the talks resumed in 1985, much more ambitious proposals became the basis of negotiations and obscured the build-down concept. Even so, a precedent had been established for effective congressional action on arms control, using the power of the purse. Not only had the administration been forced to back the Midgetman, a weapon system believed to support arms control objectives, but it also had been compelled to adopt a specific negotiating position in the talks.

Congress has persisted in its efforts to use appropriations to influence arms control ever since. The most successful of these efforts concerned antisatellite weapons. Success also has attended efforts to compel the administration to continue to adhere to limitations included in the unratified SALT II treaty. Congress failed, however, to compel a cessation of nuclear weapon tests. It is worthwhile examining these initiatives in some detail, as they illustrate the dynamics of Congress's new role in arms control.

ANTISATELLITE WEAPONS

The United States began to develop a modern antisatellite weapon in response to the USSR's testing and deployment of a system with limited capabilities in the late 1970s. By the early 1980s, the Soviet Union had ceased its tests following a very mixed record of apparent successes and failures, while the U.S. system was nearing operational testing and deployment. Many experts believed that once the U.S. system had been tested, the USSR would insist on developing and testing a system of comparable sophistication, and it would then be impossible to negotiate a verifiable ban on these weapons. Given the two great powers' growing reliance on satellites for military operations, the existence of operational antisatellite weapons would provide both sides with incentives to strike first in the event of crisis and make more difficult the termination of conflict once a war had begun. The administration refused to consider negotiating a ban on ASATs, however, believing it both impractical and unwise.[27]

Nonbinding resolutions urging negotiations on antisatellite weapons

26. Pat Towell, "Efforts to Delay Pershing II Deployment Fail," *Congressional Quarterly Weekly Report*, December 3, 1983, p. 2540.

27. See Ashton B. Carter, "Satellites and Anti-Satellites: The Limits of the Possible," *International Security*, vol. 10 (Spring 1986), pp. 46–98.

were introduced by Democrat Joe Moakley in the House in 1982. In 1983 Moakley also established the Space Policy Working Group, an informal organization consisting of members and staff, plus lobbyists from the Federation of American Scientists and the Union of Concerned Scientists, two groups working for arms control. The working group was intended to provide a forum for scientists to help educate politicians about space issues and for politicians and their aides to help scientists think politically. The working group expanded measurably following President Reagan's Star Wars speech in March 1983, with its emphasis on uses of space for military purposes.[28]

In June 1983 Democratic Representative George E. Brown, Jr., introduced a floor amendment to the defense authorization bill that would have cut funds for initial procurement from the ASAT program, but it was defeated, 177–243.[29] The anti-ASAT forces were pleased that this first binding initiative had received so much backing. Later that summer, the defense appropriations bill provided a second opportunity to stop the ASAT program. Recognizing the greater leverage afforded by having an initiative incorporated in a bill as reported out by committee, members of the working group approached Representative Matt McHugh, a member of the Appropriations Committee, whose district includes Cornell University. Kurt Gottfried, a member of the board of the Union of Concerned Scientists and a distinguished professor at Cornell, and two of his better-known colleagues, Hans Bethe and Carl Sagan, persuaded McHugh to introduce an anti-ASAT amendment to the appropriations bill. At McHugh's suggestion, the lobbyists persuaded Republican Representative Larry Coughlin to cosponsor, making the issue a bipartisan one.[30]

The bill's sponsors then set out to identify the specific constraints on ASATs that would have the best chance of gaining a majority. In the fall, lobbyists from the Union of Concerned Scientists visited six members of the Appropriations Committee, seeking support. Representative Dicks was sympathetic to the cause, but was reluctant to support a cut in the appropriation because the Boeing Company, an important subcontractor on the ASAT project, was in his district. He suggested instead a measure that would not reduce funding for the project, but would ban any tests of the system as long as the Soviets

28. Interviews; and *Congressional Quarterly Almanac, 1984*, p. 62.
29. *Congressional Quarterly Almanac, 1983*, pp. 179–80.
30. *Congressional Quarterly Almanac, 1984*, p. 62.

continued their own moratorium. When his proposal was accepted, Dicks signed on as a cosponsor.

During the committee's consideration of the amendment, however, Representative Jack Edwards, an opponent, suggested as a compromise that the proposed test moratorium be dropped in favor of a measure that would withhold expenditure of procurement funds until forty-five days after the president had submitted a report on ASATs and the prospects for ASAT arms control. In theory, if the president's report were unpersuasive, the forty-five-day withholding period would provide a new opportunity to stop procurement. Edwards's proposal eventually was adopted.[31] The anti-ASAT members would have preferred that the compromise amendment require a second vote to be held following receipt of the president's report before the procurement funds could be released, but they were not strong enough to shift the burden of proof to the ASAT proponents in this way.

As expected, the president's eventual report maintained that an ASAT test ban would not be in the United States' interest. At that point, the anti-ASAT forces decided to concentrate in 1984 on a test moratorium and were able to begin relatively early to build the broad bipartisan coalition necessary to pass any measure.

The issue was drawn in the summer of 1984 when the fiscal 1985 defense authorization bill came to the floor. The House Armed Services Committee again had approved the requested ASAT appropriation without condition. Brown and Coughlin cosponsored a floor amendment prohibiting the use of funds for testing the ASAT against objects in space until the president had certified that the Soviet Union had conducted a new test of its own ASAT system.[32] Coughlin's support proved particularly important, as he delivered an unexpected thirty-five Republicans in favor of the test limitation, and the Brown-Coughlin amendment was approved overwhelmingly.

The Senate, meanwhile, had approved ASAT funding with only the requirement that the president report on the prospect for negotiations.[33] To ensure a strong defense of their position in the conference

31. Pat Towell, "House Panel Keeps 'Big-Ticket' Defense Items," *Congressional Quarterly Weekly Report*, October 22, 1983, pp. 2169–70.

32. Pat Towell, "House Rebuffs Reagan on Anti-Satellite Tests," *Congressional Quarterly Weekly Report*, May 26, 1984, pp. 1219–20; and Towell, "ASAT Test Curb: Victory for Reagan Critics," *Congressional Quarterly Weekly Report*, June 29, 1985, p. 1263.

33. Pat Towell, "Administration Opts for Compromise on First Test of Anti-Satellite Missile," *Congressional Quarterly Weekly Report*, June 16, 1984, p. 1419.

despite the Armed Services Committee's opposition, the anti-ASAT forces persuaded Speaker Tip O'Neill to appoint Brown as a special conferee. This was an important precedent; it demonstrated for the first time the increasing impatience of the House Democratic leadership, reflecting the views of the majority of the Democratic Caucus, with the Armed Services Committee.

Even so, the House failed to secure passage of the ASAT test limitation in the conference in 1984. Believing that the ASAT program's well-known severe technical problems would require a protracted test program before the system could become operational, Brown accepted a compromise that permitted two of the four proposed tests, so long as the president first certified that the United States was endeavoring in good faith to negotiate a verifiable agreement with the Soviets that included the strictest possible limitations on ASATs. The certification requirement would clearly be no hindrance at all, as the president had already stated that verifiable ASAT limitations were not possible; the "strictest possible" limitations thus meant none at all.

The Brown-Coughlin test moratorium was added to the defense authorization bill again in 1985, but the Senate defeated a similar measure by a lopsided margin.[34] The conference again bitterly disappointed the anti-ASAT members. This time the culprit was the new chairman of the House Armed Services Committee, Les Aspin. The majority of the House conferees were senior members of the committee who generally were more conservative than most House Democrats. Apparently Aspin believed he could not persuade them to stick with the Brown-Coughlin moratorium, so he accepted a compromise on ASATs that imposed a testing moratorium for five months, required the by-then routine presidential certification, and then permitted three tests against objects in space. Because he had receded or struck weak compromises on several other controversial defense issues, Aspin's performance infuriated House members and contributed importantly to efforts to unseat him as committee chair at the start of the subsequent Congress.[35]

An ASAT testing moratorium was finally passed by Congress a

34. Towell, "ASAT Test Curb"; and *Congressional Quarterly Almanac, 1985,* vol. 41 (1986), pp. 162–64.

35. Interviews; Pat Towell, "Budget Dealing Derails Defense Bill in House," *Congressional Quarterly Weekly Report,* August 3, 1985, pp. 1532–33; and Towell, "House Accord May Clear Way for Vote on Defense Measure," *Congressional Quarterly Weekly Report,* September 14, 1985, pp. 1798–99.

few months later, however, when the continuing resolution for fiscal
1986 was considered.[36] (For a variety of reasons, in the mid-1980s so-
called continuing resolutions, or omnibus spending bills, were used
repeatedly as the legislative vehicle to appropriate funds, in place of
individual appropriation measures.) The two chambers entered the
conference on the resolution with more or less the same positions they
had held during the defense authorization debate. This time, however,
two of the House conferees, Norm Dicks and Les AuCoin, were
absolutely determined to obtain the moratorium. AuCoin, especially,
felt that if tests of the U.S. system were not stopped, the Soviets
would have every inducement to restart their own testing, and any
possibility of a verifiable ban on deployments would be lost.[37]

Circumstances also aided Dicks and AuCoin. The chairman of the
House Defense Appropriations Subcommittee, Joe Addabbo, was in
failing health and did not take part in the conference. The acting
chairman, William Chappell, wished to succeed Addabbo, but recognized that he was considered too conservative for the job by many
members of the Democratic Caucus. He was well aware, moreover,
of the disappointment with Aspin's performance in the authorization
conference and that he would be judged harshly if the House failed
again to get its views incorporated in the continuing resolution. Thus
he was determined to win on the moratorium provision in order to
gain support for his bid to become subcommittee chairman.

The Senate chairman, Ted Stevens, moveover, had many higher
priorities. The House conferees had made clear their determination to
persevere on the ASAT issue. Not caring that much about ASATs
himself, Stevens decided to trade the test moratorium for House
concessions on other issues. The final bill "prohibited the obligation
or expenditure of funds" for ASAT testing against objects in space
"until the President certifies to Congress that the Soviet Union has
conducted . . . a test against an object in space of a dedicated antisatellite weapon."[38] After three years, the House had succeeded. The
test moratorium was never seriously challenged after that; it was
enacted into law again in 1986 and 1987. In 1988 the Defense

---

36. *Congressional Quarterly Almanac, 1985*, p. 361.

37. Interviews; and David C. Morrison, "Half a Loaf on Defense Funds," *National Journal*, December 21, 1985, p. 2916.

38. 100 Stat. 341.

Department decided to terminate the ASAT program as part of a major effort to reduce defense costs.[39]

Circumstances favored the congressional effort to terminate ASAT tests. The Soviets maintained their moratorium throughout this period; there were not even allegations of Soviet cheating. The U.S. program did not fare well in development, experiencing huge cost overruns and repeated technical problems. The constituency for the program was small to begin with. Even so, to end the program was an uphill fight. The anti-ASAT side won in the end because of two factors.

First, the lobby was effective. The scientists' organizations were very good at explaining the highly technical issues related to ASAT deployments and had great credibility on the Hill. The lobbyists' approach was pragmatic, moreover; they were willing to accept smaller gains to obtain the support of key members, taking a longer-term view than is usually the case on these issues. The lobbyists' determination to obtain bipartisan backing for the moratorium paid off particularly well, taking some of the political curse off the measure, not only for House Republicans, but for the Senate majority as well.

Second, as the first arms control issue taken up seriously by liberal House Democrats, the anti-ASAT effort gained a degree of precedence and loyalty among the cadre of supporters. As small steps were achieved, moreover, the effort gained a sense of "winnability" and the momentum of success. In the early and mid-1980s, members were anxious to show some results to their constituents who supported arms control. They no doubt sought victory for personal reasons as well; enthusiasm can be maintained for only so long in the face of repeated defeats. For all these reasons, the ASAT test moratorium became the highest arms control priority of House Democrats; and as the political tides shifted, it became virtually inevitable.

STRATEGIC ARMS LIMITATIONS

The House Democrats have also given high priority to the effort to force the administration to continue to comply with the unratified SALT II treaty. When the treaty was withdrawn from Senate consideration in 1980, the Carter administration announced that its

39. Pat Towell, "The Carlucci Budget: Picking among Priorities," *Congressional Quarterly Weekly Report*, February 27, 1988, p. 524.

policy would be not to undercut the agreement so long as the Soviets exercised similar restraint. In March 1981 the Reagan administration stated that it too would not undercut existing arms control agreements providing that the USSR also exercised restraint.[40] This state of affairs continued until May 1986, when the president announced that in view of what the administration considered Soviet violations of the SALT agreement, the United States would abandon its informal compliance.[41] Scheduled deployments of cruise missiles on B-52 bombers suggested that the United States would breach the SALT limit on the total number of offensive systems with multiple warheads toward the end of the year.

Two measures to prevent such a violation of the treaty were swiftly introduced in the House. Representative Dicks moved successfully to amend the fiscal 1987 defense authorization bill to bar the use of funds for deployments above certain specified SALT limits, so long as the Soviets behaved similarly.[42] Meanwhile, the House Appropriations Committee acted to require the Navy to dismantle two missile-carrying submarines.[43] This latter measure would have had the effect of preserving the threatened limit without mentioning the SALT treaty by name.

The Senate passed no binding SALT restrictions in 1986, however, and appeared determined to defeat the House initiatives in conference. The administration's influence in the upper chamber (which was still under Republican control at that time) and the fact that many Democratic senators were more conservative than their House counterparts had the most to do with the Senate's recalcitrance. However, the Senate's position was also influenced by an unwillingess to concede the House a role in these issues. As one Senate staffer put it, "The Senate just isn't going to be prepared to see the other body get involved in treaty ratification."[44]

The issue was joined on the fiscal 1987 continuing resolution. Early meetings of the conference committee suggested a compromise along

40. *Weekly Compilation of Presidential Documents*, vol. 16 (May 19, 1980), p. 878; (June 30, 1980), p. 1159. vol. 17 (February 2, 1981), p. 66; U.S. Arms Control and Disarmament Agency, *Documents on Disarmament, 1981*, pub. 118 (GPO, 1985), p. 84; and Walter Taylor, "Haig Says U.S. Will Observe SALT Limits," *Washington Star*, March 5, 1981.

41. *Congressional Quarterly Almanac, 1986*, vol. 42 (1987), p. 462.

42. *Congressional Quarterly Almanac, 1987*, vol. 43 (1988), pp. 215–17.

43. *Congressional Quarterly Almanac, 1986*, pp. 462–63.

44. Pat Towell, "House Could Win Big Victory on Partial Nuclear Test Ban," *Congressional Quarterly Weekly Report*, August 30, 1986, p. 2038.

the lines of the House Appropriations measure: an initiative that did not mention the treaty, but required specific reductions in U.S. forces sufficient to maintain compliance with the agreement. This would have fulfilled the House's arms control objectives, but preserved at least the appearance of the Senate's prerogatives pertaining to treaties. The issue became moot on September 30, however, when plans for the Reykjavik summit were announced. At that point, continuing to insist on their position would have put the House Democrats in the politically awkward position of appearing to tie the president's hands on the eve of his meeting with the Soviet leader. Few politicians would choose to put themselves in such a position six weeks before an election. After some internal discussions, political prudence carried the day. House Democratic leaders accepted the fig leaf of nonbinding SALT language and some vague promises on nuclear testing in exchange for backing off the SALT-related weapon dismantlings and several other arms control issues.[45]

The failure of the Reykjavik summit guaranteed congressional action when the One-hundredth Congress convened in January 1987. This time, House activists stated their intention, if necessary, of putting binding SALT language on every available budget measure. When the Senate, with the Democratic majority that resulted from the 1986 election, passed its own binding measure to enforce SALT limits (a floor amendment by Senator Dale Bumpers to the fiscal 1988 defense authorization bill), Congress was poised to act decisively. The winning compromise in conference, like that contemplated before the Reykjavik announcement, did not mention the treaty: instead, it required the retirement of a strategic submarine to keep the United States close to the SALT II limits.[46] Comparable measures were also attached successfully to the fiscal 1989 defense authorization and appropriation bills.[47]

Congressional efforts to enforce SALT II constraints suffered from two political liabilities. First, the treaty itself remained something of a hot potato. It had been so thoroughly discredited during the 1980

45. Pat Towell, "Impasse over Arms Control Issues Resolved," *Congressional Quarterly Weekly Report*, October 11, 1986, pp. 2522–23.

46. *Congressional Quarterly Almanac, 1987*, pp. 216–18.

47. Macon Morehouse, "House Approves Defense Bill, Arms Provisions," *Congressional Quarterly Weekly Report*, May 14, 1988, p. 1308; and John Felton, "Pentagon Money Bill Makes Early House Debut," *Congressional Quarterly Weekly Report*, June 11, 1988, pp. 1612–13.

campaign that many members who otherwise supported arms control were reluctant to embrace the treaty itself. Second, House action on SALT II provoked spirited opposition from the Senate on jurisdictional grounds. The Senate was unprepared to concede an explicit role in treaty matters to the House. As a result, congressional actions to enforce SALT II constraints succeeded only by causing changes in U.S. military forces that de facto preserved the treaty. The compromises that emerged from House-Senate conferences made no mention of the treaty itself, so as to assuage Senate sensibilities about its unique role as arbiter of treaties. For the Senate to grant the House any explicit role concerning a treaty would be like the House permitting the Senate to initiate a tax bill. Few things are guarded more jealously in the Congress than the respective prerogatives of the two chambers.

NUCLEAR TESTING

Congress has been unsuccessful, despite repeated efforts throughout the 1980s, in forcing the executive branch to move toward a comprehensive nuclear test ban. Nonbinding resolutions calling on the administration to submit to the Senate two partial test ban treaties that were negotiated during the mid-1970s but never ratified and to resume negotiations for a comprehensive ban on nuclear testing died either in committee or in conference in 1982, 1983, 1984, and 1985.[48] There were many reasons for this, including the Reagan administration's unrelenting hostility to restrictions on nuclear testing and divisions among the measures' sponsors in the House. Moreover, because the test ban measures were nonbinding and members thus expected the administration to ignore them, there was a certain sense of futility attending the effort. Even members who were usually supporters of arms control were willing to invest only limited time and energy on behalf of measures with such poor prospects. There were clear similarities between the nuclear testing resolutions and the ill-fated freeze resolution; indeed, the test ban initiative sprang initially from a meeting called to decide what might be salvaged following the Senate's defeat of the freeze in 1983.

Political evaluations of the test ban changed importantly in August 1985 when, on the fortieth anniversary of the bombing of Hiroshima, Soviet leader Mikhail Gorbachev announced a unilateral moratorium on all nuclear tests and called upon the United States to follow suit.

48. *Congressional Quarterly Almanac, 1986*, pp. 461–62.

This encouraged Democratic Representative Patricia Schroeder, one of those who had been unenthusiastic about the nonbinding resolution, to introduce a bill that would have denied all funds for nuclear testing after a certain date, provided that the Soviet Union continued its own moratorium. Schroeder's move was not well received by the backers of the nonbinding resolution, who believed it was essential to put Congress on record in support of negotiations before seeking binding legislation. The issue was fought out in the Wednesday Morning Group, an informal organization of members, staff, and outside lobbyists, comparable to the Space Policy Working Group.

Having legislative precedence, the nonbinding resolution was taken up first. It finally was passed by the full House in February 1986, clearing the way for consideration of Schroeder's proposal. Encouraged by several extensions of the Soviet moratorium, Schroeder and Democratic cosponsor Tom Downey attempted to attach their restriction to the fiscal 1986 supplemental appropriation bill, but were defeated by procedural problems.[49]

Representative Bill Green, a liberal Republican, then attempted to amend the Department of Energy's appropriation to deny funds for weapons testing, as he had the previous year. (Funds for nuclear weapons development and testing are administered by the Energy Department.) For political reasons, however, Downey persuaded the Democratic-controlled Rules Committee to rule Green's amendment nongermane, even though it was worded strictly as a modification of the funding proposal. Downey had two purposes: he did not want to see Democratic leadership on the issue diluted, and he wanted the measure attached to the Defense Department authorization in order to force Les Aspin's hand on the testing issue. Downey was one of the members who had been disappointed by Aspin's performance in the 1985 defense authorization conference; forcing Aspin to take on the testing issue, Downey believed, would help make clear whether the new chairman deserved the continued support of the Democratic Caucus. These partisan and intraparty complications obviously did not help the test ban cause.

For several months thereafter, the nuclear test ban's sponsors sought to gain centrist support through modifications in the amendment's language. Tests with explosive yields below one kiloton were excluded, for example, and elaborate language was added concerning the verifi-

49. *Congressional Quarterly Almanac, 1986*, pp. 461–62.

cation requirements of a test ban. Aspin, the key to a group of moderates, continued to vacillate until late June, when he defied the House Democratic leadership to vote for contra aid.[50] The ensuing cries of betrayal prompted two members of the Armed Services Committee—Charles Bennett and Marvin Leath—to announce that they would contest the committee's chairmanship when the new Congress convened in 1987.[51] Downey and others made clear to Aspin that his support of the testing prohibition was essential to gain backing from pro–arms control members.

Aspin signed on in mid-July, bringing two other key moderates, Richard Gephardt and John Spratt, with him immediately.[52] The latter was particularly important, as he had gained a deserved reputation as one of the most thoughtful members on security issues. Indeed, he ended up crafting the changes that permitted the measure to pass. In the following weeks, Aspin and his colleagues worked diligently to gain centrist support and, on August 8, the test ban was passed as an amendment to the defense authorization bill by an astonishingly large margin, 234–155.[53]

The House entered the 1986 authorization conference determined to reverse the previous year's results and gain victories in each of the five contentious arms control issues, including nuclear testing. Aspin certainly had an incentive to work hard for these measures, given his upcoming struggle to remain in the chair. Speaker O'Neill, moreover, named key Democratic leaders on arms control issues as "special conferees" to make sure Aspin toed the line. In the end, as previously noted, the House position was undercut by announcement of the Reykjavik summit. Still, the outlines of a compromise had been made clear: until the summit announcement, a proposal by Senator Gary Hart to limit expenditures to only six tests a year had appeared likely to carry the day.[54]

The effort to constrain nuclear testing peaked with this aborted compromise. In 1987 the House again amended the defense bill to

50. *Congressional Quarterly Almanac, 1986*, p. 407.

51. *Congressional Quarterly Almanac, 1987*, p. 7.

52. Interviews; Pat Towell, "Stage Set for Battles over Reagan Arms Policy," *Congressional Quarterly Weekly Report*, August 2, 1986, p. 1766; and Towell, "House Reverses Reagan on Nuclear Tests," *Congressional Quarterly Weekly Report*, August 9, 1986, p. 1786.

53. *Congressional Quarterly Almanac, 1986*, p. 287.

54. Pat Towell, "Arms Control at Issue in Defense Conference," *Congressional Quarterly Weekly Report*, September 27, 1986, p. 2321.

prohibit all tests above one kiloton,[55] but circumstances had changed by then and the political momentum behind the move was less compelling. The Soviets had resumed nuclear testing, but there was progress in talks on both intermediate-range missiles and central strategic forces. More to the point, the Soviets had accepted the administration's position on nuclear testing and had agreed to talks on strengthening the verification provisions of two previously signed treaties placing partial limits on nuclear tests.[56]

The House of Representatives' efforts to curtail nuclear testing failed mainly because the greater political saliency of the testing issue appears to have tempted members to exploit this issue for partisan and intraparty political purposes, even at the expense of substantive progress. Whereas the anti-ASAT lobby courted bipartisanship, at some points the Democratic advocates of nuclear testing limits sought deliberately to undermine a visible Republican position. What limited progress was made on the testing issue in 1985 and 1986 was largely due to the coincidence of two factors. Externally, as the Soviet testing moratorium was extended repeatedly, political pressures for a positive U.S. response increased, peaking in September 1986 with the aborted compromise to limit the number of U.S. tests. Internally, the struggle for Les Aspin's chairmanship after his vote in favor of contra aid in June 1986 guaranteed his vigorous participation in the effort to constrain nuclear testing and the subsequent support of other previously reluctant key centrist members.

The New Politics of Arms Control

A massive shift in public attitudes toward nuclear weapons occurred roughly between the election in 1980 and the fall of 1981. As the public's previously inchoate fears of nuclear war began to crystallize during this period, it suddenly became evident that concern about nuclear war was becoming a powerful political force. As the antinuclear tide grew stronger in 1982 and 1983, politicians, especially Democrats, many of whom shared their constituents' concerns, also began to see personal rewards in associating themselves with the cause.

Political incentives favoring arms control operated at two related

55. *Congressional Quarterly Almanac, 1987*, p. 236.
56. "M.S. Gorbachev's Reception of George Shultz," *Tass*, April 15, 1987, pp. 1, 3, in Foreign Broadcast Information Service, *Daily Report: Soviet Union*, April 15, 1987, pp. A6–A10.

levels. On the national level, the nuclear issue appeared to be one of Ronald Reagan's two vulnerabilities (the other being the economic recession). It provided all Democrats with incentives to highlight the contrast between the administration's recalcitrance on the nuclear arms negotiations issue and their own positive stance. Nuclear freeze proponents were active within the Democratic party and quickly gained especially powerful positions in two key states, Iowa and New Hampshire, as well as among such traditional sources of Democratic campaign financing as the movie industry. With a large number of Senate Democrats interested in exploring their presidential prospects, there was a built-in cadre of support for arms control initiatives, if not for the freeze itself.

On the state and local level, the antinuclear movement appeared to have a direct effect on candidates' electoral prospects. Playing a visible role in promoting the freeze or similar antinuclear measures gained favorable reviews in home districts, aided fundraising efforts, and disarmed potential opponents. In this dimension the political impulse affected Republicans as well as Democrats, particularly those from regions of the country where the antinuclear movement was strongest, like the Northeast. These considerations affected relatively few senators, as most standing for reelection in 1982 or 1984 were in relatively secure seats. The effect on House races was far greater: many members sought means to show their ability to do something about the nuclear arms race. These political considerations added measurably to pro-arms control members' substantive concerns on the issues, triggering a concerted effort to carve a new role for the House and its Democratic majority.

The new participation of the House of Representatives in arms control issues, the most fundamental change underlying Congress's new role in arms control, is the direct result of these considerations. With the House being the one national institution remaining in Democratic hands in the wake of the 1980 election, it was natural that the Democratic Caucus and the House leadership would take the lead in this partisan effort to exploit popular unhappiness with the administration's arms control stance. Except in those cases in which the issue pertained directly to an existing treaty, the House has been the primary source of congressional arms control initiatives.

On arms control issues, like most other foreign policy issues, the Democratic members of the House are divided. Perhaps a third of the Democratic members are committed liberals and can be counted on to support most measures intended to advance arms control. The leaders of this faction, most of whom entered Congress in the post-Watergate classes of 1974 and 1976, are now in positions of rising influence, both in the leadership and in key committees. This liberal faction is confronted on many issues by a smaller group of conservatives, many of whom continue to hold key subcommittee chairmanships and other important posts, but the members of this latter group are on the verge of retirement and their strength is deteriorating rapidly.

The more important challenge to the liberals comes from the emergence in recent years of a moderate centrist bloc, responsive to antinuclear pressures and personally committed to achieving progressive arms control objectives, but also pragmatic about politics and about the international situation. Responding in part to the Democrats' defeats from 1978 through 1984 and again in the presidential election of 1988, these members seek to forge policy positions that might help the party to regain its former hold on the center of the American political spectrum. Compared with the liberals, they also tend to be more concerned with maintaining a strong military posture and more skeptical about the possibilities for rapid progress in arms control and U.S.-Soviet relations.

The key to effective action in the House on arms control has been the formation of a consensus centered on this moderate bloc. According to one Democratic member centrally involved in these issues, perhaps forty to sixty Democrats are the key players. If these people can be persuaded to support a position, it probably will also appeal to enough liberals and conservatives to pass. And support of the centrist bloc in the House is essential if the position is going to have a chance of being accepted by the more conservative Senate.

The House leadership played a key role in the formation of this consensus, particularly Majority Leader Jim Wright in the mid-1980s and, later in the decade, the majority whip, Tony Coelho. Whether Tom Foley and Richard Gephardt, the Democrats' new leaders, will play a comparably aggressive role remains to be seen.

The leadership's willingness in recent years, following pressures from the caucus, to exert leverage on key subcommittee chairmen is said to have been particularly important for the House's greater success in pressing arms control initiatives. Beginning in 1986, whip task forces were formed for those arms control issues on which a consensus could be established. Members of the task forces, appointed on a regional basis, would talk to colleagues, making clear the preferred positions, their relative priorities, and the legislative strategy being pursued. Whip task forces were not formed for issues lacking a centrist consensus.[57]

The whole process was carried out informally. Initiatives arose from individuals or groups of congressmen. Informal, nonpartisan organizations of members, staff, and outside experts and lobbyists, such as the Space Policy Working Group, helped to educate members on the issues, to craft legislative strategies, and to muster outside sources of influence to approach key members. Initiatives were sometimes discussed in meetings of the Democratic Caucus, but that organization is said not to have been central in the formation of positions, which was accomplished by individuals and staff. Similarly, the Democratic Study Group, which was important in the 1970s in formulating partywide positions, is said not to have played that role in the 1980s. The crucial role in formulating consensus positions was played by individual representatives in private discussions with their colleagues; the individuals able to speak for larger groups of members were well known.

The House's new role notwithstanding, the Senate has retained its traditional prereogatives on matters pertaining directly to treaties. As noted, to gain passage through the full Congress, the House initiative to compel the administration to continue to abide by the SALT II treaty could not mention the treaty at all; instead, it sought a de facto observance of the treaty by requiring the retirement of certain weapon systems. The Senate, moreover, was the main player in the dispute during 1987 and 1988 over the proper interpretation of the ABM treaty. The House passed amendments to funding bills denying expenditures for activities that would violate the traditional narrow definition of the treaty, but did not address the treaty interpretation issue directly.

The key procedural change in both chambers has been a shift in de facto jurisdiction over arms control matters from the Foreign Affairs and Foreign Relations committees, the traditional focus of congressional activities concerning arms control, to the Armed Services committees and, to a lesser extent, the Intelligence committees. There are a number of reasons for this change, the weak leadership of the Foreign Affairs and Foreign Relations committees being prominent among them. This was clear during the ABM treaty interpretation dispute. It was Senator

57. Interview with Les Aspin, November 21, 1988.

Nunn, chairman of the Armed Services Committee, who first compelled the administration to make available the treaty's negotiating record to Congress and then issued a report that strongly supported the traditional, narrow interpretation.[58] Once Nunn committed himself publicly to the narrow interpretation, Congress's eventual position was evident and the adminstration began to deal seriously on the issue. The Senate Foreign Relations Committee and its chairman, Claiborne Pell, played virtually no role in the dispute over what normally would have been considered a central matter of the committee's jurisdiction.[59]

The Armed Services committees' greater influence also reflects Congress's new willingness to use its power of the purse as leverage on arms control matters. To make effective use of appropriating power, proponents of arms control measures require a spending bill that the administration would find difficult to veto. Nothing falling within the jurisdiction of the Foreign Affairs Committee meets this requirement. Congress has gone for years without approving a new foreign aid bill, the largest authorization coming under the committee's jurisdiction. The committee also authorizes appropriations for the State Department and the Arms Control and Disarmament Agency, but they are relatively small bills and lack political support.

The defense authorization bill, however, is among the most "veto-proof" measures considered by Congress. There are no absolutes in the legislative business, of course, as both Presidents Carter and Reagan have demonstrated by vetoing defense authorizations. However, presidents usually are reluctant to risk any disruption in military operations or, more to the point, to appear to be willing to trifle with the nation's security because of what will appear to most people to be a dispute with the legislature over an obscure issue. For this reason, arms control initiatives have been added primarily to defense spending bills, and influence over these issues has shifted away from the Foreign Relations and Foreign Affairs committees.

In the early 1980s, Congress successfully checked an administration whose nuclear policies were increasingly deviating from the public's view of a judicious course of action. In mid-decade, Congress successfully channeled the public's dissatisfaction behind specific initiatives.

58. *Congressional Quarterly Almanac, 1987*, pp. 196–97.

59. Helen Dewar, "Senate Foreign Relations Panel Founders," *Washington Post*, October 10, 1989, p. A1.

It compelled the administration to resume arms talks and to make specific proposals in some of them, to continue to abide by existing agreements, and to take unilateral actions to maintain certain negotiating options. In accomplishing these objectives, Congress served well in its constitutionally intended role as a check on the executive branch, a means of ensuring that executive policies do not deviate too far from the popular will.

Still, as all recent administrations, Democrat and Republican, have pointed out, there is much wrong with the new congressional role in arms control. It is hard enough to negotiate detailed and highly technical arms control agreements with foreign governments; if the executive branch must first negotiate its own positions with a hostile legislature, largely in public, the negotiating task becomes daunting. Few members of Congress are knowledgeable enough about the details of negotiating issues, or have enough time to learn about them, to reach independent judgments. Moreover, when Congress is involved in the details of negotiations, there are too many opportunities for parochial interests to dominate decisionmaking and too many temptations to substitute calculations of political advantage and disadvantage for reckonings of the overall national interest. In a sense, Congress is too responsive to shifts in public opinion and thus cannot sustain the consistency necessary to prevail in negotiations.

As administration policy and public opinion about nuclear weapons have come into closer agreement—particularly since the midterm election in 1986—Congress's role has become less visible and legislative initiatives less successful. Still, having discovered its ability to foster arms control through appropriations, Congress (especially the House) seems unlikely to abdicate its new powers. Precedents have been established, expectations among members and arms control supporters have been set, and procedures and institutional arrangements have been set in motion. Although the tide of congressional successes seems to have ebbed, the bitterness of the conflict between the branches over the appropriateness of the new congressional role seems to have grown, as witnessed during the debate over President Reagan's veto of the defense authorization bill in 1988. From a national perspective, this struggle between the branches over arms control policy, particularly in its partisan implications, is extremely harmful. The discord that has dominated the national dialogue on nuclear weapons and nuclear arms control since the early 1970s has repeatedly embarrassed administrations and caused friends and foes to be unsure of this country's reliability as a negotiating partner. If it is to succeed in this field, any administration must come to terms with Congress's ability to use the power of the purse to influence arms control policy.

The solution lies in a more collaborative approach to negotiations and agreements. Despite the consultative processes and organizations that have been established since the 1970s, no administration has been willing to accept Congress as a true partner in the establishment of negotiating objectives and strategies. Both Democratic and Republican presidents have seen Congress largely as an obstacle to be overcome, not a body whose views should be a fundamental influence on the terms sought in negotiations. Consultative procedures are viewed largely as opportunities to co-opt members, to sell them on the administration's view, or to garner intelligence on the boundaries of congressional tolerance—not as a means of exchanging views and crafting truly collaborative approaches.

No formal mechanism can guarantee such collaboration. It can result only from an administration's understanding that its own interest, to say nothing of the nation's, hinges on greater cooperation between the branches on arms control policy. Not only must the administration take the lead, but it must do so in a politically astute way, making sure that the strategies it devises are likely to satisfy a comfortable working majority of each house. Forty years ago it was possible for Under Secretary of State Robert Lovett, working essentially with one senator, Arthur Vandenberg, to shape a resolution on the postwar U.S. relationship with Western Europe that, after debate and amendment on the Senate floor, commanded an overwhelming majority in the Senate.[60] While no single member can now represent the views of either chamber, moderate forces continue to control both houses. It is thus possible to work with a relatively small number of senators and representatives from both parties to design policies that will isolate the more extreme members and ensure majority support.

If the central thrust of administration arms control policies satisfies such bipartisan majorities, there will be far less maneuvering room for congressional initiatives on the details of negotiating positions or unilateral programs. No doubt such measures will continue to be

60. See Dean Acheson, *Present at the Creation: My Years in the State Department* (Norton, 1969), pp. 264, 266.

introduced, particularly when defense spending bills come to the floor, but the centrist support necessary for them to pass will be effectively undermined.

The potential effectiveness of such a consensus-building strategy was demonstrated clearly in the final stages of negotiations on the 1988 treaty on intermediate-range missiles. In April and May 1988, the Reagan administration consulted closely with Senate leaders before clarifying with the USSR certain provisions of the agreement pertaining to inspection procedures and developing a program to improve unilateral U.S. capabilities to verify Soviet compliance with the INF agreement and the prospective START treaty.[61] Once agreement was reached on these issues, congressional opposition to the treaty was confined to small minorities.

Adoption of such a collaborative approach at the outset of negotiations, or at the start of a new administration, could go a long way toward removing the basic source of friction in executive-legislative relations on arms control issues and could dampen support for legislative initiatives. The group of congressional leaders consulted in such circumstances, however, should be expanded to include the House counterparts of the senators consulted in the INF group. Indeed, Congress would do well to designate an official consultative group, as is envisioned, for example, in the 1988 bipartisan initiative to amend the War Powers Resolution (see Robert Katzmann's paper). In such an eventuality, thought might also be given to including a representative from each party in each chamber elected from the membership at large in order to provide some representation for the views of more junior members.

It is difficult for executive branch officials to concede a role in arms control policy to Congress; the vested interests of the bureaucracy, the arrogance of expertise, and long-engrained habits all get in the way. The experience of the 1980s has shown, however, that Congress will not be excluded from a policymaking role. The real choice is between a congressional role imposed by a hostile legislature against the executive's will—usually long after negotiating positions have been tabled and defended publicly—and a congressional role accepted in

61. Tom Kenworthy, "Byrd Prepared to Begin Debate on INF Treaty Today," *Washington Post*, May 17, 1988, p. A19; and Helen Dewar, "Final Hitches Resolved, INF Treaty Debuts in Senate," *Washington Post*, May 18, 1988, p. A4.

the normal course of setting policy. With both President George Bush and Senate Majority Leader George Mitchell stressing bipartisanship in foreign policy, the prospects for a cooperative approach to arms control appear high. Only time will tell if the new administration has the wisdom to accept the new congressional role.

American Diplomacy:
Around the World and along
Pennsylvania Avenue

BRUCE W. JENTLESON

AMERICAN DIPLOMACY has come to involve relations within government almost as much as relations between governments. Even the language reflects this tension. Battles are said to be fought between the president and the Congress. The president and congressional leaders meet in summits; they negotiate; they seek a truce; and they make peace.

During the Reagan years, "Pennsylvania Avenue diplomatic relations" on major issues of U.S. international diplomacy were characterized by four distinct patterns. First, on a number of issues involving regional conflicts—Nicaragua, South Africa, arms sales to Saudi Arabia and other Arab states—there was outright *confrontation*. On Nicaragua, matters degenerated to the point of virtual war between the legislative and executive branches, as battles were fought over both contra aid and regional diplomatic peace initiatives. On South Africa, the confrontation culminated in Congress's first veto override on a foreign policy issue since the 1973 War Powers Act. On the Arab arms sales, Reagan won the first round in 1981 on the Saudi AWACS sale, but only barely and only after a bruising battle. His record was more mixed on later sales: some went through, others had to be modified, and others had to be canceled.

Second, there was a worsening generalized *institutional competition* over much of the day-to-day conduct of diplomacy. Depending upon one's perspective, this amounted to either congressional micromanagement—meddlesome and nettlesome interference by the legislature in the affairs of state—or the proper and prudent exercise of checks and balances by the people's representatives to ensure executive accountability. The main examples here come from State Department authorization bills, foreign aid bills, and obstructionist procedural tactics often used by individual members, of which the best example is the

The author wishes to thank Robert J. Kurz for his helpful comments and Clint Brass for his research assistance.

persistent campaign waged against the State Department (its people no less than its policies) by Senator Jesse Helms.

Third, on two issues in particular, military aid to El Salvador and the leadership crisis in the Philippines, initial conflicts over policy were overcome and *constructive compromises* were worked out. There is a tendency to assume, in the penchant for politics stopping at the water's edge, that political conflict always is counterproductive to effective foreign policy. Yet on El Salvador the compromise policy of aid as leverage worked out in 1983 proved much preferable to either of the original more extreme positions of aid with no strings (White House) and aid cutoff (Congress). In the Philippines, while the White House continued to stand by Ferdinand Marcos, key members of Congress from both sides of the aisle and in both houses worked closely with key State Department officials to pressure Marcos and bring about an orderly yet democratic transition.

Finally, and for many observers most surprising, were those issues on which the interbranch peace was kept and a common, coordinated policy was pursued—in fact it could be truthfully said that *bipartisan cooperation* prevailed. This is more an assessment of the later years of the Reagan administration, rather than the early years; and what is especially interesting is that those issues on which bipartisan cooperation did emerge were among those that had been the most confrontational in the past: the use of military force against aggressor states in certain regional conflicts (Libya, the Persian Gulf, Afghanistan), relations with the Soviet Union (with the continuing exception of arms control issues), and development of normalized relations with the People's Republic of China.

In this chapter I will examine each of these patterns and their representative cases. The variations among them will be explained in terms of three principal factors: policy differences, public opinion and interest group pressure, and institutional power sharing.

First, it should be a truism that one of the primary causes of political conflict is substantive policy disagreement. Yet there still is a widespread tendency to look elsewhere for explanation. This may well reflect a legacy of the old "golden age" of bipartisanship, when foreign policy consensus was taken as a given and the lack of it treated as an aberration (or worse). But amid Vietnam, détente, and a host of other issues, the old cold war consensus broke wide open.[1] In the 1970s and into the

---

1. Ole R. Holsti and James N. Rosenau, *American Leadership in World Affairs: Vietnam*

early 1980s, there were very few foreign policy issues on which there
were not heated and substantial policy differences. Yet, as the above
patterns indicate, over the course of the Reagan years a significant
degree of differentiation emerged as policy conflicts intensified on some
issues but lessened on others.

Similarly, with regard to public opinion and interest group pressure,
conventional wisdom held that foreign policy was, should be, and
would remain insulated from such pressures. Leaving aside for the
moment the "should be" normative question, the objective analytic
point is that "would remain" no longer pertains as a general rule. Yet
not all issues generate the same amount or kinds of pressures.
Distinctions therefore need to be made among different issues in terms
of the degree of activation of public opinion, the alignments of interest
groups, and other domestic political pressures.

Finally, Edward Corwin's classical analysis of the constitutional
relationship between the president and Congress described it as "an
invitation to struggle for the privilege of directing American foreign
policy."[2] Richard Neustadt was even closer to the reality with his
characterization of "separated institutions *sharing* powers."[3] Because
Congress was so willingly deferential for most of the cold war, the
actual problem of institutional power sharing was minimized. The
1970s, however, changed all that. Moreover, with the ensconcing of
divided government (by 1992 the two branches will have been split
between the two parties for twenty of the past twenty-four years), the
invitation to struggle has been reissued. For any given issue, therefore,
one needs to look at the institutional power-sharing problem in terms
of its structure, or who has which policy instruments; its procedures,
or the particular decision rules by which policy is set; and its politics,
or the roles played by ideology on the one hand and statesmanship on
the other.

Taken together, the general tendencies toward intensified policy

and the Breakdown of Consensus (Allen and Unwin, 1984); William Schneider, " 'Rambo'
and Reality: Having It Both Ways," in Kenneth A. Oye, Robert J. Lieber and Donald
Rothchild, eds., *Eagle Resurgent? The Reagan Era in American Foreign Policy* (Little, Brown,
1987), pp. 41–72; and Eugene R. Wittkopf, "On the Foreign Policy Beliefs of the
American People: A Critique and Some Evidence," *International Studies Quarterly*, vol.
30 (December 1986), pp. 425–46.

2. Edward S. Corwin, *The President: Office and Powers, 1787–1957*, 4th rev. ed. (New
York University Press, 1957), p. 171.

3. Richard E. Neustadt, *Presidential Power: The Politics of Leadership* (Wiley, 1976),
p. 101 (emphasis in original).

differences, increased public pressure, and renewed struggles over institutional power sharing have caused foreign policy to be repoliticized. Like other areas of policy, foreign policy no longer is held above politics, no longer considered immune to political conflict and contention, no longer kept at the water's edge. The key point to be made here at the outset, though, is that the reasons for this repoliticization involve much more than partisan gamesmanship. To be sure, there is some I win–you lose political contesting at work in almost every presidential-congressional foreign policy dispute. But in a much more fundamental sense, the politics along Pennsylvania Avenue about U.S. diplomacy around the world are being driven by political forces much broader in scope and more deeply embedded in the American political system and contemporary society.

Confrontation

Perhaps the only point on which the Reagan administration and its congressional critics might agree with regard to such issues as Nicaragua, South Africa, and Arab arms sales is that their domestic political confrontations were counterproductive to effective foreign policy. Their interpretations of the appropriate alternative courses of action, of course, differ widely. But the negative policy consequences abroad of political warfare at home are quite apparent.

NICARAGUA

In some respects the presidential-congressional battles over Nicaragua should not have come as a surprise. First of all, the policy differences ran very deep. For Ronald Reagan, this issue embodied all that was wrong with the "Vietnam syndrome" and Carterite moralism. The Sandinistas were Soviet and Cuban allies. They professed Marxism-Leninism. Their very heritage as a movement was rooted in anti-American songs, slogans, and versions of history. And here they were right "in our backyard," running guns to comrades in El Salvador and other neighboring countries. But even more than that, their very existence was seen as a challenge to the credibility of American power. "If the United States cannot respond to a threat near our own borders," President Reagan posed the question, "why should Europeans or Asians believe that we are seriously concerned about threats to them? . . . Our credibility would collapse, our alliances would crumble."[4]

4. *New York Times*, April 28, 1983, p. A12.

Opponents of the Reagan Nicaragua policy also invoked analogies to Vietnam, although through the imagery of a quagmire rather than a syndrome. A little military aid here and covert action there, they contended, and pretty soon American troops would follow. The risks were great, the potential costs would be high, and the prospects for success were close to nil. They did not necessarily embrace the Sandinistas (some did, but not many) or deny that the United States had vital interests in the region; instead they stressed the possibilities for a negotiated settlement establishing viable terms for coexistence. After all, the Sandinistas had not even followed the usual Latin American practice of expropriating American investments. As to the credibility issue, they saw this as a matter of judgment more than resolve: what would truly be impressive would be a demonstration that the United States could distinguish a test from a trap.

Each side also saw itself as the claimant to moral and historical legitimacy. Ronald Reagan spoke from the heart when he called the contras "the moral equal of our Founding Fathers"; he smiled real smiles when he donned "I'm a contra, too" T-shirts. And the moral fervor of Lieutenant Colonel Oliver North became the stuff of summer television soap operas. North's knack for dramatics was hard to match, but Senator George Mitchell did make a powerful moral claim of his own during the Iran-contra congressional hearings in dressing North down for questioning the patriotism of those who opposed contra aid.

Second, the conflict was further fueled by the battle for public opinion, fought both at the level of elites and through the more generalized activities of movement activists and other pressure groups.[5] His inability to convert public opinion to the contra cause was one of the great failings and frustrations of the Great Communicator. Opinion polls consistently showed strong public opposition to contra aid. The margin reached better than 3–1 in the immediate wake of the Iran-contra revelations. Oliver North's televised testimony in July 1987 narrowed the gap but did not reverse the tide.[6] Among Democrats, opposition to the contras became not just a position but also a core

5. Despite this higher than usual level of activism, levels of information stayed amazingly low. One poll showed that, even by April 1986, only 38 percent of respondents could correctly identify whether the United States supported the Sandinistas or the contras. Cited in Robert A. Pastor, *Condemned to Repetition: The United States and Nicaragua* (Princeton University Press, 1987), p. 260.

6. "Opinion Roundup: Public Opinion on Nicaragua," *Public Opinion*, vol. 10 (September–October 1987), pp. 21–24.

party credo. It was a litmus test issue, one from which many single-issue voters and prospective campaign workers and contributors took their cues.

Yet the contra supporters made up in fervor what they lacked in numbers. Many conservatives literally put their money where their mouths were, donating millions of dollars to the various organizations set up by North and his cohorts to do for the contras what Congress would not. Nor did they pull any punches in pressuring Congress. The National Conservative Political Action Committee, for example, circulated a letter to all senators before one crucial contra aid vote threatening that "should you vote against Contra aid, we intend to see that a permanent record is made—a roll of dishonor, a list of shame, for all to see—of your failure of resolve and vision at this crucial hour in the struggle of millions of Nicaraguans for freedom and liberty."[7]

In addition to the substantive policy differences and the movement activism, the particular institutional power-sharing arrangements in which this issue was caught also contributed to the politics of confrontation. Each branch was the principal possessor of the policy instruments the other wanted to use. The policy instrument the executive branch needed most—money—was controlled by Congress and was subject to the annual authorization-appropriation cycle of all aid bills. Thus contra aid was initiated in 1981 and 1982 with the approval of the congressional Intelligence committees, approved by the full Congress for the first time (1983), defeated (1984), passed again but with restrictions (1985), increased and derestricted (1986), cut back and rerestricted (1987), and cut back and restricted further (1988). But even this chronology understates the problem. As a money issue, contra aid could be (and was) brought back to the floor again and again through all sorts of legislative vehicles. It was brought up through its own dedicated bills, of which there were many, and also tacked onto State Department authorization and appropriations bills, military construction bills, foreign aid bills, intelligence authorization bills, continuing appropriations, and almost anything else that conveniently came down the legislative pike. In 1987, for example, the Senate took over two dozen votes on contra aid. The issue simply never could be settled one way or the other.

7. NCPAC letter dated January 21, 1988. The regional variations in support for the contras were driven home to me on a trip to Florida, when my son and I encountered a game called "Get 'Em, Contras" in a video arcade. It had the longest line in the entire arcade.

Similarly, for its preferred policy objective of a negotiated regional peace plan (through the Contadora treaty, the Arias plan, or direct negotiations with the Sandinistas), Congress needed diplomatic authority and instruments of its own. But that remained the almost exclusive domain of the executive branch, and the Reagan administration was concerned much more with merely appearing to support peace negotiations than with seriously pursuing a negotiated settlement. An October 1984 National Security Council background paper boasted of having "trumped" the draft Contadora treaty. Another revealed the administration's approach was to "continue active negotiations but agree on no treaty and agree to work out some way to support the contras either directly or indirectly."[8] Assistant Secretary of State for Inter-American Affairs Elliott Abrams was quoted in the public press that it was "preposterous to think we could sign a deal with the Sandinistas . . . and expect it to be kept."[9] In August 1986 Philip Habib, only recently appointed as special negotiator, resigned out of frustration with the opposition and even personal condemnation he encountered within the administration for his efforts to treat peace talks as something more than just a way of providing "a plausible negotiating track" for public relations purposes.[10] Costa Rican President and Nobel Peace Prize laureate Oscar Arias was necessarily indulged because of his international prestige, but the best that could be said about the administration's actions toward the Arias plan was that they paid it lip service. Even when the Sandinistas and the contras were able themselves to reach an initial agreement on the Sapoá accord, the Reagan administration was neither encouraging nor supportive.

Yet even though these sources of conflict were at the heart of the Nicaragua issue, the virtual war between the branches that raged throughout the Reagan administration was not inevitable. The confrontation resulted because of the highly counterproductive strategies both sides opted for in handling the interinstitutional relationship.

8. Alma Guillermoprieto and David Hoffman, "Document Describes How U.S. 'Blocked' a Contadora Treaty," *Washington Post*, November 6, 1984, p. A1; James Chace, "The End of the Affair?" *New York Review of Books*, October 8, 1987, pp. 24–30; and William M. LeoGrande, "Rollback or Containment? The United States, Nicaragua, and the Search for Peace in Central America," *International Security*, vol. 11 (Fall 1986), pp. 89–120.

9. Shirley Christian, "Reagan Aides See No Possibility of U.S. Accord with Sandinistas," *New York Times*, August 18, 1985, p. 16.

10. Bernard Gwertzman, "Habib Finds Himself in a Hot Seat," *New York Times*, July 17, 1986, p. A20.

I will not here discuss at any length the Iran-contra scandal and its associated broader-scale covert operations, all of which are insightfully analyzed in Gregory Treverton's chapter. Suffice to say that whatever criteria one chooses, the verdict on Iran-contra comes out negative. The laws of the land were broken; felonies were committed. The Constitution was severely challenged, if not profoundly violated.[11] In strict political terms, the whole operation became an enormous self-inflicted wound, not only for the Reagan administration but also for the Republican party more generally. Even in strategic realpolitik calculations—the ends that were supposed to justify the means—the Reagan policy failed at its own chosen game. Many "yes, buts" and "what ifs" have been raised by Reagan, North, and others, but the facts of failure remain.

The whole operation was driven by the desire to go around Congress, to break out of the institutional power-sharing arrangement. To the extent that it still had to deal directly with Congress, the Reagan administration put enticement and even persuasion aside and instead tried to intimidate its legislative opponents and to win over key swing votes in the House by fomenting some old-fashioned ideological "thunder on the right." Edgar Chamorro, a former contra leader, later told of how the CIA trained him in how to lobby both in Washington and in the home districts of targeted representatives so as to "place them in a position of looking soft on communism."[12] Sometimes this worked in the short term, especially when the Sandinistas cooperated. For example, in April 1985, the day after the House voted down contra aid, Nicaraguan President Daniel Ortega flew off to Moscow. Two months later the House reversed itself, in large part because Ortega's trip had set off a reaction of "overwhelming support for the need to

11. The authors of the congressional Iran-contra report refer to a passage from *A Man For All Seasons*, in which William Roper says he would cut down every law in England to attack the devil. Sir Thomas More replies: "And when the last law was down, and the Devil turned round on you—where would you hide, Roper, the laws all being flat? This country's planted thick with laws from coast to coast—Man's law, not God's—and if you cut them down—and you're just the man to do it—d'you really think you could stand upright in the winds that would blow then?" *Report of the Congressional Committees Investigating the Iran-Contra Affair with Supplemental, Minority, and Additional Views*, H. Rept. 100-433, S. Rept. 100-216, 100 Cong. 1 sess. (Government Printing Office, 1987), p. 411.

12. Edgar Chamorro with Jefferson Morley, "How the CIA Masterminds the Nicaraguan Insurgency: Confessions of a 'Contra,' " *New Republic*, August 5, 1985, p. 21.

show the flag . . . [and] the lust members feel to strike out against Communism."[13]

The ideological zenith (or nadir) came the next year. A tone of disdain for Congress as an institution and for those who dared to disagree with administration doctrine was struck by White House Communications Director Patrick Buchanan, Elliott Abrams, Oliver North, and National Security Adviser John Poindexter. Buchanan took to the op-ed page of the *Washington Post* to label the Democrats "with Moscow, co-guarantor of the Brezhnev doctrine in Central America." He portrayed the upcoming vote on contra aid as the test of whether the Democrats stood "with Ronald Reagan . . . or Daniel Ortega."[14] Assistant Secretary of State Abrams not only lied to Congress in prepared committee testimony, but also could be found incessantly on the airwaves casting the debate in similar terms of whose side are you on. North and Poindexter struck above-the-law and higher-truth postures during the ensuing congressional and independent counsel investigation of the Iran-contra operation.

Whatever its seeming short-term benefits, over the longer term the Reagan administration's anticommunist bashing did more to antagonize than to build a coalition. As one congressman put it, commenting on the difference in dealing with the Bush administration on this issue, "It's nice to sit down with an Administration official . . . and not be considered an enemy of your own country."[15] There is a zero-sum aspect to conflicts cast in ideological terms that makes them particularly difficult to resolve. This type of conflict challenges not just opponents' positions as constructed through rational argumentation, but also their fundamental values and beliefs about right and wrong. It seeks cooperation through intimidation rather than through accommodation. It is inherently far more difficult to find terms for compromise when issues are defined so absolutely and when such antagonistic tactics are chosen. It may be good movement politics and even good electoral politics—but it is highly counterproductive as Pennsylvania Avenue

13. Representative William V. Alexander, Jr., chief Democratic whip, quoted in Steven Roberts, "Anti-Managua Aid Is Seen as Likely," *New York Times*, May 5, 1985, p. A4.

14. Patrick J. Buchanan, "The Contras Need Our Help," *Washington Post*, March 5, 1986, p. A19.

15. David Obey, quoted in Robert Pear, "Bush's Courting Splits Democrats," *New York Times*, March 16, 1989, p. A8.

politics. The Reagan administration sought confrontation, and that is what it got.

Yet Congress too must come in for a share of the blame, in at least two respects. First is the charge of inconsistency, of the on again–off again manner in which it handled the contra aid issue. Reagan, North, and others repeatedly defended their actions as a response to congressional inconsistency. They have a point, although not necessarily the one they intended. Surely, as a defense of their activities, it is as weak as any other rationalization about the ends justifying the means. Moreover, one can just as easily argue that Congress should have been more consistent, but in terms of sticking by its opposition to the contra aid policy. What Congress lacked, from this perspective, was not so much will and resolve to stay the course as the political courage and stamina to define and follow through on an alternative course.

A second charge, leveled in particular at Speaker Jim Wright, was of meddling. Critics of Congress often raise the specter of "535 secretaries of state" gratuitously and as political cover for a policy disagreement. In the case of Speaker Wright's November 1987 attempt at "alternative track diplomacy," however, the charge holds to a greater degree than usual. Wright injected himself directly into the peace process as a combination mediator and negotiator. He met not only with Ortega but also with the contra directorate and Nicaraguan Cardinal Miguel Obando y Bravo, who was the agreed-upon mediator of the internal discussion between the Sandinistas and the contras under the terms of the Arias plan. These meetings went on over a three-day period in Wright's office in the Capitol and at the Vatican Embassy. The Reagan administration was excluded from the meetings and received its information only through the media. Yet these were more than the normal consultative or informational sessions. Substantive negotiations were being conducted.

This was another ends-means situation. In addition to his outrage over the Iran-contra scandal, and reflecting the sentiments of many House Democrats, Wright was quite frustrated over the Reagan administration's lack of seriousness about pursuing a diplomatic solution. But irrespective of the ends being pursued, the costs and risks are quite serious when an official of the U.S. government attempts to set himself up as a full-fledged alternative track of diplomacy circumventing the president. Wright's efforts, quite rightly, ran into a storm of protest, which included even some who agreed with his position but strongly objected on procedural grounds. Congress can have an important and constructive diplomatic role, as the Philippines case in particular shows. But when the Speaker of the House starts receiving heads of state from countries with which the United States is engaged in conflict, and acts in direct counterpoint to the president of the United States, there is a serious procedural and political problem. It is not ever in the interest of the United States to have the leader of another country brag, as Ortega did, that his meetings with the principal officer of the U.S. Congress would "leave the Administration totally isolated."[16] The immediate effects, as well as the precedents thus set, cannot be healthy ones for the practice of American diplomacy.

In September 1988 Wright made more headlines when he cited CIA testimony in accusing it of covert destabilization operations within Nicaragua. Wright contended that the information to which he referred was already part of the public record. The administration took the dual position that it was a revelation of classified material, but that no such operations were going on anyway. Motivations, intent, and accuracy all can be debated, but politically they were less important than the effects, which evoked images of congressional parochialism and harmed the reputation for professionalism and statesmanship that Congress in general wanted (and needed) to cultivate.

SOUTH AFRICA

In the late 1970s, partly through Carter administration diplomacy and partly through congressional initiatives, American policy toward South Africa began to take an antiapartheid turn. Previous administrations never had explicitly endorsed apartheid, but, whatever their rhetoric, their actions inclined toward tacit alliance with South Africa in the context of global containment. The Carter administration, however, was much more vocal in its condemnations of apartheid and also took a number of concrete actions, including voting for a United Nations mandatory arms embargo, endorsing the Sullivan code on fair labor practices, curtailing official sports contacts, and taking a lead role in UN efforts to gain independence for Namibia. Where the Carter administration still stopped short, as with continued Export-Import Bank loan guarantees to South Africa, Congress acted to increase the antiapartheid pressure.[17]

16. John Felton, "Nicaragua Peace Process Moves to Capitol Hill," *Congressional Quarterly Weekly Report,* November 14, 1987, p. 2789.
17. Donald Rothchild and John Ravenhill, "From Carter to Reagan: The Global

As in the case of Nicaragua, the Reagan administration came in with the intent of reversing policy. "Constructive engagement" was hailed by Secretary of State Alexander Haig as being about "old friends . . . who are getting together again." It had two central premises, one about influence and the other about interests. Influence against apartheid was said to be more effective by being a good and reliable friend than through criticism or coercion. However, in truth realpolitik considerations superseded moral concerns, and the overriding American interest was in ensuring that this strategic country was ruled by a friendly regime. Thus in May 1981 the Reagan administration invited a delegation of South African military officers to Washington, as much for a symbolic contrast with the Carter administration as for specific consultations. It also restored the U.S. role as a supplier of military-related equipment: by 1984 American exports of aircraft, computers, communications equipment, and other military-related goods had increased 100 percent over Carter administration levels.[18]

By 1984–85, however, the Reagan administration had very little in the way of constructive results to show for its engagement. Despite Reagan's own claim that the Botha regime was genuinely "reformist" and his supporting contention that segregation had been "eliminated,"[19] the antiapartheid protests within South Africa had so intensified that the Botha regime resorted to declaring a state of emergency. It cracked down against political demonstrations, school boycotts, labor stoppages, and rent strikes. It arrested key leaders of black labor unions and of the antiapartheid United Democratic Front. By late 1985, as the situation became increasingly violent, the reported death toll was 3.5 lives a day.[20]

Within the U.S. foreign policy debate, like that over Nicaragua, there was a fundamental substantive disagreement over who was friend and who was foe in a situation of third world instability. It was not simply a matter of liberal moralism versus conservative realpolitik. Both sides laid claim to democratic traditions, interpreted on the one side as standing up for racial equality and majority self-determination and on the other side as protecting yet another third world country

Perspective on Africa Becomes Ascendant," in Kenneth A. Oye, Robert J. Lieber, and Donald Rothchild, eds., *Eagle Defiant: United States Foreign Policy in the 1980s* (Little, Brown, 1983), pp. 337–65.

18. *Washington Post (National Weekly Edition)*, December 24, 1984, p. 24.
19. Interview with WSB Radio of Atlanta, Georgia, August 26, 1985.
20. *Washington Post (National Weekly Edition)*, October 28, 1985, p. 17.

from descending into the depths of rule by ruthless Marxist-Leninists. Both sides also claimed to be geopolitical realists, with the one stressing the long-term risks to U.S. interests of yet again being on the wrong side of political change and the other side drawing its historical analogy to the damage done to American interests by the late 1970s "reforms" the United States helped to engineer in Iran and Nicaragua.

On this issue, even more so than on Nicaragua, public opinion was unambiguously one-sided. For a period from late 1984 through early 1987, the antiapartheid movement captured the public imagination in the United States like no other protest movement had since the Vietnam War. In fact, compared with the antiwar movement with its hippies and yippies and flagburners, the antiapartheid movement with its members of Congress, civil rights leaders, mayors, religious leaders, and other prominent citizens peacefully (and dramatically) submitting themselves to arrest struck a much more sympathetic chord. The contrast with the footage being beamed into American living rooms from the townships and streets of South Africa (that is, until the South African government imposed stricter censorship) was particularly striking.

Corporate and business groups worked the other side of the issue, but even among congressional Republicans they made limited headway. The main reason, as Senate Majority Leader (and prospective presidential candidate) Robert Dole observed, was that the issue had become a "domestic civil rights issue."[21] Prime Minister Pieter Botha was Governor George Wallace; Bishop Desmond Tutu was the Reverend Dr. Martin Luther King, Jr.; and the Anti-Apartheid Act was the Civil Rights Act. Republicans, looking more than ever to recruit blacks into their party, thus voted for the Anti-Apartheid Acts of 1985 and 1986 by margins almost as huge as the Democrats.

There were a number of reasons economic sanctions were turned to as the policy instrument of choice against South Africa. They were a tangible means for bringing pressure for change to bear against the Botha government. They also had a powerful symbolic effect as an expression of U.S. solidarity with the antiapartheid cause. And there was no problem of possession of policy instruments: Article I, Section 8, of the Constitution vested in Congress the power "to regulate commerce with foreign nations." This was not like urging the executive branch to negotiate in good faith with the Contadora countries or to

---

21. *Congressional Quarterly Almanac, 1986,* vol. 42 (1987), p. 372.

otherwise try to condition and constrain the diplomacy options available to the executive. It was for Congress to take the action itself, to use its institutional share of the shared powers to set the basic terms of U.S. policy.

The Anti-Apartheid Act of 1985 passed with veto-proof margins in both chambers: 380–48 and 80–12. As noted, and as the numbers substantiate, these were not party-line votes. When the White House threatened to veto this bill, a group of thirty House Republican conservatives sent a joint letter to the president stating their intention to join their liberal colleagues in an override. Senate Foreign Relations Committee Chairman Richard Lugar also warned the administration it would lose a veto fight.

As a last gambit, on the eve of what was billed as a major speech by Prime Minister Botha, National Security Adviser Robert McFarlane was dispatched to Vienna for direct talks with South African Foreign Minister Roelof Botha. McFarlane even gave public assurances after this meeting that the prime minister's speech would include major new reforms. However, the heralded speech proved to be little more than more business as usual—and the Reagan administration once again was left embarrassed by the intransigence of the government it claimed to have constructively engaged.

The White House then showed some pragmatism in its interbranch political strategy. It preempted Congress by issuing an executive order imposing its own economic sanctions. These were more limited than those in the House or Senate bills, and the president dubbed them "active constructive engagement." He also dropped his praise for purported reform and denounced apartheid as "deliberate, systematic, institutionalized racial discrimination." While many Democrats were not totally satisfied, the strategy worked: support was sufficiently dented that the congressional bill died.

In 1986 Congress once again passed sanctions legislation. The House version, sponsored by Representative Ron Dellums, would have moved to comprehensive sanctions, including corporate disinvestment. But House leaders agreed even without convening a conference committee to accept the Senate bill, which went further than Reagan's 1985 executive order but stopped short of disinvestment. The 308–77 House vote on the Senate bill sent two messages. To those advocating comprehensive sanctions, the message was that the support was not there. To the White House, contemplating a veto, the message was that support for an override was there.

The same message also was delivered up Pennsylvania Avenue more directly. Key Senate Republican leaders such as Senators Dole, Lugar, and Nancy Kassebaum (chair of the African Affairs Subcommittee) all appealed to the White House for political pragmatism. But their message was not heeded. Instead Reagan directly confronted Congress by vetoing the bill. And he paid the price: for the first time since 1973 and the War Powers Act, a presidential veto on a foreign policy issue was overridden. At 313–83 in the House and 78–21 in the Senate, the margin was not even close.

Reagan kept coming back to his highly ideological view of the situation. There was only "one group" within South Africa that favored economic sanctions, he told a press conference, and that was the African National Congress, whose real agenda was to encourage "the disruption that would come from massive unemployment and hunger and desperation of the people, because it is their belief that they could then rise out of all that disruption and seize control."[22] Press reports indicated that the White House staff was split on the issue, with Chief of Staff Donald Regan and Patrick Buchanan reinforcing the president's ideological view and prevailing over the more pragmatic recommendations from others within the White House, from the State Department, and from the Republican congressional leadership. Senator Lugar later lamented that the president "didn't take my advice the first, second, third or even fourth time." From the House side Minority Leader Robert H. Michel commented, "To put it in the mildest terms, . . . the administration has been less than brilliant in handling this issue."[23] Unlike his strategy in the previous year, but like that in the Nicaragua issue, Reagan's chosen response was confrontation. Once again it was the ramrod approach to making foreign policy: intimidate, attack, condemn, even when it is members of your own party (as, for example, Patrick Buchanan did in singling Senator Lugar out for purported disloyalty).[24]

As was the case with Nicaragua, presidential-congressional conflict was probably not avoidable, but the degeneration into confrontation was. And here, too, the policy consequences were highly counter-

22. *Washington Post*, August 13, 1986, p. A15.
23. *Congressional Quarterly Almanac, 1986*, pp. 360, 373.
24. Addressing a rally of movement conservatives, Buchanan derisively quoted from King Lear to attack Lugar: "How sharper than a serpent's tooth, to have a thankless child." *Congressional Quarterly Almanac, 1986*, p. 373.

productive.[25] The next two years were spent battling over the Reagan administration's lackluster enforcement of the sanctions and whether Congress would move to fully comprehensive sanctions. Each side blamed the other, and neither accepted accountability. Meanwhile, events within South Africa itself continued to drive home the reality that while Pennsylvania Avenue may get gridlocked, foreign policy problems do not stand still.

SAUDI AND JORDANIAN ARMS SALES

The first major foreign policy confrontation between the Reagan administration and Congress occurred in late 1981 over an $8.5 billion arms sale to Saudi Arabia. Under the terms of the 1976 Arms Export Control Act, Congress could block any major arms sale through the "legislative veto" of a concurrent resolution of disapproval passed by simple majorities in both houses. During the Ford and Carter administrations, this legislative veto was never explicitly exercised, although its very existence undoubtedly had some deterrent effect. The 1981 Saudi arms sale was the closest the legislative veto came to actually being used. The arms package proposed by the Reagan administration included five advanced-technology AWACS (airborne warning and control system) radar planes, as well as tanker equipment and missiles that would significantly increase the capabilities of the Saudi fleet of F-15 fighter jets (the sale of which had precipitated an earlier heated debate in 1978). Reagan won, but barely, by a three-vote margin in the Senate.

On ensuing arms sales, however, he did not fare as well. The administration proposed three consecutive deals with Jordan between 1983 and 1985: one to arm and train elite Jordanian army units as a rapid deployment strike force, another to sell shoulder-fired Stinger antiaircraft missiles, and one to sell advanced warplanes and missiles. Each had to be withdrawn without a vote because of overwhelming opposition in Congress.

The next major deal with the Saudis (more F-15s, M-1 tanks,

25. The one achievement was the Angolan-Namibian disengagement accord signed in late 1988. Yet, in terms of credit claiming, not only was the role of Soviet leader Mikhail Gorbachev and his "new thinking" to be accounted for, but those advocating sanctions could make at least as strong a claim as those pushing constructive engagement, arguing that it was only after Pretoria saw that the United States was serious about pressure that it was willing to make concessions.

Stinger missiles, Sidewinder air-to-air missiles, and Harpoon air-to sea
missiles), first proposed in 1985, would also have gone down to defeat
had it not been for the 1983 Supreme Court *Chadha* decision striking
down the legislative veto. *Chadha* required that presidents be able to
veto resolutions of disapproval (which thus became joint rather than
concurrent resolutions) as they could other regular legislation, and that
Congress then be required to garner a two-thirds majority in both
houses to override. The new Saudi deal was voted down in both
houses; that is, a joint resolution of disapproval was passed. Reagan
then vetoed this resolution, and Congress failed by one vote in the
Senate to override. This was even after the arms package had been
scaled back to include only the Sidewinder and Harpoon missiles. The
next year (1987), while the administration got Congress to agree to
twelve F-15s on a replacement basis and some electronic upgrades, it
had to withdraw its proposal to sell 1,600 Maverick antitank missiles.

Why was virtually every one of these arms sales so confrontational?
Most analyses start with the influence of "the Jewish lobby" and of
the American-Israel Public Affairs Committee (AIPAC) in particular.
For the Jewish community, the Saudi AWACS sale was a key issue—
our "principal legislative priority," according to the American Jewish
Committee—for a number of reasons.[26] Coming so early, it was seen
as a test case of the pro-Arab leanings of the new administration. The
Jewish community had stuck with Jimmy Carter, despite their mis-
givings about him, over Ronald Reagan in the 1980 election (although
this explains why Reagan's percentage of the Jewish vote exceeded
that of other recent Republican presidential candidates). They also had
doubts about key appointees such as Defense Secretary Caspar Weinberger, a former top executive of Bechtel, known for its many contracts
and clients in the Arab world. There also was concern about the size
of the sale and the type of equipment involved. The $8.5 billion value
of the 1981 package was almost as much as the total weapons sales to
Saudi Arabia over the previous six years. Moreover, the combination
of the AWACS as the most advanced air defense surveillance technology
and the F-15 offensive capability upgradings were feared to infringe
on the margin of military superiority considered crucial to the credibility
of the Israeli deterrence posture.

It would be naive and even disingenuous not to acknowledge the

26. Bill Keller, "Stopping Sale of AWACs to Saudis Is Top 1981 Priority of Israel
Lobby," *Congressional Quarterly Weekly Report*, August 22, 1981, p. 1524.

influence that AIPAC and the Jewish lobby do have. Whether one interprets it as an attribution of credit or blame, AIPAC does lobby with great skill and effectiveness. It is known for being particularly adept at organizing at the grass roots through its local chapters and contacts. The Jewish community also is one of the key sources of political fundraising, especially for Democrats. Yet on this very high-priority issue, and despite its concerted effort, AIPAC lost on the Saudi AWACS sale.

Two other factors came into play. One was the countervailing political pressure exerted by AWACS proponents. The usual caricature of AIPAC as Svengali imputes a greater degree of one-sidedness to Middle East policy issues than was the case in this instance. The Saudi government retained high-priced and well-connected Washington lobbyists (such as the former assistant secretary of state for congressional relations in the Kennedy and Johnson administrations). American corporations with major interests in trade and investment in Saudi Arabia and the rest of the Arab world mounted their own quite substantial lobbying campaign (including, for example, Mobil's well known "box" on the op-ed page of the *New York Times*). In addition, the White House was also part of the countervailing pressure. It used the argument (as Jimmy Carter had four years earlier over the Panama Canal treaties) about permanently crippling a president's overall foreign policy credibility by handing him a major defeat in his first year. Where that was not enough, it got right down to horse trading: a U.S. attorney appointment for the friend of one senator, a coal-fired power plant for the state of another, a hospital for another, and a promise not to campaign against another.[27]

But as important as the interest groups and horse trading were, there also was a substantive policy side to the AWACS politics. At issue were conflicting concerns about the security of two valued allies. AIPAC aside, few members of Congress questioned the basic proposition that Israel required technological military superiority to deter Arab attack. But at no time before or since has strategic concern about Saudi security been as intense as it was in 1981. The Soviet invasion of Afghanistan was still then seen by many as the latest step in Russia's historic march toward the Middle Eastern oilfields. Moreover, in the wake of the fall of the shah of Iran and amid the rising tide of Islamic

27. Bill Keller, "Reagan Team May Draw Key Lessons from Difficult Struggle over AWACs," *Congressional Quarterly Weekly Report*, October 31, 1981, p. 2099.

fundamentalism, there was even more fear about a mullah-led regional domino theory. This fear was made palpable by the assassination of Anwar Sadat by Islamic extremists right at the height of the congressional debate. In fact, two Republican senators who had been original cosponsors of the resolution of disapproval switched positions the next day—cutting the number of cosponsors from fifty to forty-eight and thus shifting the balance just enough for the AWACS sale to go through.

The proposed Jordanian arms sales did not fare as well because both the interest group politics and the substantive policy debate cut differently. Mobil and its allies were not as concerned about Jordan. King Hussein did not have the kinds of lobbyists on retainer that King Fahd did. The strategic argument also was weaker. The rationale for the arms sale was less one of an imminent security threat than a hope of obtaining political leverage to make Jordan more cooperative with U.S.-led regional peace plans. This, however, was fast becoming a discredited argument. A number of past arms sales had been justified in terms of political leverage, but King Hussein was yet to be particularly forthcoming. From the king's perspective, his caution may have had its justifications, but it surely was not helping the search for an Arab-Israeli peace.

For similar reasons, by 1986 the policy debate also had shifted against the Saudis. Because AIPAC took a hands-off position on the 1986 Saudi arms package, one might have expected more of it to go through. But the Saudis also had yet to come through in significant ways to support American efforts to restart the peace process. They had opposed the Camp David accords, the 1982 Reagan plan, the 1983 Israel-Lebanon treaty, and virtually every other U.S.-led regional peace plan. Accordingly, the argument that arms sales would produce diplomatic leverage lost much of its credibility.

Where the Saudis were cooperating was with the Reagan administration's global anticommunist crusade: they supported the Afghan mujaheddin and, as later came out, helped to fund the contras. As far as Congress was concerned, however, the contra connection didn't have much redeeming value. The Afghan cause was more popular, but those concerned about peace in the Middle East were not about to accept it as a substitute for Saudi support and cooperation within the region. In fact, to some it looked like the Reagan administration, self-professed hardheaded realism and all, was being cleverly manipulated at the game of realpolitik by a smaller ally. Thus the 1986 Saudi arms sale package, even in its scaled-back form, got through only after having been disapproved by both the House and the Senate, rescued by a presidential veto, and then saved by a one-vote failure to override in the Senate. And, as noted, the 1987 arms package also had to be significantly scaled back.

In a certain respect, given all those sources of conflict, what needs to be explained is not why the interbranch relations on the issue were so conflictual, but why it did not end up, like Nicaragua and South Africa, in total stalemate. Two factors, one institutional and the other political, were key.

What differentiated the institutional relationship governing these arms sales was that, although powers were shared, the decision rules required that the issue be resolved one way or the other. The procedures were very specific, as distinct from the multiple bills, attachment of riders, and general legislative freelancing common to most issues. The decision time period was fixed (thirty calendar days for Congress to act after formal notification by the executive), as distinct from the normal elastic schedule of each Congress. If the votes were there, there would be no arms sale. If they were not, the arms sale would go through. The issue might (and did) resurface, and conflict might (and did) recur, but each time it could be treated as a discrete issue that could be decided, one way or the other.

The political factor was that the congressional strategy pursued by the White House was pragmatic rather than ideological. The 1981 arguments about the credibility of the presidency being on the line worked well at the time, but were more difficult to reuse. The horse trading done in 1981 to get the AWACS through, as it leaked to the press, did not sit well and was to be avoided as much as possible as being unpresidential. But on this issue the Reagan administration showed impressive adaptability. It saw in 1986 that it could get the Sidewinder and Harpoon missiles through Congress, but not the F-15s, the M-1 tanks, or the Stinger missiles, so it took these out. In 1987 it dropped the Maverick antitank missiles in order to get the replacement F-15s through. This strategy of trade-offs and coalition building contrasts sharply with the administration's legislative strategy on both Nicaragua and South Africa and reflects a pragmatism that settled for half-loaves instead of risking none.

Half-loaves, to be sure, have their policy problems. They leave unresolved how the United States will balance its concerns over the security of two allies who themselves are adversaries. Will the United

States be a reliable supplier of arms for Saudi Arabia? How can the Saudis be influenced to play a more constructive role in the next round of efforts at finding a Mideast peace? These are all policy questions that remain open and are becoming more pressing and less settled all the time. But that brings one back to the original proposition that where there are policy differences, there will be political conflict. The key in such situations is to try to manage those differences along Pennsylvania Avenue as well as possible, to try at a minimum not to exacerbate the policy effects of political conflict.

SOURCES OF CONFLICT, UNAVOIDABLE AND AVOIDABLE

All these cases have in common three reasons why at least some presidential-congressional conflict was unavoidable. First, all three tapped basic substantive policy differences over how the United States should define and defend its interests in various regions around the world. Second, public and interest group pressures were quite intense on all three; constituencies were watching. Third, all three issues involved shared powers; neither institution could act independently.

What was avoidable, though, was the extreme to which the conflicts degenerated, especially in the Nicaragua case. Of course presidents need not always avoid confrontation with Congress. Leadership often requires the courage of one's convictions and the willingness to take political risks. That's why even the Framers, their fears of executive power notwithstanding, gave the president the veto and required the two-thirds margin for a legislative override. That's also why the "bully pulpit" has been so important to presidents as a political strategy for reaching out to the public and thereby pressuring Congress to fall in line. This has always been true, but has become especially so in an age of divided government.

But the key to strong and effective presidential leadership is to know when to push and keep pushing, and when to pull back and start dealing. What so often dumbfounded the critics of Ronald Reagan, both as governor of California and as president, was how frequently he did show flexibility, despite his strongly proclaimed ideology. But on the Nicaragua issue he was inflexible and ideological—so much so that rather than deal with Congress, he resorted to the machinations and unconstitutional activities of the Iran-contra operation.

The point here is the need (for scholars as analysts and for elected leaders as practitioners) to distinguish between the avoidable and the unavoidable, and the dysfunctional and the potentially functional, aspects of presidential-congressional foreign policy conflict. The other two issues add further to the argument. On South Africa, the question that remains is why did the administration take the uncompromising stand on sanctions in 1986 after the successful co-opting in 1985? The general sentiment, especially among Senate Republicans, was that the 1986 veto override defeat, with its consequences both for policy and more generally for the administration's reputation, did not have to happen. The political history of the issue may have been as a partisan one, but by 1985–86 many Republican conservatives had joined the more traditionally Democratic antiapartheid movement. Thus it is even easier on this issue to discern potential compromises: they were, after all, proposed to the White House by a number of Republican congressional leaders. On the Saudi arms sales, while political conflict was not avoided, it was contained and reasonably effectively managed. In fact, congressional support for arms sales to Saudi Arabia was eroding as time went on. But on this issue the Reagan administration showed flexibility, adaptation, and a willingness to compromise. It did not get all that it wanted, but it got some—and, by settling for that, it avoided another confrontation that would have damaged all concerned.

Ideology surely has its place in presidential leadership on foreign policy issues, but when there is a need to build governing coalitions in support of policies that already have their sources of conflict, pragmatism works much better. Statesmanship abroad requires statesmanship at home.

Competition

A second principal pattern in presidential-congressional foreign policy relations was a generalized institutional competition in which Congress sought to exert influence and to hold the executive accountable on a range of issues involving the ongoing conduct of diplomacy, while the executive protested against congressional micromanagement. These issues were not the high drama of confrontations over Nicaragua, South Africa, and Saudi arms sales. They were much more the everyday business of foreign relations—authorizations of State Department operations, appropriations of foreign aid, and appointments requiring Senate confirmation. But as such their politics were as much about who would decide as what would be decided, that is, about assertions of institutional prerogatives as much as substantive policy conflicts or public pressure. Three examples from the Reagan years demonstrate the dilemma and illustrate the tension between ensuring executive accountability yet avoiding congressional micromanagement.

THE 1987 STATE DEPARTMENT AUTHORIZATION ACT

Any time eighty-six amendments are added to a bill on the Senate floor, something must be wrong with the process. Either the bill produced by committee is so bad that it needs such extensive "perfecting," or it is the old "Christmas tree" habit, in the past confined more to domestic spending on pet projects, now manifesting itself in a foreign policy form. Or, of course, a little of both.

State Department authorization bills used to be about as routine as legislation gets. A 1956 law requiring an explicit congressional authorization before the State Department could spend any of its appropriations meant that in every session some bill had to be passed. Catchall continuing resolutions thus were not an option for State. This helped protect State Department authorization bills from onslaughts of amendments, which tended instead to be concentrated on the foreign aid bills. Ironically, though, in 1987, when the foreign aid bill was deadlocked, this very requirement that a bill be passed had the reverse effect of attracting amendments to the State Department authorization bill. And it was quite an array of amendments, including protection of human rights in Tibet, a new position of ambassador at large for Afghanistan, sanctions against Toshiba, cost-cutting closings of some U.S. consulates abroad, closer congressional oversight of the State Department's Office of Public Liaison, drug and lie detector testing for certain State personnel, limitations on diplomatic immunity, an official residence for future secretaries of state, and limits on U.S. contributions to the United Nations.

One of the hottest issues, which itself gave life to over ten of its own amendments, was the controversy over the new embassies the United States and the Soviet Union were building in each other's capitals. The controversy had been set off by the revelations that U.S. Marine embassy guards in Moscow had been arrested on charges of espionage and that the new American embassy under construction contained Soviet electronic bugs. The marine spying case appeared to be an enormous breach of security and to point to major systemic problems beyond just the misjudgments and disloyalties of the three young guards. As for the new U.S. Moscow embassy, it struck many as incredible that State Department officials had allowed the concrete columns and beams to be precast off the construction site and out of supervision by American officials. This contrasted strongly with the fact that the new Soviet embassy in Washington had been built on one of the few elevated sites in the city, a location quite suitable to enhanced electronic espionage.

In April 1987 Representatives Daniel Mica and Olympia Snowe, chairman and ranking minority member of the Foreign Affairs Sub-committee on International Operations, led a committee delegation on an inspection tour of the U.S. embassy site in Moscow. Even in the existing embassy, concerns about bugging led the delegation members to bring along children's "magic slates" to communicate on. (Later that month, while in Moscow for arms control negotiations, Secretary of State Shultz resorted to working out of a mobile van.)[28] Mica and Snowe issued a blistering report, condemning both the new embassy building and the marine guard scandal. Their report had all the more impact because Democrat Mica was not a "usual suspect" liberal critic and Republican Snowe was usually a staunch party loyalist. Upon their return they cosponsored an amendment prohibiting use of the Moscow site, calling for the Soviets to reimburse the costs incurred, and prohibiting the Soviets from opening their new Washington embassy. The amendment was approved 414–0.

While the Mica-Snowe amendment did establish some conditions subject to presidential discretion that could allow the two embassy projects to go ahead, the Senate approved a tighter amendment requiring full abrogation and renegotiation of the 1969 and 1972 accords on embassy construction. The State Department opposed both amend-ments, citing a report it commissioned from a team headed by former Defense and Energy Secretary James R. Schlesinger. Schlesinger was highly critical of the blunders made thus far, but he contended that the new U.S. embassy required only partial dismantling to be debugged and then could be completed. He also dismissed the espionage concerns about the site of the new Soviet embassy.

When the two bills reached conference committee, the restrictions were softened so as to leave the president the discretion to decide whether to go ahead with either or both embassy sites. In so doing, Congress ended up striking a reasonable balance of asserting account-ability without micromanaging. This truly was an issue on which the State Department had made a series of major errors and had allowed

28. *Congressional Quarterly Almanac, 1987*, vol. 43 (1988), pp. 148–49.

serious breaches of security. Congress was justified in focusing public
attention on this issue and served a useful role in doing so. There
could be no doubt that any future arrangements or actions would be
watched closely. Yet in the end, Congress stepped back from the kinds
of restrictions and abrogations that might have felt good but would
not help solve the problem.

On another controversial issue raised as an amendment to the State
Department authorization bill, however, the charge of micromanagement is more justified. This was the closing of the New York office
of the Palestine Liberation Organization (PLO). Under congressional
pressure the Reagan administration already had closed the PLO's
Washington office. The New York office posed a more complicated
issue because the PLO had official observer status at the United
Nations. The original agreement locating the UN in the United States,
in its letter and especially in its spirit, had sought to minimize the host
country's self-interested interference in the operations of the international body. Both on these legal grounds and as a calculation that such
a move would be counterproductive to U.S. diplomacy, the State
Department opposed closing the PLO's New York office. The Senate
bill, however, included a provision requiring the office to be closed.

The most pertinent point for the present discussion is neither one
of international law nor one of foreign policy strategy, but rather the
terms of the debate through which Congress took its action. A reading
of the *Congressional Record* shows the dominant sentiment expressed by
member after member was the desire to lash out at terrorism. This
was not even taken up as an order of strategy. It was posed more as a
matter of whether members were for or against allowing a terrorist
organization that killed an old crippled American (Leon Klinghoffer)
and little children in airports (Rome and Vienna in December 1985)
to have a propaganda office in the United States. Cast in such terms,
how is a member of Congress to vote? Do citations of international
law or even considerations of strategy have any chance of standing up
to this line of argument? In the end, once the issue got out of the
limelight and into small-group executive-legislative final bargaining
sessions, the PLO office provision was diluted sufficiently to give the
executive discretion. But this kind of taking an issue out of its fuller
deliberative context is one of the stronger charges made by micromanagement critics.

Two final points brought out by the State Department authorization
bill concern the human resource and time perspective problems created

by this whole process. The number of times the secretary of state and top officials must come to Capitol Hill to testify, the number of reports that have to be written, the number of negotiating sessions that have to be held, the amount of congressional staff time invested, the days of floor debate taken up—all of these come out of a finite stock of time and energy. The eighty-six Senate amendments have already been mentioned; when the Senate and House bills finally went to conference committee, there were 170 differences between the two chambers' versions. The State Department had to prepare over 175 position papers to cover not only these issues but also those on which the two bills were in accord but State objected. Anyone who has seen the process at work knows that most of the people in both branches work long and hard at their jobs. Moreover, in terms of policy planning, it is often asked why it is so difficult to give attention to long-term problems and issues such as global environmental problems, worldwide poverty, or long-term invigoration of democratic institutions. The answer in part lies with how much time is spent on the business of the day: one more hearing to attend, one more amendment to offer. The micro must be brought under better control if there is to be any chance to begin to grapple with the macro.

FOREIGN AID

Foreign aid, historically a troublesome issue for the two branches, has been made even more so by being caught in a triple squeeze of fiscal constraints, conflicts over policy priorities, and increased resort by both institutions to nondiscretionary "earmarking."

The fiscal constraints have been a function of the broader federal budget problems and the deficit-reduction stringencies of the Balanced Budget and Emergency Deficit Control Act of 1985 (Gramm-Rudman-Hollings). Total foreign aid had increased 65 percent between 1981 and 1985, from $10.1 billion to $16.7 billion. But under the Gramm-Rudman-Hollings regime, in each of the next three years aid was cut, falling to $14 billion in fiscal year 1988, in real terms no greater than the aid level back in 1981. Those pushing hardest for the aid cuts, in a striking break from the past, were congressional Democrats. Democrats used to defend foreign aid programs from the "give-away" charges of Republicans. But in the context of the fiscal constraints and as a consequence of divided government, the terms of debate shifted. The Reagan administration wanted foreign aid increases to further pursue its global foreign policy strategies. Since it remained adamant in refusing to raise taxes, this meant increased pressure to find budget cuts in domestic social programs. For congressional Democrats, this transformed the political significance of foreign aid. Now it was largely serving foreign policy objectives with which many Democrats disagreed. As David Obey, chairman of the House Appropriations Foreign Operations Subcommittee, put it, it was "very difficult to make a persuasive case for an increase in foreign aid while funds for domestic programs are being cut. Members of Congress, particularly the traditional proponents of foreign aid, will weigh their support for aid abroad according to the administration's proposals on domestic programs."[29]

The conflict over policy priorities primarily involved the relative shares going to military aid and economic aid. The Reagan administration's extremely strong emphasis on military aid, coming within the context of the shrinking overall budget pie, made this conflict even more acute than it traditionally had been. Under Reagan the relative share of security-related aid (economic support fund, foreign military sales program, military assistance program) increased from 50 percent to 62 percent of total U.S. aid. The relative share of bilateral economic development assistance (economic, food) fell from 35 percent to 29 percent.[30] In addition, there were disputes over strategies of economic development. The Reagan administration not only placed a lower priority on economic development, it also pushed for free-market-oriented programs over public ones and opposed family planning and other social and community programs. Here too the conflict was intensified because of the limited resources available.

The third part of the squeeze has been caused by the proliferation of "earmarking," the foreign aid equivalent of domestic entitlements. Earmarking comes in two forms: country earmarks, allocating specific amounts of aid to particular countries, and development functional category earmarks, allocating aid among such programs as population planning, agricultural and rural development, child survival, and AIDS prevention. There is a logic to earmarking, especially under conditions of budgetary stringency; limited funds should be directed to priority purposes. The problem, though, is the same as with the overall federal budget. Given the multiple priorities injected into the process by individual members of Congress, the various executive branch actors

29. David R. Obey and Carol Lancaster, "Funding Foreign Aid," *Foreign Policy*, vol. 71 (Summer 1988), p. 149.
30. Obey and Lancaster, "Funding Foreign Aid," p. 143.

with interests in foreign aid, and powerful interest groups, very little nondiscretionary foreign aid is left. In fiscal 1989, 98 percent of the economic support fund aid and 92 percent of military aid was earmarked. The percentage for development aid was only 49 percent, but half the funds that were left nondiscretionary in country terms were regulated by functional category earmarks.[31]

Although earmarking is not totally new, the problem has become one of excess. As recently as the mid-1980s, only about 50 percent of security assistance funds were earmarked. Congress is partly to blame. Some of its earmarks are in response to interest group pressure, such as aid to Greece ($7 for every $10 sent to Turkey) and some of the aid to Israel. Some also reflect its micromanagement, such as the House version of the 1988 foreign aid authorization bill, which imposed set figures for U.S. contributions to each of twenty international organizations—far more detailed than even the old practice of setting amounts by broad functional or regional categories. But the executive also does more than its share of earmarking. By far the largest claimants to U.S. foreign aid are Egypt and Israel, whose earmarks were established as part of the 1978 Camp David accords. Base rights countries such as Greece, the Philippines, Turkey, and Spain have insisted on lucrative guaranteed aid packages in negotiations to renew military base agreements. And the earmarking for strategically designated countries such as El Salvador and Pakistan has been very much a case of the executive branch proposing and the legislature disposing.

By the end of the Reagan administration, this problem was attracting increased attention. Voices in both Congress and the Bush administration began to acknowledge the policy problems created by their institutional competition. The Foreign Assistance Authorization Act was in desperate need of an overhaul and streamlining. It had not been rewritten since 1961, and no systematic review and change had been successfully completed since 1973. Instead incrementalism and cumulation had been the order of the day. Accordingly, the law listed some thirty-three "policy objectives," which not only spread its priorities much too thin but also in some instances were outright contradictory. The Agency for International Development (AID) elaborated these into seventy-five "priorities," robbing the term of any

31. Department of State, Bureau of Public Affairs, *FY 1990 Security Assistance Program*, Current Policy no. 1159 (Testimony of H. Allen Holmes, Assistant Secretary of State for Politico-Military Affairs, March 8, 1989); and Rochelle L. Stanfield, "Built without a Blueprint," *National Journal*, April 8, 1989, p. 848.

useful meaning. A further problem was the number of congressional reporting requirements that AID must meet, estimated at 288 by early 1989. Only the Department of Defense has more, yet it has a budget fifty times greater.[32]

A report issued in early 1989 by a task force of the House Foreign Affairs Committee, chaired by Lee H. Hamilton and Benjamin A. Gilman, made a number of important and innovative proposals. It called for an end to "most of the conditions, restrictions, directives and earmarks" and the formulation of "a new premise, a new framework, and a new purpose to meet the challenges of today."[33] It proposed reducing the thirty-three objectives to four: economic growth, environmental protection, fighting poverty, and promoting democracy. It also was self-critical enough to take Congress itself to task and offered to cut back on congressional earmarking if in turn the executive branch would involve Congress more in the broad setting of policy goals.

Although the Hamilton-Gilman report received a great deal of attention and was greeted warmly by Secretary of State James Baker, the ink was barely dry when old practices resumed and new fights began breaking out. Representative Obey repeated his insistence on symmetry between Gramm-Rudman-mandated cuts in domestic spending and comparable cuts in foreign aid, which in effect meant a 10 percent cut ($1.4 billion) in the Bush administration's proposals. In addition, earmarks hardly went away. The fiscal 1990 foreign aid budget submitted by the Bush administration still was loaded with earmarks. Numerous others were added during House committee markups, causing Hamilton to lament, "We really have not succeeded in persuading committee members to drop earmarks." On the floor, upwards of 170 amendments were proposed.[34] Thus, while there was some agreement on the diagnosis of the problems being caused by institutional competition, there still was not a genuine willingness to carry out serious reform.

---

32. Lee H. Hamilton, "To Make Foreign Aid Work," *Washington Post*, April 2, 1989, p. C7.

33. Cited in David B. Ottaway, "Foreign Aid: Sweeping Change Debated," *Washington Post*, February 27, 1989, p. A7.

34. John Felton, " 'Earmark' Tradition Shows Staying Power on Hill," *Congressional Quarterly Weekly Report*, April 22, 1989, pp. 903–04; Felton, "Intention to Change System Encounters Hill Reality," *Congressional Quarterly Weekly Report*, May 27, 1989, p. 1265; and Felton, "For Bush, Problematic Measure May Be Best Alternative," *Congressional Quarterly Weekly Report*, July 8, 1989, pp. 1705–09.

PROCEDURAL OBSTRUCTIONISM

A third aspect of the institutional competition involves "procedural obstructionism" as practiced by individual members of Congress with particular policy agendas (or, in less neutral terms, axes to grind). This long has been a practice in domestic affairs, for example, the Senate filibusters used to block civil rights legislation in the 1950s and early 1960s. Increasingly, and distressingly, it also has become a practice in foreign affairs.

No senator in recent years has used procedural tactics as often, or in as masterful a fashion, as Jesse Helms. A Senate foreign policy aide from the late 1970s recalls having to make many a call home about being late for dinner because Senator Helms was stalling, maneuvering, or otherwise extending the session into the evening. Nor, as the Reagan administration discovered, were these tactics reserved just for a president of the other party.

Helms was particularly antagonistic toward Secretary of State George Shultz. According to one account, he "used every opportunity to undermine Shultz, with the apparent goal of getting him fired."[35] He even went so far as to block Shultz's request for authority to build an official residence for *future* secretaries of state. Helms also blocked any number of Reagan State Department appointments, delayed others, pushed hard for his own favored candidates (including a number of his own former staffers), and even broke tradition by using an endorsement signed by twenty-two ambassadors (all political appointees) in his 1984 reelection campaign.

Helms also was not averse to interfering directly in diplomacy. In 1978 he sent an aide to London in an effort to disrupt the Lancaster House negotiations for black majority rule in Zimbabwe-Rhodesia. In 1984 he accused the CIA of financing Jose Napoleon Duarte's presidential campaign in El Salvador as a means not just of beating the left (who in fact were boycotting the election), but also of staving off a challenge from the rightist Arena party and its leader, Roberto D'Aubuisson. Helms's charges were true, but they hardly were what the Reagan administration wanted to be aired in public.

In 1985, as the Reagan administration was beginning to distance itself from and put pressure on the Chilean government of General Augusto Pinochet, Helms personally sought to block any such policy

35. *Congressional Quarterly Almanac, 1985*, vol. 41 (1986), p. 37.

changes. He called on Reagan to fire his new ambassador, Harry G. Barnes, Jr., and accused Barnes and the State Department more generally of not being sufficiently anticommunist. Helms and a senior aide also were accused of leaking intelligence information to the Pinochet government, a charge they denied.

I make these points less as a commentary on Helms and his particular policy goals than as an example of individually based, rather than institutionally rooted, executive-legislative conflict. Even if the competition at the institutional level were to be ameliorated, the problem of the manipulation of the shared-powers system by individual members of Congress would remain. Courtesy holds on executive appointments requested by even one senator are exceedingly difficult to change in an institution that values its individual perquisites as much as the U.S. Senate does. The same is true of filibusters, intentional floods of amendments, and other procedural tactics individual representatives and senators can use to obstruct the foreign policy-making process. No institutional reforms can preclude this possibility of procedural obstructionism and even personal attacks by individual members. These always will be dependent on the individuals involved and the political calculations they make.

THE TENSION BETWEEN ACCOUNTABILITY
AND MICROMANAGEMENT

Few would question that by the early 1970s the executive branch needed to be made more accountable and less "imperial" in its formulation and conduct of foreign policy. But the greater congressional oversight, budgetary control, and overall involvement in not just the headline issues but also in the steady and continuing business of global diplomacy, which was to be the solution to that problem, became a problem in its own right. By the end of the 1970s, as I. M. Destler observes, "much of the bloom had left the congressional rose." Congress had established a greater degree of executive accountability, but in the process had made much more difficult "settling on specific goals and pursuing them consistently."[36]

The three examples discussed here thus have wider implications than simply as conflicts situational to the Reagan years. They were

---

36. I. M. Destler, "Executive-Congressional Conflict in Foreign Policy: Explaining It, Coping with It," in Lawrence C. Dodd and Bruce I. Oppenheimer, eds., *Congress Reconsidered*, 3d ed. (Washington: Congressional Quarterly Press, 1985), p. 344.

competitive assertions of institutional prerogatives that, although fed by substantive policy differences and group-based political pressures, were most fundamentally rooted in the power-sharing structure of the foreign policy process. As retiring Senator Daniel Evans chided his colleagues, it was a "trivializing" of America's world stature to attach eighty-six amendments to a State Department authorization bill.[37] It is both telling and in its own way troublesome that the Hamilton-Gilman report on reforming foreign aid ran over 300 pages. And surely the personal attacks and procedural obstructionism to which members of Congress increasingly resort are but another sign of the declining civility in current politics.

How, then, can the congressional micromanagement problem be reduced while the necessary executive accountability is still ensured? This question and its attendant issues lack the high drama of many of the "high politics" issues of foreign policy. But in many respects this pattern of institutional competition over the prerogatives of the normal conduct of international diplomacy may bode even more trouble for the future.

Compromise

Thus far the discussion has focused on the negative policy consequences of political and procedural conflict. As such, it is consistent with the usual view that there is too much presidential-congressional conflict over foreign policy, and this conflict is bad. However, two other cases from the Reagan period, El Salvador and the Philippines, demonstrate the policy benefits of a nondeferential Congress.

EL SALVADOR

The Reagan administration wasted no time in 1981 responding to the dire situation it perceived in El Salvador. What was happening there, according to Secretary of State Haig, was "a textbook case of indirect armed aggression by Communist powers through Cuba."[38] Accordingly, Haig and others in the administration pushed for a response that was essentially military in nature: increased military aid, more military advisers, expanded military training programs. Plans for

---

37. *Congressional Quarterly Almanac, 1987*, p. 152.

38. Department of State, Bureau of Public Affairs, *Communist Interference in El Salvador*, Special Report no. 80 (February 23, 1981).

direct U.S. military intervention were disavowed, although never absolutely or unconditionally.

The initial congressional response was one of skepticism but acquiescence. Congress approved the full increase in military and economic aid, although it did add a provision requiring semiannual certifications that the Salvadoran government was improving its human rights record, cracking down on the infamous right-wing "death squads," and moving ahead with land reform.

In 1982 and 1983, however, the interbranch conflict intensified. The Reagan administration increased its aid requests and complied with the certification requirements in form only. It issued the required reports with the requisite findings, even though its favorable assessments were quite inconsistent with most other sources. House Speaker Thomas P. (Tip) O'Neill, Jr., called the July 1982 certification "simply unbelievable."[39] Congress cut the fiscal 1983 military aid request by 40 percent.

The issue came to a head in late 1983. President Reagan vetoed the bill renewing the certification requirement for future aid. The death squads were still running rampant, but Reagan offered the view that these killings could well be the work of Marxist guerrillas trying to frame the government.[40] Those who insisted on linking military aid to human rights were "either naive or downright phony." They were naive in failing to recognize that this was "a power play by Cuba and the Soviet Union, pure and simple."[41] And they were phony in not acknowledging the significance of the freely elected Constituent Assembly as evidence that the Reagan policy was working.

Protests against the veto came from both sides of the aisle and in both chambers. Senate Foreign Relations Committee Chairman Charles H. Percy expressed concern that the veto "sends a confusing signal to El Salvador just at a time when we are trying to send a strong, clear signal that political violence must cease." Michael D. Barnes, chairman of the House Foreign Affairs Subcommittee on Western Hemisphere Affairs, was less diplomatic, calling the veto "just unbelievable."[42] More important, Congress found alternative policy instruments for keeping the linkage between human rights and military aid. Through

39. *Congressional Quarterly Almanac, 1982*, vol. 38 (1983), p. 139.
40. *Congressional Quarterly Almanac, 1983*, vol. 39 (1984), p. 154.
41. Speech to Cuban-American leaders, *Weekly Compilation of Presidential Documents*, vol. 20 (March 26, 1984), p. 383.
42. *Congressional Quarterly Almanac, 1983*, p. 156.

separate legislation it made 30 percent of the military aid contingent on progress in the investigations of the 1980 murders of four American churchwomen. It also cut Reagan's fiscal 1984 military aid request for El Salvador by 25 percent.

Four years later, during the 1988 presidential campaign, George Bush cited his December 1983 trip to El Salvador, in which he informed the Salvadoran military that their aid was increasingly in jeopardy unless they genuinely cracked down on the death squads, as evidence both of his own diplomatic skills and of the success of the Reagan-Bush administration's policy. There is no reason to dispute the first point. But on the second point at least 51 percent of the credit lies with Congress. Bush delivered the warning only because Congress had forced the administration to do so. Once Congress had convinced the administration that it had no choice, the administration convinced the Salvadoran military of the realities of its relations with the United States. Salvadoran Defense Minister General Eugenio Vides Casanova stated that they then realized that "in order to receive U.S. aid, we had to do certain things."[43] Had it not been for Congress, the Salvadoran military would not have had to do those certain things.

A final point in Congress's favor is that in balancing the administration's more extreme tendencies it reflected the prevailing opinion of the American public. Support for the administration's policy was low—less than 30 percent. As one pollster observed, this is "almost as low as Presidents ever record for their handling of specific issues": lower than President Carter's rating on handling inflation, lower than President Ford's rating on the Nixon pardon, and only slightly higher than President Nixon's rating on Watergate.[44] Moreover, the intensity of public opposition correlated with the intensity of American involvement. When asked about sending more American military advisers, 59 percent disapproved. When asked about more military aid, 72 percent disapproved. And when asked about American troops, upwards of 80 percent disapproved. Moreover, 59 percent agreed that poverty and human rights abuses were the main causes of the unrest. Only 25 percent cited the Soviet Union, Cuba, or Nicaragua. To the public, then, as well as to Congress, this was something other than a textbook

43. James McClatchy, "Inside Central America," *Sacramento Bee*, September 17, 1985, p. A20.

44. Barry Sussman, "On Central America, Reagan Is Consistently Unpersuasive," *Washington Post (National Weekly Edition)*, May 14, 1984, p. 37.

case of monolithic communist aggression—and should be dealt with accordingly.

Any success that was achieved in establishing democratic structures in El Salvador was thus because of, not in spite of, Congress's assertion of its role in the setting of U.S. policy. The recent resurgence of the death squads and the uncertain political future El Salvador faces show the limits of what was achieved. But in the shorter term, Congress's role was a highly constructive one that probably helped avert a crisis on El Salvador during the Reagan presidency.

THE PHILIPPINES

The orderly transition of power from Ferdinand Marcos to Corazon Aquino is widely considered one of the great successes in American foreign policy in recent years. Most of the credit, to be sure, goes to Aquino, other Filipino leaders, and the Filipino people. If one were to allocate the credit on the American side, it would go first to the State Department, next to Congress, and only last to the president.

Ferdinand Marcos was one of the few world leaders Ronald Reagan knew personally when he became president. He had gone to Manila in 1969 while governor of California, and he and Mrs. Reagan were "dazzled" by Imelda Marcos's opulent parties. Reagan also was quite impressed by Marcos's stories of his alleged heroism as a World War II anti-Japanese guerrilla. He considered Marcos, one of his aides was later quoted as saying, like "a hero on a bubble gum card he had collected as a kid."[45]

As president, Reagan "embraced Marcos more closely than had any previous president since Johnson."[46] When in January 1981 Marcos went through the charade of lifting martial law but retaining the authority to rule by decree, the Reagan administration played right along. The elections held the following June were blatantly fraudulent; Marcos claimed some 86 percent of the vote. Yet while Japan and other countries protested by sending low-level representatives to the inauguration, Vice President Bush arrived with a message of "warmest congratulations" from President Reagan. "We stand with you," Bush

45. Stanley Karnow, "Setting Marcos Adrift," *New York Times Magazine*, March 19, 1989, p. 50.

46. Richard J. Kessler, "Marcos and the Americans," *Foreign Policy*, vol. 63 (Summer 1986), p. 56.

declared. "We love your adherence to democratic principle and to the democratic processes."[47]

Reagan himself received Marcos in September 1982 in his first official state visit since 1966. Amid more than the usual pomp and circumstance, Reagan hailed "the superb relationship between our two countries" and touted Marcos as "a respected voice for reason and moderation" and for his "dedication to improving the standard of living of your people." No mention was made of how small the group of Marcos's people was whose standard of living had been improved (that is, his cronies) or of how the overall Philippines economy was severely deteriorating.

On August 21, 1983, the mix of confidence and complacency that thus far had characterized the Reagan policy was shattered by the assassination of Benigno Aquino as he returned from exile. President Reagan's scheduled visit to Manila had to be canceled, although more out of fear for Reagan's safety than as a rebuke to Marcos. Reagan personally wrote Marcos to reassure him of their "warm and firm friendship," adding that "I've always had confidence in your ability to handle things."[48]

More important in terms of its lasting effects on policy was the issuance of a national security study directive creating an interagency group for a comprehensive review of U.S. policy. The directive that came out of this review called for increased pressure on Marcos for political, military, and economic reform. The strategy was to try "to influence him [Marcos] through a well-orchestrated policy of incentives and disincentives." However, as also was explicitly stated, "while President Marcos at this stage is part of the problem, he is also necessarily part of the solution." Marcos needed to be influenced to the point where he would begin to "set the stage for peaceful and eventual transition to a successor government whenever that takes place." But "the U.S. does not want to remove Marcos" from power.[49]

47. Raymond Bonner, *Waltzing with a Dictator: The Marcoses and the Making of American Policy* (New York: Times Books, 1987), pp. 303–07; Lela Garner Noble, "Politics in the Marcos Era," in John Bresnan, ed., *Crisis in the Philippines: The Marcos Era and Beyond* (Princeton University Press, 1986), pp. 106–08; and Kessler, "Marcos and the Americans," p. 57.

48. Stanley Karnow, *In Our Image: America's Empire in the Philippines* (Random House, 1989), p. 408.

49. Walden Bello, "Edging Toward the Quagmire: The United States and the Philippine Crisis," *World Policy Journal*, vol. 3 (Winter 1985–86), p. 36.

The State Department took the lead in pressuring Marcos. Under Secretary of State Michael Armacost, Assistant Secretary of State Paul Wolfowitz, and Ambassador to the Philippines Stephen Bosworth all openly criticized Marcos for not moving ahead with reforms. Efforts also were stepped up to go around Marcos. Ambassador Bosworth increased contacts with leaders of the moderate opposition, especially Corazon Aquino and Jaime Cardinal Sin. Both the U.S. embassy and the Defense Department secretly funded the Reform the Armed Services Now Movement. AID threatened to channel food and development assistance through the Catholic church unless Marcos cracked down on the rampant corruption and waste. State and Treasury both supported a delay by the International Monetary Fund in disbursing the next $113 million loan installment pending serious economic reform. The signals got mixed and diluted, however, by the White House's insistence on increasing military and economic aid. Moreover, Marcos knew Reagan was "on his side" and so he "refused to budge."[50]

In Congress, however, there was an emerging consensus, both bicameral and bipartisan, that Marcos was part of the problem and *not* the solution. The principal policy instrument available to Congress was military aid, which it cut almost in half. The Democrat-controlled House wanted even deeper cuts; the Republican-controlled Senate withstood these, but also was not disposed to approve the levels recommended by Reagan. Two key Senate Republicans, Foreign Relations Committee Chairman Lugar and Intelligence Committee Chairman David Durenberger, took leading roles along with Democrat Stephen Solarz, chair of the House Foreign Affairs Subcommittee on Asia and a longstanding Marcos critic. The position they shared was not solely based on human rights considerations. They also stressed the importance of maintaining the Clark and Subic Bay bases and of defeating the communist guerrilla New People's Army. But they felt the best way to achieve these objectives was by getting rid of Marcos. One might argue that theirs was a far more strategic view than the president's, much less locked in by the inertia of existing commitments and untouched by sentimentality for the Marcoses.

Marcos tried to co-opt the pressure by calling in October 1985 for a snap election in early February 1986. The problem, though, was that Corazon Aquino won this election, and Marcos then resorted to electoral fraud. Reagan's reaction was that any fraud probably was

50. Karnow, "Setting Marcos Adrift," p. 50.

committed "on both sides." But in Congress the Senate passed 85–9 a resolution censuring the election, and the Solarz subcommittee voted unanimously to suspend all military aid. And an official American observer team in the Philippines, headed by Senator Lugar, vehemently protested against Marcos's effort to steal the election. When Lugar heard Reagan's "fraud on both sides" apologia, he bluntly stated "the President was misinformed."[51]

A key role also was played by Senator Paul Laxalt, Reagan's closest personal friend in Congress. Laxalt had gone to the Philippines as a personal emissary of the president in October 1985, again to plead for Marcos to change his ways. Then during the electoral crisis, it was Laxalt whom Marcos called, and who could credibly deliver the message from President Reagan to "cut and cut cleanly. The time has come."[52] Reagan came to this position very late, but he finally did.

Congress thus had influence through both formal and informal instruments. It acted in truly bipartisan fashion: Democratic and Republican legislators worked together, and the legislative institution worked with the executive branch, especially the State Department. The members of Congress who took the lead minimized any demagoguery and acted quite responsibly in their exercise of power. They set as their priority pushing for an effective policy, rather than engaging in a fight just to score points against the president.

Congress pushed the administration when it was complacent and then helped force its decision when crisis was at hand. The president, on the other hand, was a prisoner of personal friendships, past commitments, and a persisting ideological world view (to throw Marcos "to the wolves," he argued, would be to give rise to "a Communist power in the Pacific").[53] Had policy been left to the president, the results almost certainly would have been less favorable (defined in terms of both democratic values and American diplomatic interests). Reagan even waited two months before calling President Aquino to congratulate her. He refused to grant her the full honor of a state visit on her late 1986 trip to the United States. And it was Congress, far more than the president, that put together the new increased aid package to help President Aquino try to reconstruct the Philippines

51. Bonner, *Waltzing with a Dictator*, p. 422.
52. Paul Laxalt, "My Conversations with Ferdinand Marcos (A Lesson in Personal Diplomacy)," *Policy Review*, vol. 37 (Summer 1986), p. 5.
53. Karnow, "Setting Marcos Adrift," p. 50.

from the effects of Marcos's autocracy, corruption, and crony capitalism.

WHEN PRESIDENTIAL-CONGRESSIONAL CONFLICT IS CONSTRUCTIVE

The experiences in El Salvador and especially the Philippines should dispel the generalization that deference by Congress always is beneficial to U.S. diplomacy. There are indeed situations, of which these two cases are examples, in which "debate, creative tension and review of policy can bring about decisions and actions that stand a better chance of serving the interests and values of the American people."[54] The president does not always know best. To the contrary, and even leaving aside the specific policy preferences of Reagan or any other particular president, one of the problems inherent in the presidency is a tendency to feel locked in to existing commitments to preserve continuity and credibility. The United States should not take its reputation for reliability lightly. But it also must be able to discern when short-term concerns about credibility can be counterproductive to longer-term strategic interests, to say nothing of considerations of human rights and democratic values.[55]

The Philippines case in particular shows how important it is for pragmatism and statesmanship to prevail over ideology and partisanship in executive-congressional relations. The leadership from both branches— Senator Lugar, Representative Solarz, Ambassador Bosworth, Under Secretary Armacost, Assistant Secretary Wolfowitz, Secretary Shultz— was eminently responsible in its handling of this issue. There was very little posturing, very few cheap shots, very little grandstanding in either Congress or the State Department. The initial policy differences thus were bridged, and American policy was that much stronger for it. It was truly an exemplary instance of the separate branches sharing their powers in a constructive fashion.

Cooperation

The conflicts between the Reagan administration and Congress were so dramatic as to overshadow the substantial bipartisan cooperation

54. Lee H. Hamilton and Michael H. Van Dusen, "Making the Separation of Power Work," *Foreign Affairs*, vol. 57 (Fall 1978), p. 28.

55. For a fuller analysis of this problem, see Bruce W. Jentleson, "American Commitments in the Third World: Theory vs. Practice," *International Organization*, vol. 41 (Autumn 1987), pp. 667–704.

that was achieved in three issue areas: the use of military force against aggressor states in certain regional conflicts, overall relations with the Soviet Union, and development of normalized relations with the People's Republic of China. The fact that these issues in the past had been among the most confrontational made them all the more interesting, in themselves and in their implications. Moreover, in the first few months of the Bush administration this new bipartisan cooperation was put to the test by the continuing initiatives as well as the upheaval of Mikhail Gorbachev's Soviet Union and, even more so, by the brutal repression of the "democracy movement" in China.

REGIONAL CONFLICTS AND THE USE OF FORCE

The principal legacy of the Vietnam War had been to call into question the utility of military force as an instrument of U.S. foreign policy. This was one of the defining policy conflicts along which the old cold war consensus split open, over both the normative questions about ends and means as well as the quite practical ones about the scope and limits of the utility of military force. The issue also raised fundamental questions regarding institutional power sharing, which, as Robert Katzmann discusses, the War Powers Act has not been able to resolve.

I already have discussed Nicaragua and how the option of using military force, even through the surrogate of the contras, could not gain sustainable support either in Congress or among the general public. The 1982-84 deployment of the marines to Lebanon had a similar, albeit less severe, political problem. But on a number of other issues pertaining to the use of force—notably the arming of the Afghan mujaheddin, the 1986 bombing of Libya, and the 1987–88 naval deployment against Iran in the Persian Gulf—both Congress and the public were more supportive. For example, public opinion poll data show a level of support for Reagan's Nicaraguan policy ranging from a high of 43 percent to a low of 22 percent. For Lebanon, the range was 44 percent to 27 percent. But for the Persian Gulf reflagging and naval deployment, support reached 53 percent and did not go below 43 percent. For the bombing of Libya, the range was 77 percent to 53 percent.[56] And while no comparable public opinion data are available

---

56. *Public Opinion*, vol. 6 (August–September 1983), p. 37; *Public Opinion*, vol. 10 (September–October 1987), p. 24; *National Journal*, July 28, 1984, p. 1450; *National Journal*, March 8, 1986, p. 600; *National Journal*, May 17, 1986, p. 1224; *National Journal*, June 27, 1987, p. 1682; and *National Journal*, September 19, 1987, p. 2366.

for the Afghanistan policy, the reason appears to be that pollsters considered it to be such a strongly consensual issue that it was not worth dedicating a question to it.

The same pattern holds for congressional support. On Nicaragua, Congress was always reluctant at best to vote for aid to the contras. But on Afghanistan it was Congress that repeatedly pushed the Reagan administration to take a harder line than it appeared inclined to do.[57] Initially the Reagan administration had kept aid and other covert assistance to the mujaheddin at the relatively low levels set by the Carter administration. The first major increase in aid came at the behest of Democratic Representative Charles H. Wilson, who in the fall of 1983 sponsored a secret amendment reallocating $40 million in Defense Department funds to the CIA for the Afghan operation. In fiscal 1985 Congress acted to nearly triple the Reagan administration's aid request.[58] The next year Congress set up a Special Task Force on Afghanistan and chose as its chair Republican Senator Gordon H. Humphrey, a staunch conservative. When press reports indicated in late 1987 that the State Department was considering conceding to Soviet demands for a cessation of U.S. aid to the mujaheddin as part of the withdrawal accords, the Senate voted unanimously for a Humphrey resolution opposing any such concession and pressuring the administration to stand tough on linking U.S. aid to the mujaheddin to Soviet aid to the Kabul regime.

The comparison between the use of the War Powers Act in the cases of Lebanon and the Persian Gulf cuts in the same direction. On Lebanon Congress was willing to go along with the marine deployment as part of the second multinational force, but only through a carefully crafted agreement that, while technically stopping short of a formal invocation of the War Powers Act, made the troop commitment politically subject to congressional renewal or termination. Thus support was there, but it was tenuous and tentative, ready to be tipped in the other direction by some unforeseen event—which is precisely what happened with the marine barracks bombing. In the case of the Persian Gulf reflagging and naval operations, the opposition in Congress never could muster the critical mass to take constraining action. The

57. Bob Woodward, *Veil: The Secret Wars of the CIA* (Simon and Schuster, 1987), pp. 316–18; Rosanne Klass, "Afghanistan: The Accords," *Foreign Affairs*, vol. 66 (Summer 1988), p. 934; *Congressional Quarterly Almanac, 1982*, pp. 166–67; and *Congressional Quarterly Almanac, 1984*, vol. 40 (1985), pp. 118–19.

58. *Washington Post (National Weekly Edition)*, January 28, 1985, pp. 14–15.

House passed a ninety-day delay on reflagging in early July 1987, but the Senate failed to follow suit. A number of senators tried in a variety of ways to invoke the War Powers Act or to pass other restrictive measures. But when the Senate finally passed a heavily watered-down version (the Byrd-Warner amendment), this time it was the House that failed to act.

In the Libyan case the president consulted congressional leaders before the April 1986 bombing. The consultation was more informational than advisory, but both Democrats and Republicans assured him of their personal support. Some liberal Democrats protested, but many others raced to get on the syndicated talk shows to bash Qaddafi. Congress never seriously considered any condemnatory or restrictive action.

What this points to is a sharp contrast that has developed within American politics between the political legitimacy of using military force for imposing foreign policy restraint on an aggressor state, as distinct from using military force to overthrow or otherwise remake the internal composition of the government of another state.[59] In brief, there are three principal reasons for this pattern. First, there is a sharp contrast in the level of threat posed to the United States: blatant violations of national sovereignty and the concomitant echos of Munich (Afghanistan), immediate threats to vital American geopolitical and economic interests (Persian Gulf), and direct aggression against American citizens (Libya), compared with deposing the government of a tiny country because of a largely hypothetical threat (Nicaragua) and keeping somebody else's peace (Lebanon).

Second, efforts to coerce foreign policy restraint are more apt than efforts to reconstitute governments to allow for assertiveness without extended involvement, shows of strength without lasting commitments. As such, they embody what William Schneider calls the pervasive desire of Americans in the 1980s for "peace and strength, yes; involvement, no."[60] Peace and strength through shows of force that do not entangle either because of their indirectness (Afghanistan) or their quickness (Libya) are much easier for Congress and the public to support than open-ended wars, even by surrogates (Nicaragua). The Persian Gulf case was more direct and less quick, and thus caused

59. For further elaboration of the distinctions described in the text, see also Bruce W. Jentleson, "Force and Diplomacy: Lessons from the Reagan Record," paper prepared for the 1989 annual meeting of the American Political Science Association.

60. Schneider, " 'Rambo' and Reality," p. 45.

greater tension within public opinion, although not nearly as much as the even more direct and entangling Lebanon commitment.

Third, the two types of objectives also differ in the international legitimacy they can claim. Principles of nonaggression, national self-determination, and the rights of sovereignty, however abused in practice they have been, are the closest the international system has to a universal set of rules and norms. Uses of force mounted to restrain an aggressor nation in defense of these basic principles therefore can draw upon historical tradition as well as canons of international law for their justification. Moreover, at least during the Reagan years, these issues tended to involve foreign leaders who ranked high in the rogues' gallery of American public opinion, notably Qaddafi and Khomeini. Daniel Ortega was hardly an American hero, and the Lebanese terrorists who bombed the American Marine barracks would undoubtedly have engendered enormous hatred, if they ever had been identified. But Qaddafi and Khomeini in particular are figures for whom no member of Congress was about to express understanding, let alone sympathy.

A note of qualification needs to be made so that this contrast is not taken too far. This distinction between the principal objectives of foreign policy restraint and governmental reconstitution is not posited as being absolutely determinative of the U.S. domestic politics of the issue. The Reagan administration did also make headway in getting Congress to repeal the 1975 Clark amendment and to fund the anticommunist forces of UNITA in Angola. But this still was low-level funding and did not involve either the direct use of American force or a declaratory policy commitment to the extent given in Afghanistan. Then there is the 1983 invasion of Grenada. In many respects Grenada is a special case from which it is difficult to generalize. The initial critical outcry in Congress did fade very quickly; Speaker Tip O'Neill, for example, changed his position from protest to support, albeit qualified by criticisms that the War Powers Act was not invoked.[61] But the main implications of this discussion are that there tends to be significant bipartisan support for the use of American military force when American interests are threatened by the aggressive actions of another government. This represents a substantial shift from the late 1970s, when the disinclination to use military force was more generalized.

61. *Congressional Quarterly Almanac, 1983*, p. 135.

U.S.-SOVIET RELATIONS

There is some irony in the fact that détente began as the policy of a Republican president, which encountered substantial Democratic opposition in Congress (for example, by Senator Henry Jackson) but ended up as the albatross around the neck of a Democratic president and the Democratic majority in Congress. By 1980 the Democrats had come to be associated with cuts in defense spending, the less than popular SALT II treaty, the Cuban troops in Angola, the mysterious Soviet brigade in Cuba, and ultimately the Soviet Union's brazen invasion of Afghanistan. For Ronald Reagan, who long had been a leader of the antidétente wing within the Republican party, what had been a detriment limiting the scope of his political appeal now became an asset. Nor did it work only for Reagan. Their association with détente was among the factors that helped defeat enough incumbent liberal Democratic senators to turn the Senate over to Republican control for the first time in twenty-six years.

Reagan sought to transform the tone of U.S.-Soviet relations no less than he sought to change the actual policies. He spared few words in doing so, especially in his first three years in office. In his very first press conference as president, Reagan accused the Soviets of "reserv[ing] unto themselves the right to commit any crime, to lie, to cheat." In June 1982, addressing the British Parliament, he stated his goal of pushing "Marxism-Leninism on the ash-heap of history." In March 1983 he labeled the Soviets "the focus of evil in the modern world." A few months later, when the Soviets shot down Korean Air Lines Flight 007, he dismissed the possibility of an accident and concluded instead that "it was an act of barbarism born of a society which wantonly disregards individual rights."[62]

On the policy front, as Barry Blechman discusses in his chapter, Reagan and Congress clashed over numerous issues of arms control, weapons development, and defense spending. The other major early clash came over economic sanctions against the Siberian natural gas pipeline.[63] The ostensible reason for the sanctions was Soviet complicity

62. *Weekly Compilation of Presidential Documents*, vol. 17 (February 2, 1981), pp. 66–67; vol. 18 (June 14, 1982), p. 769; vol. 19 (March 14, 1983), p. 369; and vol. 19 (September 12, 1983), p. 1200.
63. See Bruce W. Jentleson, *Pipeline Politics: The Complex Political Economy of East-West Energy Trade* (Cornell University Press, 1986).

in Polish martial law. In fact, though, as statements by administration figures such as Secretary of Defense Caspar Weinberger and Assistant Secretary of Defense Richard Perle made clear, the real agenda was to "squeeze" the Soviet economy. Congress responded at both levels, trying to overturn the embargo for its direct economic costs to American exporters and as a more general rejection of the economic squeeze strategy.

The next year, when the Export Administration Act (the principal authority for export controls) came up for renewal, the Reagan administration proposed much more highly restrictive criteria as a matter of general policy. A version of this proposal passed the Senate, but with fifty-two Republicans crossing over, the House passed a more trade-liberalizing measure. This set up what proved to be the Ninety-eighth Congress's longest running conference committee and its least successful one: no agreement was reached, and the old legislation had to be given an emergency extension.

One issue on which Congress and the Reagan administration did agree was grain trade with the Soviet Union. Reagan promised during the 1980 campaign to lift the Carter grain embargo. In March 1981 this became one of the first major intraadministration disputes. Secretary of State Haig was opposed to lifting the grain embargo without a significant quid pro quo from the Soviets.[64] Reagan's political advisers urged him to keep his campaign promise and were reinforced by heavy lobbying from Capitol Hill. Thus, at a time when on virtually every other front he was pushing hard-line anti-Soviet policies, Reagan lifted the grain embargo. In 1983 a new grain trade agreement was signed in which the United States pledged never to impose a grain embargo again. Some conservatives criticized it, but the president and most of Congress hailed it. In 1985 the administration even agreed to subsidize Soviet purchases of U.S. grain. Secretary of State Shultz strongly objected, but he too was overwhelmed by the political pressure group considerations shared by both the White House political advisers and Congress.

By 1984 the distance between Reagan and Congress on issues involving the overall U.S.-Soviet political relationship had begun to narrow. A number of diverse forces were at work. First, as part of his reelection strategy, Reagan shifted somewhat toward the center. His

64. Alexander M. Haig, Jr., *Caveat: Realism, Reagan, and Foreign Policy* (Macmillan, 1984), pp. 110–16.

campaign strategists read the electoral climate as conducive to moderation. The themes of strength and caution were retained, but the emphasis was more on glorifying America than on condemning the Soviet Union.

Second, a significant part of the Democratic party moved (or at least tried to move) from the other direction and toward the center. It had become exceedingly difficult to maintain any semblance of validity for any remnants of détente amid both the actions and the images of Brezhnev's last years and the paralysis of the Andropov-Chernenko interlude. More than ever the Soviets came across as blustering, stagnating, antagonistic—in effect, as one big *nyet*. The presidential candidacy of Walter Mondale did not push this centrist shift very far, but the initiative was taken up in particular by the Democratic Leadership Council, which was centered around such congressional leaders as Senators Sam Nunn and Albert Gore, Jr., and Representatives Les Aspin and Richard Gephardt.

The third force at work was the rise of Mikhail Gorbachev. *Nyet* became *da*. Where they had stormed out of negotiating sessions and into Afghanistan, the Soviets now were the ones putting forward proposals for new negotiations and withdrawing their troops from Afghanistan. Gorbachev was almost universally regarded, in British Prime Minister Margaret Thatcher's phrase, as a man "with whom the West can do business." He also was enormously attractive as a personal leader, cracking old stereotypes and drawing in Western publics from Washington and New York to Bonn, London, and Paris.

Thus, over the course of Reagan's second term, a new operative consensus of moderation in U.S.-Soviet relations emerged. Mikhail Gorbachev and Ronald Reagan together had legitimized the reinjection of serious diplomacy into U.S.-Soviet relations. To be hopeful was no longer to appear naive; one could now acknowledge the prospects for progress while still being considered prudent and a realist. Accordingly, it now was possible for the conservative Republican president, the Democratic Congress, and the Soviet general secretary to coexist in the same political space.[65]

Of course, the political converse was that the target left for Congress

65. The main dissent came from the right, who felt let down (and worse) by their hero. Upon Reagan's signing of the INF treaty, New Right leader Howard Phillips branded him a "useful idiot for the Soviets." Even earlier, see Norman Podhoretz, "The Reagan Road to Detente," *Foreign Affairs*, vol. 63 (America and the World 1984), pp. 447–64.

to aim at during the second Reagan term was much smaller and more sporadic. By no means, though, was there agreement on all issues. Nor did Congress revert to its old deferential role or pass up opportunities to criticize the president. As Blechman discusses, arms control disputes continued and came to a head on a number of issues. The fiasco of the Reykjavik summit also left Reagan vulnerable for attacks from the left (for being so stubborn on "Star Wars" that he passed up the chance to move toward true disarmament), the right (for even thinking about disarmament), and the center (for his apparent lack of knowledge about the basics of deterrence). Also, the Moscow embassy and other spy scandals stirred congressional oversight and offered some irresistible opportunities for pointing fingers at executive branch shortcomings.

The bounds of this newly consensual middle were curiously defined during the 1988 presidential campaign by Democratic candidate Michael Dukakis's efforts to claim that he, not George Bush, was the rightful claimant to Reagan's legacy in U.S.-Soviet relations. More than one eyebrow was raised when at his last presidential news conference Ronald Reagan expressed his view that yes, he could even foresee the possibility that the United States and the Soviet Union might become allies someday. And Democrats, especially those mentioned early for the 1992 presidential sweepstakes, set out to forge positions that would make them part tough-talking Harry Truman, part tough-dealing John Kennedy, and part engagingly patriotic Ronald Reagan.

Yet it also is a fragile consensus, potentially vulnerable on both its flanks. If Gorbachev were to fall and be replaced by "old thinking" leaders (or if somehow Gorbachev himself were to evidence substantial contradictions between his "new thinking" and his actions), the splits of the 1970s might reopen. Expectations have been dashed too often in the past for the possibility to be dismissed that the conservative critique might once again hold sway. However, to a much greater extent than in the past there is also political pressure for bolder, faster, and more far-reaching moves toward building a new, more cooperative relationship with the Soviet Union. These pressures are particularly acute within the NATO alliance, notably from West Germany. But there are also indications of a much more substantial American political constituency than ever before in favor of dramatic change in the U.S.-Soviet relationship. The domestic criticisms of the Bush administration's early extensive policy review producing only a strategy of "status quo plus," and then of its understated responses to Eastern Europe's self-liberation, were manifestations of this new attitude. Bush's bold proposals for conventional force reductions at the May 1989 NATO summit, and then the initiatives at the December 1989 Malta summit with Gorbachev, effectively neutralized the criticisms, at least for the moment. But this sentiment favoring greater cooperation with the Soviet Union could still cause Bush political problems if his efforts slow down, fail, or otherwise are outshone by Gorbachev.

RELATIONS WITH THE PEOPLE'S REPUBLIC OF CHINA

The normalization of relations with China was a truly bipartisan enterprise in the 1970s. Democrats in Congress worked with and supported Republican Presidents Nixon and Ford. Republicans in Congress were more split: the majority were supportive under Carter as well as Nixon and Ford, but staunch conservatives such as Senator Barry Goldwater even took to the courts to oppose the policy. But when President Ronald Reagan pledged to end arms sales to Taiwan and started selling them to the People's Republic of China and then visited "Red China" itself, it showed how wide the embrace of this new policy consensus had become.

The Reagan administration had been conducting secret talks with China since late 1981. A preliminary decision was made in January 1982 not to sell Taiwan the advanced FX fighter. In August 1982 a joint communiqué was issued in which China pledged to seek peaceful reunification and the Reagan administration pledged to limit and ultimately end arms sales to Taiwan. Liberal Democrats such as Representative Solarz praised these actions as "wise and statesmanlike," while Goldwater and other conservatives decried them as "duplicity."[66] In June 1983 the Reagan administration lifted a number of restrictions on sales to China of high-technology equipment with military applications. Later that year Defense Secretary Caspar Weinberger led a delegation to Beijing to discuss possible military cooperation. This visit was reciprocated in March 1984 by a Chinese military delegation, which held extensive meetings at the Pentagon and with American defense contractors. The Potomac, not the Yalu, was the river now being crossed.

Then in 1984 Reagan himself journeyed to the Inner Kingdom. The television shots of his toasts with Deng Xiao-ping and of him climbing the Great Wall were, true to the Chinese expression, worth

66. *Congressional Quarterly Almanac, 1982,* pp. 140, 142.

a thousand words. In more substantive terms, the main outcome of the Reagan trip was an initial agreement for the United States to sell China nuclear fuel, equipment, and technology. A thirty-year nuclear cooperation agreement was signed the following year. This was the first nuclear sales agreement the United States had ever signed with any communist country and its first bilateral nuclear sales agreement with a country that was an acknowledged possessor of nuclear weapons.

The Reagan administration's thinking followed the well-worn path of the strategic triangle. This was still pre- and early Gorbachev, and so the enemy (China) of my enemy (Soviet Union) was my friend. But as often happens with strategic triangle thinking, strategists focus so much on the "big picture" that they pay too little attention to the specific details of the particular agreements. Such was the case, as far as Senator John Glenn and others in Congress were concerned, with the lack of safeguards against nuclear proliferation in the U.S.-China nuclear cooperation accord. In another striking role reversal, it was liberal Democrats who accused Ronald Reagan of having given away too much to the Chinese. Unlike conservatives such as Barry Goldwater and Jesse Helms, who opposed the agreement per se, Democrats such as Glenn were concerned with the lack of strict safeguards against nuclear proliferation. China allegedly had been assisting Pakistan in developing its nuclear bomb and also was a major exporter of nuclear equipment and technology to such nonsignees of the nonproliferation treaty as Argentina and Brazil. With this in mind, Glenn and others criticized the administration for not insisting on the usual International Atomic Energy Agency inspections and reporting requirements.

The Senate went so far as to pass a Glenn amendment to require a formal nonproliferation certification from the president. But when it became clear through both administration and Chinese protests that such a requirement would kill the agreement, Congress was pragmatic enough to drop it in conference committee. In its stead a series of conditions were attached to the joint resolution of approval, which did not go as far as Glenn and others wanted but did add greater oversight for both Congress and the International Atomic Energy Agency. By adding some conditions and restrictions but drawing the line at a damaging amendment, Congress managed to modify the policy without undoing the agreement. In so doing it showed that it had learned how to be nondeferential yet cooperative.

This was further evident in Congress's approval at virtually the same time of the first U.S. government arms sale to China. The $98

million deal included both equipment and technology for the construction of ammunition and explosive factories. Then in 1986 Congress
approved an even larger arms package, $550 million in sophisticated
technology to enhance China's fleet of F-8 warplanes. In effect, while
both U.S. and Chinese officials were circumspect about acknowledging
it, the U.S.-China relationship had moved under the Reagan administration from simple normality to tacit alliance. This was a truly
historic transformation, yet there were few dissenting voices within
American politics.

This broad consensus was severely tested beginning in June 1989
with the Chinese government's brutal repression of the "democracy
movement" and in particular its massacre of student protesters in
Tiananmen Square. The Bush administration was severely criticized
in Congress, from both sides of the aisle, for its muted response to
Tiananmen Square and for imposing only limited economic sanctions.
Efforts at compromise were hampered by further disputes over visa
extensions for Chinese students, and then by revelations of two secret
trips to China by top administration officials. If the Bush administration
reorients its approach to be more consistent with the cooperative
procedures, the spirit of consultation, and the policy balance between
strategic concerns and democratic values that built the bipartisan
consensus in the first place, that consensus still can be sustained. If it
does not, China may become Bush's South Africa, if not his Nicaragua,
in his relations with Congress.

FOREIGN POLICY POLITICS IN A CHANGING WORLD

The new areas of congressional-executive cooperation that emerged
during the Reagan years on certain key issues of U.S. diplomacy may
be best understood (however ironically) in terms of a Marxian-Hegelian
dialectic of thesis-antithesis-synthesis. The old cold war policies were
the theses: intervention in third world conflicts as the norm, conflict
with the Soviet Union as inexorable, and Red China as the enemy and
Taiwan as the friend. The 1970s provided the antitheses: post-Vietnam
retreat from interventionism, détente with the Soviet Union, and
normalization of relations with China and rejection of Taiwan. In the
early 1980s theses and antitheses clashed intensely. But by the late
1980s syntheses, integrating elements of both, emerged: a greater
capacity to distinguish between those third world conflicts in which
force should and should not be used, a combination of a sober and
cautious attitude toward continuing security needs with a sense of a

potentially historic opportunity in relations with the Soviet Union, and a relationship with China, which while still seeking to be grounded in common interests, was also becoming more realistic as to both its scope and its limits.

These areas of newly cooperative politics were important both as a direct contribution to more effective policy and as a more general tempering of the Vietnam era's pessimism about the intractability of the domestic politics of foreign policy. Congress (the Democratic House included) proved that it was not automatically against the policies of Republican presidents.

Thus, albeit with costs and conflicts along the way, the American political system came out of the period in which we had come to see ourselves as "our own worst enemy" with some successes as well as failures.[67] These successes are not to be exaggerated in terms of either their generalizability or their durability: much remains to be seen in both these regards. But in drawing conclusions from the Reagan years and looking at the Bush years, they also should not be ignored.

Conclusion: Diplomacy Starts at Home

There is a natural human tendency, especially when feeling beset by problems of the moment, to hark back to the "good old days." There is a great deal of such longing for the "golden age of bipartisan-ship," that period usually delineated as stretching from the Truman Doctrine to the early days of the Vietnam War. But as understandable as such sentiments are, as the basis for serious discussions about how to improve presidential-congressional relations in the making of U.S. foreign policy, they are highly misleading.

Without getting into a full historical discussion, three points are key. First of all, from a longer historical perspective, the foreign policy politics of the 1947–65 period were more the exception than the rule. One must go back to Corwin's analysis of the Constitution as an invitation to struggle, or to Louis Henkin's more recent assessment of it as a "starkly incomplete, indeed skimpy . . . blueprint for the governance of our foreign affairs."[68] Throughout American history—

67. I. M. Destler, Leslie H. Gelb, and Anthony Lake, *Our Own Worst Enemy: The Unmaking of American Foreign Policy* (Simon and Schuster, 1984).

68. Louis Henkin, "Foreign Affairs and the Constitution," *Foreign Affairs*, vol. 66 (Winter 1987–88), p. 287; and Arthur M. Schlesinger, Jr., *The Imperial Presidency* (Houghton Mifflin, 1973).

from the Jay treaty to the Versailles treaty, from the Mexican war to the 1930s neutrality acts, across many administrations and over many issues—presidents and Congresses repeatedly have vied with one another in trying to fill in the details of that blueprint. Second, the reality of the golden age was not as purely golden as is remembered. It did, after all, include the visceral experience of McCarthyism. The country also learned the hard way, in Vietnam and elsewhere, the risks of bipartisanship when it means Congress writes out blank checks of discretionary authority for presidents. Third, there is no going backward. Would anyone today invoke Clinton Rossiter's classic metaphor of the 1950s of the president as a "magnificent lion who can roam widely and do great deeds," and against whom checks and balances only needed to be kept tight enough to ensure that "he does not try to break loose from his broad reservation"?[69] Would any congressional committee chairman, current or prospective, share the view of Thomas (Doc) Morgan, chairman of the House Foreign Affairs Committee in the 1960s, of his committee "in *all* matters, as the subordinate partner in a permanent alliance with the executive branch"?[70] What of the venerable J. William Fulbright, chairman of the Senate Foreign Relations Committee, who as late as 1961 reflected on whether "the time has not arrived, or indeed already passed, when we must give the Executive a measure of power in the conduct of our foreign affairs that we have hitherto jealously withheld," only to later be among the leading voices condemning "the growth of presidential dictatorship in foreign affairs"?[71]

A substantial role for Congress in U.S. international diplomacy is a given. It is that point from which all serious discussion about how to make the process work better should begin.

The basic structural problem of institutional power sharing thus remains. Of particular importance in this regard is the need for the executive branch to institutionalize the practice of early and genuine consultation with congressional leaders on key issues of U.S. diplomacy.

69. Clinton Rossiter, *The American Presidency*, rev. ed. (New York: New American Library, 1960), pp. 68–69.

70. As characterized by Richard F. Fenno, Jr., *Congressmen in Committees* (Little, Brown, 1973), p. 71 (emphasis in original).

71. Compare J. William Fulbright, "American Foreign Policy in the 20th Century under an 18th-Century Constitution," *Cornell Law Quarterly*, vol. 47 (Fall 1961), pp. 1–13, with his "Congress and Foreign Policy," included in *Commission on the Organization of the Government for the Conduct of Foreign Policy*, vol. 5 (GPO, 1975).

This should not just be intermittent when crises break out, but should be on a more systematic and continuing basis. Coordination needs to come as part of, rather than after, policy formulation. In this way there may be less crossing of swords, each branch wielding the policy instruments at its disposal in pursuit of inconsistent and at times conflicting policy objectives. Those who have been in on the planning of policy are less likely to criticize its results.

In this regard the "open hand" that President George Bush offered in his inaugural address was a positive start. When Ronald Reagan called for bipartisanship, for "Republicans and Democrats standing united in patriotism and speaking with one voice," the one voice was meant to be the president's, with Congress merely joining in at the refrains.[72] President Bush and his Secretary of State, James A. Baker III, early on showed that they genuinely had in mind a more balanced two-way conception. For example, much was made in the early days of the Bush administration of the personal style of the new president. The Speaker of the House was invited for a weekend at Camp David, other key congressional Democrats were invited for White House dinners, and President Bush even showed up for workouts in the House gym. Secretary of State Baker made bipartisanship the central theme of his confirmation hearings. In substantive terms the most important early manifestation was the March 1989 bipartisan accord on Nicaragua. In contrast to the Reagan administration, the Bush administration did not bash its congressional opponents, it negotiated with them. The result was that within two months it accomplished what the Reagan administration could not in eight years, a genuine presidential-congressional agreement that avoided further self-destructive political conflict over policy toward Nicaragua.

However, it is not just a matter of cooperation between the institutions themselves. There also is the broader political environment to consider, in particular the reality that interest group pressure is now a normal part of the foreign policy-making process, and it is unlikely to slacken in the foreseeable future. Increasing numbers of groups have interests that are affected by international events and policies. For example, it was once mainly the Polish-Americans and the Jewish-Americans whose ethnic allegiances led them to seek to influence U.S. diplomacy. Now it is also the Greek-Americans, the African-Americans, the Arab-Americans, and the Filipino-Americans. There has also

72. *Weekly Compilation of Presidential Documents*, vol. 20 (April 9, 1984), p. 496.

been a tremendous growth—on both the left and the right ends of the political spectrum—in religious, human rights, ideological, and other activist groups. And on economic matters, where once just a few industries had interests at stake (textiles, steel, and then autos), there are now few sectors of the American economy that are not affected by the international economy.

Most important, the normalcy of substantive disagreements over foreign policy needs to be recognized. When a nation faces a clear and present danger, as the United States did after Pearl Harbor and arguably in the early days of the cold war, it then is quite logical that its politics stop at the water's edge. But under less extreme conditions, it is altogether logical that there be full, substantive debate. It is precisely because foreign policy issues so often raise such vital concerns and pose choices involving such core American values that they take on such political importance. It is thus all the more encouraging that more common ground exists today on relations with the Soviet Union than at any point in the postwar era. There are, as noted, no guarantees that the politics will stay this way, nor does this mean that conflicts over specific issues are precluded. But it is, nevertheless, a hopeful development.

The most contentious foreign policy issues are likely to continue to concern the proper responses to third world instability. In the 1970s there were disputes over Vietnam, Cambodia, Chile, Angola, and Iran; in the 1980s there was Nicaragua, South Africa, El Salvador, and the Philippines; and in the 1990s there inevitably will be many other as yet unspecified countries facing major problems of instability. Although each case will continue to have its unique aspects, recent experience shows a common pattern to the types of choices posed for the United States and accordingly to the terms of debate within American politics. Surely one lesson of the Reagan years is that there are both constructive and counterproductive ways of dealing with these types of issues. On the Philippines and El Salvador, Congress played an enormously important and constructive role. In both cases, as I have argued, U.S. policy was much better off because of the compromises struck than if the Reagan administration's original policy preferences had carried the day. On Afghanistan, Libya, and the Persian Gulf, Congress dispelled the notion that it was intrinsically averse to using military force. It did not write out 1950s-style blank checks of discretionary authority, but it did provide the administration with broad bipartisan cooperation.

On Nicaragua, however, the Pennsylvania Avenue politics made a difficult issue that much worse. To be sure, presidents should try to rally the country around their views and positions. That is what leadership is all about. But the Reagan years proved how politically destructive, diplomatically counterproductive, and even constitutionally threatening such breakdowns in relations between the executive and legislative branches can be. Some political conflict was unavoidable, but it was exacerbated because ideology was allowed to prevail over pragmatism, and partisanship over statesmanship.

An additional concern, which has only been touched on here, is less one of policy conflict than of policy inattention. Both Congress and the executive branch have an extremely difficult time dealing with issues that have long time frames. For example, during the Reagan years both branches failed to deal effectively with the third world debt crisis. The administration involved itself periodically, as in putting together special bailout packages for Mexico. And Congress did hold hearings and issue various studies and reports. A substantial number of people in both branches shared the view that if something was not done, the consequences (political and strategic as well as economic) could be severe. But these would happen later—not on the Reagan administration's watch, and surely not before the next congressional election. The problem, though, for enduring U.S. interests is that if everyone waits until the governments start to topple, it will be too late.

A similar problem is posed by global environmental issues. The warning signs have been evident for some time. A dwindling number of people or organizations are denying or belittling the problems. But mobilizing for systematic action remains exceedingly difficult. The policy logic of a particular administration and Congress taking action to deal with the problem before it gets much worse is overwhelmed by the political logic of hopes that some future administration and Congress will have to face the consequences and pay the bills.

In addition to these issues, other new places, issues, and conflicts also are likely to arise on which the president and Congress will have to try to avoid confrontation and competition and find bases for compromises and cooperation. But that is what diplomacy is all about— at home as well as abroad.

Trade Policy:
Refereeing the Playing Field

PIETRO S. NIVOLA

IN THE PAST decade presidents and legislators have changed the tenor of American trade policy. Through most of the postwar period policymakers deemed it in the nation's economic and strategic interests to tolerate flaws in the international trading order. That tolerance has since been displaced by the notions that trade can be harmful unless it is "fair" and that the government should intervene, frequently and unilaterally, to secure fairness. Thus one industry after another has sought designated market shares or special protection on the grounds that foreign competitors price their products improperly or that foreign governments subsidize exports or deny access to home markets. Increasingly stringent rules are being enforced against the worst offenders. This new emphasis is sustained by more than an insistent Congress; it involves an intricate political minuet between the legislative and executive branches.

The broad context of the new stance has been the country's changing economic position in the world. Driven by an overvalued currency, the nation's merchandise trade deficit ballooned from $24 billion in 1980 to an imposing $139 billion in 1986, and imports rose from 10 percent of GNP to 14 percent, while exports fell from 12 percent to 10 percent.[1] To finance this surfeit of consumption over domestic production, foreign claims on U.S. assets rapidly increased. Net external borrowing stood at $264 billion in 1986 and is headed for the

I wish to thank Claude E. Barfield, Martha Derthick, J. Michael Finger, Robert G. Gilpin, Jr., Steven I. Hofman, Gary N. Horlick, Robert A. Katzmann, Robert Z. Lawrence, Robert E. Litan, Robert A. Pastor, Steven S. Smith, and Joseph White for their constructive comments on an earlier version of this paper. I gratefully acknowledge research support from the Earhart Foundation and the Lynde and Harry Bradley Foundation.

1. Bureau of the Census, *Highlights of U.S. Export and Import Trade*, series FT-990 (November 1987), p. A-3 (1986 figure adjusted to reflect undocumented exports to Canada); and, for imports, *Statistical Abstract of the United States: 1988*, p. 407 (based on 1982 dollars).

$1 trillion mark in the early 1990s if trends continue.[2] Although exchange rates accounted for most of the import penetration and losses of overseas orders, the relative decline in the competitive position of U.S. industry also reflects a long-term shift in the global distribution of productive resources and technological capabilities. The United States is still the world's preeminent economy, but new rivals are catching up, and the mounting trade deficits of the 1980s have been viewed with alarm as signs that the country's industrial might is waning. As with leaders of any great power losing some of its competitive edge, U.S. policymakers fear that other countries are practicing devious economic statecraft, and that left unchecked, their connivances could soon force the United States to trade places with its rivals. Therefore their clever commercial tactics presumably call for a policy response; some would be emulated, others combated.

Parts of this diagnosis and prescription have been somewhat perplexing. Fashionable theories of American decline notwithstanding, the real economic growth of the United States averaged nearly 4 percent a year between 1982 and 1988, roughly the same pace as Japan's and a better rate than in most of Western Europe.[3] (Roles were in fact reversed: in the 1970s, growth in Japan and most of Europe had consistently surpassed that in the United States.) And for all the talk of soaring trade deficits costing jobs, 14 million new jobs were created in the United States and unemployment plunged from 9.5 percent in 1982 to 5.7 percent at the end of 1987, the lowest point in fourteen years. Meanwhile, unemployment rose 17 percent in Japan and 16 percent in the European Community.[4] The vigorous, noninflationary U.S. expansion, moreover, fueled the export economies of Europe and Asia, which would have grown more sluggishly without the strong American demand for imports. Indeed, apart from currency misalignments, a leading reason for the trade imbalance has been the economy's comparatively high and steady rate of growth, which allowed the United States to suck in imports faster than the outside world could absorb its exports.

2. Peter G. Peterson, "The Morning After," *Atlantic Monthly*, October 1987, pp. 49, 50.
3. Calculated from International Monetary Fund, *International Financial Statistics*, vol. 41 (April 1988), pp. 524–25.
4. *Economic Report of the President, February 1988*, pp. 284–85; and OECD Department of Economics and Statistics, *Report of Main Economic Indicators* (March 1984), p. 18; (June 1989), p. 22.

Nor has the United States been deindustrializing. Manufacturing has continued to represent about 20 percent of GNP, the same share it has held for the past forty years.[5] Employment in manufacturing has been improving, and so has productivity. Growing at an annual rate of 3.1 percent, U.S. manufacturing output per hour of labor, although lamentably lower than Japan's, was greater in the first half of the 1980s than at any time in the past three decades and did not compare unfavorably with the levels of some other principals—West Germany, for instance.[6] Slowdowns in labor productivity growth have occurred in every major industrial country since 1950. In fact, in most the growth has slowed more than in the United States.

Contrary to the popular view, U.S. exports, particularly of high-technology manufactured goods, did not uniformly collapse even when the dollar was at its peak. In 1984 the United States accounted for 25 percent of world exports in high-tech products, which was close to its share in the 1960s.[7] After the dollar began to decline in value in mid-1985, American exports of all kinds started booming again. With the overall U.S. share of the world market projected to reach 18 percent in 1989, compared with West Germany's 13 percent and Japan's 12 percent, there should be no doubt that external markets are not closing.[8]

Finally, although the country's foreign debt is huge, it is in the hands of diverse foreign creditors who own no more than 5 percent of the assets in an economy that produces $4.5 trillion worth of goods and services a year.[9] The debt is broadly distributed. Japan, for

5. Robert Z. Lawrence, *Can America Compete?* (Brookings, 1984), p. 18. More recent statistics continue to confirm this figure. In 1986, manufacturing accounted for 21.9 percent of GNP (in constant 1982 dollars). *Statistical Abstract of the United States: 1988*, p. 409.

6. Martin Neil Baily and Alok K. Chakrabarti, *Innovation and the Productivity Crisis* (Brookings, 1988), pp. 3–5. Measured in terms of annual rates of GDP growth per worker, however, U.S. productivity growth from 1980 to 1987 did lag behind the rates of Japan, Canada, France, West Germany, Italy, and the United Kingdom. Whether this is cause for concern about America's competitiveness in international trade is not entirely clear. Barry P. Bosworth and Robert Z. Lawrence, "America in the World Economy," *Brookings Review*, vol. 7 (Winter 1988–89), p. 44.

7. Rachel McCulloch, "The Challenge to U.S. Leadership in High-Technology Industries (Can the United States Maintain Its Lead? Should It Try?)," Working Paper 2513 (Cambridge, Mass.: National Bureau of Economic Research, February 1988), table 2.

8. Robert J. Samuelson, "The Asia-Bashing Impulse," *Newsweek*, February 22, 1988, p. 53.

9. Robert D. Hershey, Jr., "Foreign Stake in U.S. Rose to Record in '87," *New York Times*, June 31, 1988, p. D1.

instance, held only 12 percent of the cumulative total invested by
foreigners in hard assets at the end of 1988. While commentators have
raised the specter of foreign money buying America, few have taken
stock of the other side of the ledger: the magnitude of American
investments overseas, the book value of which is probably three times
as large as the value of foreign direct investment in the United States.[10]

If the United States is no longer the world's foremost economic
power but only one among equals, it has shown few signs of shrinking
into anything less. Thus the rest of the world will continue to look to
it for economic leadership. Whether this leadership will be provided
by the domestic political process, which has seemed to respond
primarily with complaints of foreign unfairness, is an important
question. For while coping with unfair trade is an unavoidable concern
of policymakers, their intense absorption with the issue has appeared
to distract attention from other primary tasks. One of these is for the
federal government to reduce the budget deficit and lift the national
rate of savings. A second is to take strong steps to maintain the quality
of the American work force. And a third is to recognize that the
success of America's foreign economic relations rests in no small part
on the continuing ability to resist unilateralism. Up to a point, threats
of retaliation such as those mandated in the 1988 trade law might
promote some commercial expansion in selected industries by challenging alien trade barriers. But in a finely integrated world economy,
amicable relations cannot be conducted by trading partners wielding
sticks and offering few carrots. Over the long haul the global trading
system is unlikely to prosper under a confrontational, lone-judge-and-
jury approach to trade frictions, but will require patience, cooperation,
and a willingness to live with imperfections.

The growth of U.S. trade regulation has been puzzling in some
other respects as well. It has accelerated during a decade of heightened
awareness and sophistication as to the limitations of other economic
regulatory programs. While government has been policing more and
more international commerce, it has simultaneously been curtailing its
regulatory role in important sectors of the domestic economy—
transportation, energy, telecommunications, banking. And while policymakers have favored regulatory retrenchment in national antitrust

10. Estimated by Stephen S. Roach of Morgan Stanley, in Gene Koretz, "The
Buying of America: Should We Be Worried?" *Business Week*, May 9, 1988, p. 36. For a
more alarmed view, see Martin Tolchin and Susan Tolchin, *Buying into America: How
Foreign Money Is Changing the Face of Our Nation* (Times Books, 1988).

law, the trade laws have moved in the opposite lane, authorizing regulators to battle more discriminatory business practices abroad.[11]

For the most part the movement toward stricter regulations for foreign trade has not been mandated by new tariffs, quotas, or other distinctly protectionist statutes. Since 1930 Congress has artfully avoided such enactments. Instead, much of the recent regulatory impetus came from the Reagan administration. And curiously, it received the blessing of a president who, like every other chief executive after 1932 (only more so), professed confidence in the beneficence of unfettered world market forces.

Although protectionist laws remained out of favor, Congress provided overwhelming bipartisan support for administrative sanctions against unfair trading (in 1987–88 a 200-member conference committee toiled for nine months on a massive piece of legislation aimed primarily at strengthening available remedies). Moreover, every candidate in the 1988 presidential race affirmed a need to take action against unfair traders.[12] None questioned the practicability of pursuing that aim by unilateral law enforcement nor raised the possibility that an exertion of this sort might cause more trouble than it was worth. At the same time, nearly everyone conceded that the nation's trade gap had little to do with foreign commercial policies and that even the most energetic attack on trade inequities would close the gap only a little.[13]

In short, during a period of sustained economic prosperity, the goal of fair play in international trade has been pushed into the spotlight. It has become a recurring theme in national elections, it inspired an ambitious regulatory venture in a Republican administration dedicated to deregulation, and it was the top legislative priority of Democratic leaders in the One-hundredth Congress. Yet alongside all the attention has been an equally clear consensus that achieving fairness would make only a small difference in U.S. trade performance.

So how can the preoccupation with "leveling the playing field" be understood? Various reasons are considered here. One is that the

11. See Robert H. Bork, *The Antitrust Paradox: A Policy at War with Itself* (Basic Books, 1978), chap. 20; and Robert A. Katzmann, "The Attenuation of Antitrust," *Brookings Review*, vol. 2 (Summer 1984), pp. 23–27.

12. Council on Competitiveness, *Competitiveness and Campaign '88* (Washington, January 1988), pp. 85–93.

13. Even Representative Richard A. Gephardt admitted that at least four-fifths of the U.S. global deficit was "our own fault" and could not be alleviated by bringing foreign practices into conformity with American preferences. Gephardt, "The Carrot and Stick in Foreign-Trade Relations," *New York Times*, July 15, 1987, p. 27.

regulatory effort may amount to a kind of affirmative action campaign concerned with equity more than efficiency. A second is that the exercise has been largely symbolic, useful in foiling protectionist domestic political pressures by modestly assuaging aggrieved interests. Another is that an increasingly active and frustrated bureaucracy makes trade policy. Though each of these interpretations might be helpful in explaining the contemporary politics of trade remedy administration, the most distinctive catalyst of this intensely political process may be quite simple: it affords rich opportunities for redressing constituents' complaints while permitting policymakers to take cover from the perils of trade actions. Especially in a time of budgetary austerity, any government program that creates such opportunities is bound to flourish. With a perceived economic predicament—the vulnerability of the American economy in a more competitive world—helping to justify it, the program could expand all the more. The original intent was to create a system of administrative remedies for unfair trade that was supposed to safeguard a liberal trade regime, not compromise it. But the recent interplay of legislative and executive roles in trade decisionmaking has sustained other incentives and has seemed increasingly unconstrained by the old policy premises.

Affirmative Action?

There is no question that significant segments of American industry and agriculture have been hammered by foreign competition, particularly in the years when the value of the dollar was high. As their ability to price their products competitively deteriorated (and even after 1985, when the dollar had depreciated but companies were still scrambling to reclaim eroded markets), more and more industries ran to the government for relief from imports or assistance in pushing exports.

But there are established channels for requesting relief that do not depend on having to prove that competitors are unfair. The right of industries to gain temporary breathing room has long been recognized in the General Agreement on Tariffs and Trade (GATT). The "escape clause" (under U.S. law, section 201 of the 1974 Trade Act) is supposed to serve this purpose. Yet amid the growing number of trade casualties the government has attended to, relatively few have been treated through the escape clause. The great majority have sought help on grounds that overseas rivals have been not only injurious but unjust. In 1986, for example, administrative agencies charged with investigating complaints of unfair or unreasonable foreign trade practices ruled on 121 cases, but decided only 4 escape clause cases.[14]

Maybe the outside world has been trading with the United States more unfairly in the 1980s than before. If, for instance, American businesses are systematically victimized by predatory pricing, the United States could be expected to defend its home industries, regardless of whether the defense appreciably alters aggregate trade statistics. Likewise, if markets are being closed to American exporters, U.S. officials would be justified in demanding fair access for these businesses, no matter how little it affected the nation's overall import-export balance.

Such decisions may indeed leave the current account largely unchanged and still serve the interests of individual firms. The Department of Commerce has repeatedly insisted that Japanese market distortions were blocking at least $10 billion a year in purchases of U.S. products.[15] Even if all those transactions were suddenly realized, a lopsided Japanese trade surplus would persist. Japan's surpluses ultimately reflect the country's conservative spending patterns. Given any level of income, production, and spending, increased imports would displace Japanese spending on Japanese goods, creating, at least in the near term, an excess supply. Japanese manufacturers would probably lower their prices to sell more abroad. Thus the increase in Japanese imports would boost Japanese exports, a result reinforced by the weaker yen that would accompany the heightened demand for imports. A large share of those exports would be absorbed by the United States, and without a substantial change in Japanese spending patterns, much of the improvement in the trade figures between the two countries would soon be offset. Yet even though in the end the balance of trade might be little changed, the *composition* of trade could shift, and if so, the

14. The 121 included antidumping, countervailing duty, and section 301 cases (alleging "unjustifiable, unreasonable, or discriminatory" trading). J. Michael Finger and Andrzej Olechowski, eds., *The Uruguay Round: A Handbook on the Multilateral Trade Negotiations* (Washington: World Bank, 1987), pp. 259, 265; David B. Yoffie, "American Trade Policy: An Obsolete Bargain?" in John E. Chubb and Paul E. Peterson, eds., *Can the Government Govern?* (Brookings, 1989), p. 129; and I.M. Destler, *American Trade Politics: System under Stress* (Washington: Institute for International Economics; New York: Twentieth Century Fund, 1986), p. 245.

15. Edward J. Lincoln, *Japan: Facing Economic Maturity* (Brookings, 1988), p. 232.

stakes for particular American industries (such as construction, citrus fruits, and beef) would be significant.[16]

In practice, wider opportunities to compete abroad often have a maddening way of falling short of fetching the volumes of business envisioned. The scales are not easily tipped by threats to promote product-by-product conquests of foreign markets. If hints of retaliation clear away some barriers, others are soon discovered. Some are public policies that continue to elude the grasp of U.S. negotiations, but many tend to be unofficial obstructions—tight bonds between foreign buyers and their local suppliers, stiff competition from third countries trying to seize a larger share of a newly liberalized market, exchange rate realignments, or differences in the propensity or ability to consume. (Perorations of the 1988 presidential primaries notwithstanding, it would take a miracle for Chrysler to sell many $10,000 K cars in South Korea, even if tariffs were bashed to nothing. With an average per capita income of $2,100, Korea has only eight automobiles for every 1,000 people).[17]

Nonetheless, companies have often welcomed government efforts. In the spring of 1989, for example, on behalf of the Motorola Corporation, U.S. Trade Representative Carla A. Hills accused Japan of excluding American cellular telephones from the Tokyo market. Even if Hills's crowbar succeeded in prying open that lucrative market, the effect on the trade deficit would be slight. Like other American multinationals, Motorola manufactures products abroad. The phones to be sold in Japan could come from a factory in Illinois or a plant in Malaysia.[18] There was no guarantee that more Japanese purchases would simply translate into more exports from the United States. Yet to Motorola the possibility of moving into a market worth more than $2 billion in the next ten years was alluring.

In disputes like this, other countries have typically backed down in

16. When the United States finally settled its acrimonious dispute over beef sales to Japan, the National Cattleman's Association estimated that the agreement could result in an additional 53 million pounds being shipped each year. Assuming that other competitors, such as Australia, do not grab a substantial share of the expanded market, the size of the American beef industry's world export market could double. This would still represent a small share (about 4 percent) of total U.S. beef production, and a minuscule fraction of the overall trade deficit, but potentially something "very exciting" to the beef industry. Gary Klott, "A Doubling of Some Exports Is Seen," *New York Times*, June 21, 1988, p. D6.

17. Bruce Stokes, "Coping with Glut," *National Journal*, November 1, 1986, p. 2614.

18. Robert B. Reich, "Members Only," *New Republic*, June 26, 1989, p. 14.

the face of American ultimatums. But when they do not retreat and the threatened punishment has to be meted out, retaliation becomes indistinguishable from protection for specific products: the U.S. current account balance remains roughly the same, but some domestic producers gain short-run relief from competing imports. Thus there are firms that consider themselves near-term winners in a retaliatory campaign, whether it succeeds or fails and regardless of its effect on the national trade accounts.

Whether such firms have deserved to win this protection (or promotion) of their interests, however, has depended on whether they could claim to be losers in a global economy that had become increasingly unfair. Measuring the extent of unwarranted foreign trade restraints is for all practical purposes impossible. The United States would have to somehow scrutinize all national practices, including cultural habits and informal or secret understandings within or among industries, that may directly or indirectly determine export pricing and market access. That the world remains a far cry from the open trade ideals of David Ricardo is undeniable. But the best efforts to study today's barriers provide no indication that discrimination against U.S. products worsened sharply after 1981 (the year the U.S. current account turned negative).[19]

On the contrary, obstacles to trade with key commercial challengers have gradually been coming down. The Japanese and Korean markets, for example, are less protected than they were a decade ago.[20] Residual

19. Perhaps the most exhaustive research ever attempted on nontariff protection, a study prepared by the World Bank in 1988, found that the percentage of imports covered by hard-core barriers increased somewhat among selected OECD countries from 15.1 to 17.7 percent between 1981 and 1986. Interestingly, the biggest percentage increase was not recorded among the usual suspects—the European Community or Japan—but in the United States. These data measure only import coverage, not actual restrictiveness; unlike the comprehensive tariffs of the past, today's product-specific quantitative controls are often remarkably porous, and in any case the marginal increase in protection identified by the study almost certainly has been offset by continuing duty reductions under the Tokyo round. Sam Laird and Alexander Yeats, "Quantitative Methods for Trade Barrier Analysis" (Washington: World Bank, 1988), pp. 130, 133.

20. The United States sent a larger fraction of its manufactured exports to Japan in 1986 (10 percent) than it did in 1981 (6 percent). Robert Z. Lawrence and Robert E. Litan, "The Protectionist Prescription: Errors in Diagnosis and Cure," *Brookings Papers on Economic Activity*, 1:1987, p. 293. (Hereafter *BPEA*.) Between 1985 and 1988, U.S. exports to Japan increased 66.8 percent, from $22.6 billion to $37.7 billion. Robert Z. Lawrence, "The Japanese Market: How Open Is It?" statement before the Joint Economic Committee, October 11, 1989, p. 18. Korean tariffs, formerly among the highest, were

constraints need to drop further and faster, but vexing as the pace of improvement in these and other economies can be, the United States has also experienced difficulty in ridding itself of import restrictions. Amid the clamor to accelerate reforms for everyone else, protection here expanded between 1975 and 1985 from less than one-tenth of import volume, according to one estimate, to more than one-fifth.[21]

Have exports to the United States had undue advantages? Competition from low-wage countries, many accused of violating the standards of the International Labor Organization, has often been singled out as particularly unequal.[22] Yet while the U.S. trade deficit vaulted to $140 billion, the share of manufactured imports from these less developed countries did not increase appreciably; it was 25.0 percent in 1981 and 25.9 percent in 1986.[23] Even ardent advocates of worker rights amendments to U.S. trade laws have not presumed that the greatest threat facing American businesses is from nations with low wage rates.

If cheap labor has not been the unfair edge, what about other kinds of price distortions? Have foreign pricing strategies and subsidies posed a growing problem? Under U.S. law, foreign sales at less than full average cost of production are grounds for imposing antidumping penalties. Yet discount pricing can be normal—indeed efficient—business behavior for firms with substantial fixed costs and fluctuating demand. (It is worth recalling that the first antidumping law was enacted in 1904 by Canada against the U.S. Steel Corporation for periodically unloading surpluses at cut rates.) Why firms should be enjoined from doing in international markets what they can freely try in domestic markets has remained a mystery to most economists. The double standard might be defensible if it could be shown that discounting is intended methodically to drive out all competition. But careful studies have unearthed few examples of such plainly predatory

---

rolled back an average of nearly 50 percent between 1978 and 1986. Rudiger Dornbusch and Yung Chul Park, "Korean Growth Policy," *BPEA*, 2:1987, p. 443. By late 1988 Commerce Secretary C. William Verity's assessment was that Asian markets had become "far more open today." David E. Sanger, "The Asians Have Given In and Still Prevailed on Trade," *New York Times*, September 18, 1988, p. E3.

21. Paula Stern, "Promoting Competitiveness in the Trade Laws," statement for the Subcommittee on Economic Stabilization of the House Committee on Banking, Finance, and Urban Affairs, March 10, 1987, p. 10.

22. John M. Culbertson, "The Folly of Free Trade," *Harvard Business Review*, vol. 64 (September–October, 1986), p. 123.

23. Lawrence and Litan, "Protectionist Prescription," p. 291.

dumping and virtually none of dumping that succeeded in eliminating enough competition to impose monopolistic pricing.[24]

If predatory price cutting is ever sustainable, it could only be possible for firms with exceedingly deep pockets. There may thus be a link between discriminatory pricing of commodities and financial cushions provided by government subsidies.[25] But to what degree other advanced nations subsidize their industries more than the United States does, whether those foreign subsidies increased anomalously in the 1980s, and what difference it has made is not obvious. Barring some breakthrough in how to define and measure "subsidy," comparative estimates of subsidization, let alone its net effects on competition, are often misleading. Mere comparisons of explicit export subsidies (for example, export credits), which countries such as Japan, France, and Great Britain routinely use far more often than the United States, are inadequate.[26] A nation with relatively few direct subsidies can, through less visible means such as tax preferences and selective procurement, still skew as much commerce as a state practicing brazen trade control.

Attempts in GATT to differentiate between innocuous domestic support programs and illegal subsidies that buoy exports have not been simple. As an extreme example, a country can even be assisting its exporters by subsidizing imports. Such may have been the case in the 1970s when the U.S. petroleum price and allocation controls in effect subsidized imports of crude oil to the short-term benefit of some petrochemical producers and certain other export industries using petroleum-based feedstocks. In fact, virtually every action of government can be regarded as a subsidy for someone, and almost all can

24. Richard Dale, *Anti-dumping Law in a Liberal Trade Order* (St. Martin's Press, 1980), pp. 16, 31.

25. See, for example, Stephen S. Cohen and John Zysman, *Manufacturing Matters: The Myth of the Post-Industrial Economy* (Basic Books, 1987), pp. 248–49; Paul R. Krugman, "Introduction: New Thinking about Trade Policy," in Paul R. Krugman, ed., *Strategic Trade Policy and the New International Economics* (MIT Press, 1986), pp. 6–7; Michael Borrus, James E. Millstein, and John Zysman, "Trade and Development in the Semiconductor Industry: Japanese Challenge and American Response," in John Zysman and Laura Tyson, eds., *American Industry in International Competition: Government Policies and Corporate Strategies* (Cornell University Press, 1983), pp. 240–44; and Alan Wm. Wolff, "International Competitiveness of American Industry: The Role of U.S. Trade Policy," in Bruce R. Scott and George C. Lodge, eds., *U.S. Competitiveness in the World Economy* (Harvard Business School Press, 1985), pp. 314–19.

26. See, for instance, Gary Clyde Hufbauer and Joanna Shelton Erb, *Subsidies in International Trade* (Washington: Institute for International Economics, 1984), pp. 6–7.

affect exports. As one analyst wrote, "Even a requirement that domestically manufactured flags be flown on government buildings provides assistance for flag makers. By giving a secure home market and promoting economies of scale, such a regulation may assist potential exporters."[27]

The proposition therefore that subsidy levels have remained trivial in the United States compared with those in other industrialized countries depends partly on definition. The disparity widens if entire categories of governmental involvement, such as tax credits and depreciation allowances, defense-related funding of research and development, NASA programs, and promotional electrification, are assumed not to underwrite any commercial ventures that could ultimately displace imports or assist exports. Relaxing that implausible assumption, the United States may look more like other active practitioners of industrial policy. Indeed, by some measures the role of government is comparatively large.[28]

Whatever the case, evidence does not point to a growing subsidies gap; industrial subsidies in Europe have generally diminished in recent years and have never been a prominent feature of Japanese industrial targeting.[29] Even in the most abrasive export sector, agriculture, severe budgetary constraints may finally put downward pressure on the European Community's uncontrollable spending for crop supports and export restitutions.[30] In the meantime the farm programs of the United States have swelled. Relatively sophisticated efforts by the OECD to weight average producer subsidy equivalents as a ratio, with all income transfers to farmers in the numerator and total agricultural income in the denominator, have placed the U.S. ratio well above Australia's (9

27. Richard H. Snape, "Export-Promoting Subsidies and What to Do about Them," Working Paper 97 (Washington: World Bank, Research Administration, September 1988), pp. 3–4.

28. Gary R. Saxonhouse, "What Is All This about 'Industrial Targeting' in Japan?" *World Economy*, vol. 6 (September 1983), pp. 255, 258, 268.

29. Robert Z. Lawrence, "Structural Adjustment Policies in Developed Countries," paper prepared for United Nations Conference on Trade and Development, October 26, 1988, pp. 46, 48, 49; Philip H. Trezise, "Industrial Policy Is Not the Major Reason for Japan's Success," *Brookings Review*, vol. 1 (Spring 1983), p. 18; and Robert S. Ozaki, "How Japanese Industrial Policy Works," in Chalmers Johnson, ed., *The Industrial Policy Debate* (San Francisco: Institute for Contemporary Studies, 1984), p. 61.

30. David M. Curry, "Farm Trade: A European View," *Europe* (April 1986), p. 45. The Europeans have taken some limited administrative steps to curb subsidy-induced overproduction and to lower support prices for such commodities as dairy products, wine, and cereals.

percent) and on a par with Canada's and New Zealand's (22 to 23 percent). The EC's rank was higher (33 percent). However, the figures predate the Food Security Act of 1985, which boosted U.S. farm subsidies substantially. Only Japan, where the ratio of subsidized to total income for farmers averaged 72 percent between 1982 and 1984 (but where farmers do not compete in third markets), remained a distant outlier.[31]

But do subsidies necessarily create comparative advantage in export pricing? The special case of agricultural trade aside, evidence is at best mixed. Although some foreign targeting has been aimed at innovative high-technology sectors such as aeronautics, telecommunications, and electronics that could yield important externalities, most of the subsidies have flowed toward antiquated, high-cost industries that rarely earn high or even normal rates of return.[32] Government grants or equity infusions for the French, Belgian, or Italian steel industries have not resulted in major expansions of capacity or in promotional export prices but have largely sustained inefficient management, uncompetitively high wages, and mounting debt payments.[33] In fact, heavily subsidizing industries has often meant prices above competitive levels—high ticket prices on European airlines are an obvious illustration. The theory that the competitive position of nations rests on the lavishness of their industrial policies is unsubstantiated. Recent studies of French export targeting have found that "export-credit subsidisation wastes France's scarce public resources in the promotion of the wrong industries exporting the wrong products to the wrong markets." Similarly, "German subsidization policy mostly redistributes money from structurally strong sectors to weak ones."[34] Although the lesson is more complicated, Japan's trade pattern can be explained in part by an anti-

31. See Robert L. Paarlberg, *Fixing Farm Trade: Policy Options for the United States* (Cambridge, Mass: Ballinger, 1988), pp. 62–63. The cost of agricultural intervention by the U.S. government went from $3 billion in 1980–81 to $11.9 billion in 1984 and an estimated $20 billion a year in 1986–88. World Bank, *World Development Report, 1986* (Oxford University Press, 1986), p. 122.

32. Paul R. Krugman, "The U.S. Response to Foreign Industrial Targeting," *BPEA*, 1:1984, pp. 114–15.

33. Robert W. Crandall, "The EC-US Steel Trade Crisis," in Loukas Tsoukalis, ed., *Europe, America and the World Economy* (Oxford: Basil Blackwell, 1986), p. 28.

34. Patrick A. Messerlin, "Export-Credit Mercantilism à la Francaise," *World Economy*, vol. 9 (December 1986), p. 386; and Karl H. Jüttemeier, "Subsidizing the Federal German Economy—Figures and Facts, 1973–1984," Working Paper 279 (Kiel, Germany: Institute of World Economics, January 1987), p. 21.

import bias but also in large part by the national savings rate, the quality of the labor force, and geographic factors rather than subsidized export drives.[35]

For nearly two decades American politicians have been asserting that "the rest of the world hides behind variable levies, export subsidies, import equalization fees, border taxes, cartels, government procurement practices, dumping, import quotas, and a host of other practices which effectively bar our products."[36] The commercial playing field at the end of the 1980s is certainly not as smooth as such politicians wish it would be. Whether it has become rougher for American firms because the rest of the world is suddenly cheating more is another matter. That perception is flawed but politically expedient.

Ghost Busters?

If at times the U.S. assault on foreign trading practices may seem quixotic, one explanation could be that making trade policy is often more symbolic than consequential. The paradigm would run as follows: Since the debacle of the 1930 Tariff Act, the legislative and executive branches have shared a common commitment to liberalizing trade. They have sought to prevent renewed protectionist reflexes from eroding the postwar system of open trade. A favored technique has

35. Saxonhouse, "What Is All This about 'Industrial Targeting'?" p. 271. Japan's Ministry of International Trade and Industry (MITI) and Ministry of Finance played more than a negligible role in steering investment in important export industries (most notably electronics) during an earlier, high-growth phase. See Chalmers Johnson, *MITI and the Japanese Miracle: The Growth of Industrial Policy, 1925–1975* (Stanford University Press, 1982), chap. 6. But with the economy well beyond the catch-up stage, MITI's glory days may have passed. Increasingly, the commercial policy decisions of the vaunted Japanese bureaucracy evince politicization rather than strategic planning as parliamentary and party politics begin to show more signs of interest group pluralism. Kozo Yamamura, "Caveat Emptor: The Industrial Policy of Japan," in Krugman, ed., *Strategic Trade Policy*, pp. 190–92. The role of geographic variables in accounting for Japan's trade position is recognized even by critics. Japan imports almost all its oil, for example. As the price of oil in dollars declined during the 1980s, so did the price of dollars in yen. Whereas Japan spent more than 5 percent of its gross national product on imported oil at the beginning of the decade, oil now costs Japan less than 1 percent of GNP—a huge windfall that has increased the Japanese trade surplus. See James Fallows, "Containing Japan," *Atlantic Monthly*, May 1989, p. 43.

36. Russell B. Long's opening statement in *The Trade Reform Act of 1973*, Hearings before the Senate Committee on Finance, 93 Cong. 2 sess. (Government Printing Office, 1974), pt. 1, p. 2.

been to divert the complaints of special interests into regulatory agencies and courts: the International Trade Commission (ITC), the International Trade Administration of the Commerce Department (ITA), the Office of the U.S. Trade Representative (USTR), and the Court of International Trade (CIT). Operating under clear rules, these bodies are supposed to adjudicate the claims of interest groups and in legitimate cases offer limited temporary protection. The theory in Congress has been that the administrative and judicial shields deflect political heat from Capitol Hill and diminish the odds of another Smoot-Hawley-style lawmaking experience. Put another way, by ceding power to an independent system of trade ombudsmanship, Congress has restrained itself from misbehaving—not unlike the criminal who, finally giving himself up to the police, says "stop me before I kill again." Meanwhile, the White House has assumed that the system supplies enough relief to keep troubled industries off the president's back but not so much as to approximate the degree of protectionism Congress might otherwise legislate (and that the president would be forced to veto to avoid wholesale violations of international obligations).

Much of the revived interest in fair trade administration might be viewed merely as an extension of this process, as a stepped-up effort to give aggrieved petitioners their day in court and to pacify them with enough token payoffs to defuse demands for much more drastic measures. Regulating the commercial habits of other countries cannot relieve U.S. trade troubles, but presumably it does ease domestic political pressures.

There is something to be said for this thesis. Up to a point the agitation to get tough on foreigners engaging in improper trade practices is only grandstanding as Congress and executive agencies play to key clients or jockey to strengthen their negotiating hands (with one another as well as with interested parties abroad). The play unfolds predictably. After hearing from enough noisy constituents about the invidious commercial tactics of the latest Pacific tiger, Congress decides to send a message to the other end of Pennsylvania Avenue: it holds hearings, adopts strongly worded resolutions, and even passes some punitive bills. In the meantime the constituents have requested, under section 301 of the 1974 Trade Act, an investigation of the "unjustifiable, unreasonable, or discriminatory" behavior in question. Officials of the appropriate regulatory bureaucracy—in this case the USTR—take up the dispute, warning the offending nation of dire consequences ("Congress might take matters into its own hands!") if concessions are not forthcoming. After months of tedious talks, the tiger makes a few ceremonial concessions–enough to calm Congress and, however briefly, quiet the constituents but not the kinds that can substantially narrow its big bilateral trade surplus.

Notice the tacit rules of the game. The American negotiators gain leverage by talking up the shots Congress has fired across their bow, and the legislators also claim some credit for their labors. But every player knows that, except for an unlikely settlement that offers no face-saving results whatsoever, the cannonades from Capitol Hill are mostly blanks: the hearings only make a record, the resolutions are nonbinding, and the bellicose trade bills are guaranteed to be tamed in conference or to fall short of commanding enough support to override a veto. Thus the furor is harmless and concludes with a collective sigh of relief when the threat of draconian legislation and of a trade war recedes.[37]

A superficial look at the data on administrative trade cases might seem to confirm this generalization. Between 1980 and 1986, rising numbers of formal requests were filed for action under section 301, antidumping penalties (section 731 of the 1930 Tariff Act), and duties to countervail export subsidies (section 701 of the 1930 act). Completed investigations leapt from 59 to 121 a year. On average nearly 60 percent of the cases resulted in tariffs, quotas, or other identifiable sanctions. But striking as the numbers are, the quantity of imports successfully challenged amounted to only a small fraction of the total, suggesting to some analysts that the outside world considered the U.S. statutes little more than a nuisance.

The trouble with concluding, as a former ITC chairman has, that the laws probably have "an imperceptible impact on our trading partners" is that several of the partners have found the impact anything but imperceptible.[38] The European Community, for instance, has repeatedly included U.S. antidumping, countervailing duty, and section 301 regulations high on a lengthy list of barriers that cause "a considerable loss for European businesses," and in the negotiations over the U.S.-Canadian free trade agreement, by far the thorniest

37. Robert Pastor, "The Cry-and-Sigh Syndrome: Congress and Trade Policy," in Allen Schick, ed., *Making Economic Policy in Congress* (Washington: American Enterprise Institute for Public Policy Research, 1983), pp. 158–95.

38. Paula Stern, "Stop the Trade Bill Hysteria," *New York Times*, December 15, 1987, p. A31.

issue was Canada's "security of access to the American market as measured by relief from the operation of U.S. trade remedy laws."[39]

The reasons for these concerns are straightforward. To begin with, duties or quantitative restraints that seem small in relation to total imports can pose serious difficulties for foreign vendors that depend heavily on the U.S. market. Canada exports approximately one-third of everything it produces, almost 80 percent of it to the United States, while only 20 percent of U.S. exports go north. Thus the effect of a 5 percent tariff on Canadian products would be the equivalent of a 20 percent Canadian levy on American products. Second, with the possible exception of Australia, no other major trading nation has resorted to more antidumping and countervailing duty actions than the United States. If the numerous investigations discontinued or resolved through withdrawal of petitions, often after price increases on the dumped or subsidized goods, were added to the number of cases that culminated in official import fees, U.S. antidumping and countervailing duty administration would enter a league of its own. The frequency with which these and other instruments of litigation are used suggests that the domestic private interests they serve think the actions well worth paying for. The millions of dollars in legal and lobbying bills paid by American businesses pressing charges of unfair trade have almost certainly bought more than just an even chance of hitting competitors with formally administered sanctions; a larger quotient of unwanted competition has been blunted indirectly by harassment.

Finally, it is misleading to assess the amount of trade inhibited through these means without recognizing that the outcomes of big cases have tended to be far-reaching restraint agreements, not narrowly gauged duties or price undertakings. In 1983 a countervailing duty petition aimed at textile imports from China resulted in tighter restrictions on East Asian textiles generally. In 1984 a barrage of dumping and countervailing duty complaints filed by the steel industry led to negotiated export restraints with virtually every major producing country. In 1986 charges that the Japanese were selling computer chips below fair value spawned not only a "voluntary" system of administered prices for chips but a full-fledged market-sharing arrangement.[40]

39. "E.C. Issues Updated List of U.S. Trade Barriers," *European Community News*, no. 9. 87 (April 2, 1987), p. 1; and Philip H. Trezise, "At Last, Free Trade with Canada?" *Brookings Review*, vol. 6 (Winter 1988), p. 20.

40. Semiconductor Industry Association, *One and One-half Years of Experience under the U.S.-Japan Semiconductor Agreement* (Cupertino, Calif.: March 1, 1988), pp. 9–14.

In a word, in the 1980s the crackdown on countries said to be taking unfair advantage of the United States in international trade became more than rhetorical.

Zealous Bureaucrats?

When regulatory programs appear to acquire a life of their own with few conspicuous links to legislated mandates, it is natural to wonder whether internal administrative imperatives may be powering them. And indeed, there may be a kernel of truth in the idea. Most of the major trade-managing schemes since World War II began with the decisions of executive agencies under powers consigned to them by Congress, not with legislated intervention such as statutory quotas or tariffs, the preferred methods of protection before the war. Triggering the administrative actions in most instances were formal requests from distressed industries seeking refuge under the various legal safeguards against unfair trading (or, when unfairness was impossible to claim, under the escape clause, section 201). Yet in recent years a number of important cases have not commenced this way. In 1985 the USTR, aided by the Commerce Department, ostensibly started moving on its own against a half-dozen countries suspected of dealing improperly in goods ranging from pasta to motion pictures, sweaters, and supercomputers.[41] The flurry of self-initiated investigations made enforcers of fair trade seem to resemble other types of federal law enforcement authorities—those whose bureaucratic organizations have distinct missions and fairly autonomous operating procedures.

Why would the trade bureaucracy wish to drum up business for itself? Perhaps administrators, exasperated by the results of trade negotiations, had begun to embrace activist doctrines. There were in fact signs that increasingly unorthodox views of how nations ought to carry on their commercial relations were gaining currency in trade agencies. For instance, Clyde V. Prestowitz, Jr., a top Commerce Department trade negotiator in the early 1980s and author of an important book based on his experiences, has asserted that the United States should "negotiate a market share or a specific amount of sales"

41. Clayton K. Yeutter, "The President's Trade Policy: An Update," in *Comprehensive Trade Legislation*, Hearings before the Subcommittee on Trade of the House Committee on Ways and Means, 100 Cong. 1 sess. (GPO, 1987), pt. 1, pp. 166–70.

with countries such as Japan.[42] Another former Commerce and USTR official writes, "There is . . . no reason to conclude that . . . free trade is necessarily good and protection is necessarily bad. Both policies represent legitimate options that the United States should employ depending upon the prevailing state of the U.S. economy and the international trading system."[43] Exponents of such views might well have been growing impatient with the inertia they perceived in the midst of a trade crisis and urged the various investigative agencies to roll up their sleeves.

The fact is, however, that administrative activism on trade has by no means been an independent bureaucratic phenomenon. Most has been a response to political signals from Capitol Hill or the White House. The Reagan administration's trade offensive, which became especially spirited with Clayton K. Yeutter's appointment as U.S. trade representative in 1985, was mainly a reaction to congressional pressure. Against the backdrop of widening trade deficits that reached $108 billion in 1984, restless lawmakers voiced a long-standing ambition to get a fairer shake for American manufacturers and farmers. Hundreds of bills were introduced between 1981 and 1985, with one chamber or the other eventually adopting several that contained strict reciprocity standards or provisions to beat back competition in the domestic market through buy-American and local-content requirements. By early 1985 the calls to ensure equitable market opportunities reached a feverish pitch, and the House and Senate each passed near-unanimous resolutions urging the administration to curb Japan's mercantilist policies. Later two major pieces of legislation began wending their way through Congress: a measure to expand textile quotas and a proposal to levy a 25 percent surcharge on imports from Japan, Taiwan, South Korea, and Brazil. Hoping to head off such developments, the executive resolved, in Yeutter's words, "to deal vigorously and decisively with trade problems" through available administrative mechanisms.[44]

The ensuing burst of energy at the USTR and from Commerce

42. Clyde V. Prestowitz, Jr., *Trading Places: How We Allowed Japan to Take the Lead* (Basic Books, 1988), p. 322.

43. John Greenwald, "Protectionism and U.S. Economic Policy," *Stanford Journal of International Law*, vol. 23 (Spring 1987), p. 236.

44. Quoted in Raymond J. Ahearn and Alfred Reifman, "U.S. Trade Policy: Congress Sends a Message," in Robert E. Baldwin and J. David Richardson, eds., *Current U.S. Trade Policy: Analysis, Agenda, and Administration* (Cambridge, Mass.: National Bureau of Economic Research, 1986), p. 123.

Secretary Malcolm Baldrige's strike force has been described as a "turnaround" in President Reagan's "noninterventionist" trade policy.[45] Actually the maneuver was just another in a series of interventionist decisions designed partly to deflate congressional initiatives and partly to serve other political purposes.

Rejecting the International Trade Commission's advice, the administration had chosen in 1981 to negotiate limits on imports of Japanese automobiles. The voluntary restraints were meant to forestall a move widely supported in the Senate to set mandatory quotas. In addition the restraints fulfilled a campaign vow in which Reagan pledged to try "to convince [the] Japanese . . . [that] the deluge of [their] cars into the United States must be slowed."[46] In 1982 the administration reimposed import quotas on sugar, a concession that appeared to be part of a deal with southern Democratic House members in which the president agreed to support the price of sugar in exchange for votes on the 1981 budget reconciliation.[47] In 1983 the administration raised quotas on specialty steel and tightened restrictions on textile imports—in the latter case after the president, taking his political cues from Baldrige, discarded a cabinet committee vote (11 to 1) opposing the idea. Senators Strom Thurmond of South Carolina and Jesse Helms of North Carolina, who were coming up for reelection in 1984, had made their wishes known, and the White House evidently listened, making good on an earlier commitment "to moderate the growth of textile imports."[48] Reagan also heeded a plea from the motorcycle industry for "a little breathing room" and ordered a tenfold increase in duties on heavy bikes.[49] The action was unusual in that the domestic industry in this instance consisted of a single company, Harley-Davidson. Yet the context was that the Democrats had picked up twenty-six House seats in the previous fall's midterm election and had begun to stress the growth of imports as a sign of weakness in the administration's economic policy.

In 1984 the administration capitulated to carbon steel producers,

45. Ahearn and Reifman, "U.S. Trade Policy," p. 103.

46. Quoted in Stephen D. Cohen and Ronald I. Meltzer, *United States International Economic Policy in Action* (Praeger, 1982), p. 75.

47. Elizabeth Wehr, "Administration Dairy, Sugar Plans Draw Fire," *Congressional Quarterly Weekly Report*, May 8, 1982, p. 1071.

48. Destler, *American Trade Politics*, p. 130.

49. Sally Jacobsen, "Tariffs Raised on Imported Cycles," *Washington Post*, April 2, 1983, p. C7.

promising to seek more restraint agreements with steel-exporting nations. The political exigency this time was to decontaminate a comprehensive trade bill toxic with neoprotectionist amendments for steel and a half dozen other commodities. Moreover, 1984 was a presidential election year, and the White House played it safe by stealing some of Walter Mondale's thunder. (Mondale stumped the Rust Belt vowing to "get tough, and I mean really tough" on trade. Calling for sharp limits on steel imports, he declaimed, "We've been running up the white flag when we should be running up the American flag. What do we want our kids to do, sweep up around the Japanese computers and spend a lifetime serving McDonald hamburgers?")[50]

In 1986 protection was extended to three more crucial industries: microchips, machine tools, and lumber. In each instance congressional or electoral reverberations affected the administrative proceedings. A probe of the charge that Japan was dumping memory chips quickly widened after a trade panel of the Joint Economic Committee, steered by Senator Pete Wilson, held animated hearings on the Japanese practice of selling chips below average production cost.[51] When machine tools became a candidate for negotiated restraint, the president timed his announcement to dilute support for another disagreeable trade package nearing a vote on the House floor.[52] And in the most politically charged case of all—the campaign to impose countervailing duties on Canadian softwood—the Commerce Department suddenly found provincial stumpage programs to be a form of export targeting. Canadians suspected that the verdict was a price exacted by members of the Senate Finance Committee, which had come within a hair's breadth of denying the administration fast-track negotiating authority for the U.S.-Canada free trade pact.[53] Arriving in mid-October, the contro-

50. Quoted in Steven Schlossstein, *Trade War: Greed, Power, and Industrial Policy on Opposite Sides of the Pacific* (Congdon and Weed, 1984), pp. 3–4.

51. *United States-Japan Trade: Semiconductors*, Hearings before the Subcommittee on Trade, Productivity, and Economic Growth of the Joint Economic Committee, 99 Cong. 1 sess. (GPO, 1985).

52. *Congressional Quarterly Almanac, 1986*, vol. 42 (1987), p. 343. The machine tool decision may also have been linked to the horse trading with Congress to round up votes for the 1986 tax reform. See Jeffrey H. Birnbaum and Alan S. Murray, *Showdown at Gucci Gulch: Lawmakers, Lobbyists, and the Unlikely Triumph of Tax Reform* (Random House, 1987), p. 172.

53. Harold Hongju Koh, "A Legal Perspective," in Robert M. Stern, Philip H. Trezise, and John Whalley, eds., *Perspectives on a U.S.-Canadian Free Trade Agreement* (Brookings, 1987), p. 98.

versial decision also suited the interests of several Republican senators in lumber-producing states—for example, Steven D. Symms of Idaho and Mack Mattingly of Georgia—who were facing uphill reelection fights in November.[54]

In sum, administering succor and safeguards was more often inspired by political or tactical needs than by bureaucratic fervor. And the inspiration was more often provided by presidential politics and interbranch friction associated with Congress's partial delegation of trade policy-making authority than rooted in policy prescriptions for trade deficits.

The Ups and Downs of Delegation

Whatever else remedial trade regulation may do, it allocates benefits and costs not only among groups but among policymakers. Typically the benefits are narrowly concentrated: particular petitioners collect economic rents (in the case of protection) or possible sales abroad (in the case of negotiations to increase market access), and particular elected officials can claim credit for arranging the favors. The allocation of costs is more complicated. At best, from the vantage point of the politicians and their clients, costs will be so widely dispersed as to go unnoticed by the electorate. But the proponents of an aggressive trade agenda may run significant political risks—countersanctions against specific American exports, for example, or the onus of being labeled protectionist by the news media, or even the possibility of a backlash at the polls when buyers wake up to find the prices of key imports grossly inflated.

Historically the political pitfalls in trade decisions that go awry have been real enough to give pause. More than a half century after the passage of the Smoot-Hawley Act, Congress remains haunted by the swift retaliation the act provoked: twenty-five nations reduced their purchases of U.S. exports by two-thirds and thereby deepened the Great Depression. At that time, the volume of exports was small compared with what it is now, when some $230 billion in American export sales would be on the line.[55] Export-dependent manufacturers and agricultural producers are sensitive to this arithmetic. Multinational

54. Andy Plattner, "Democrats See Political Gold in Trade Issue," *Congressional Quarterly Weekly Report*, September 21, 1985, p. 1856.

55. *Highlights of U.S. Export and Import Trade*, series FT-990 (November 1987), p. A3.

corporations with extensive intrafirm trade flows are particularly wary of higher trade barriers at home that can disrupt global production strategies, raise input costs, and possibly bring reprisals against exposed fixed assets abroad.[56] These interests have often thrown their considerable political weight against the sponsors of patently restrictive trade proposals.

For those on whom the lessons of 1930 may have been lost, electoral omens throughout the 1980s have repeatedly underscored the political uncertainties of reckless or overly strident appeals to economic nationalism. On the eve of the 1980 primary in South Carolina, candidate John B. Connally, former secretary of the treasury, railed, "It's time we said to Japan: 'If we can't come into your markets with equal openness and fairness as you come into ours, you had better be prepared to sit on the docks of Yokohama in your little Datsuns . . . while you stare at your own little TV sets . . . because we've had all we're going to take.' "[57] This type of political oratory, playing on supposed fears of American economic decline and frustration over rising imports and trade deficits, had become familiar. So had its futility. Connally was promptly trounced by Ronald Reagan, there and elsewhere, and ended up at the Republican convention with a single delegate. Four years later Mondale's attempt to strike the same chord ("If you try to sell an American car in Japan, you better have the United States Army with you when they land on the docks") proved similarly ineffectual.[58] And four years after that, even amid record-breaking trade deficits, the trade hardliners in both parties—Richard Gephardt, Robert Dole, and Pat Robertson—were routed in the early presidential primaries.[59]

Because trade actions can reap penalties as well as rewards, decisionmakers seek strategies that avoid risk. One way to accomplish this

56. Yoffie, "American Trade Policy," p. 125.

57. Quoted in "Talking Tough on Trade," *Newsweek*, March 14, 1988, p. 18.

58. Quoted in Schlossstein, *Trade War*, p. 3.

59. It is true that the campaigns of each of these candidates labored under other, more basic handicaps, but the limited appeal of economic nationalism was evident throughout the 1988 contests. In the South Carolina primary, Senator Dole campaigned in support of a pending textile quota bill that Vice President Bush opposed. Dole was soundly defeated. The Democratic presidential nominee, Governor Michael S. Dukakis, adopted some of Representative Gephardt's shrill rhetoric, enabling Bush to accuse him of "protectionist demagoguery." Dukakis failed to carry a single Rust Belt state—not even Gephardt's Missouri. Stuart Auerbach, "Dukakis' Tough Trade Stance Moves Him Far from GOP Line," *Washington Post*, October 9, 1988, pp. H1, H10; and "Meet Militant Mike, The Tough Talker on Trade," *Business Week*, October 24, 1988, p. 37.

is by delegation.[60] The U.S. Constitution is explicit: the power to regulate commerce with foreign nations belongs to Congress. But with the exercise of that power comes responsibility, and blame or ridicule for obvious blunders (as dozens of incumbents found out in the tumultuous elections of 1932). So starting with the Reciprocal Trade Agreements Act of 1934, Congress began entrusting more of its constitutional privileges to the executive branch. Presidents gained new authority to negotiate tariff revisions, to grant or deny escape clause relief, and through cabinet appointees to decide how vigorously and decisively to perform other administrative duties. But legislators did not wholly relinquish their ability to deliver selective benefits. Rather they invented new methods of getting the job done while achieving considerable cover from accusations of serving special interests or practicing protectionism.

Of course, as presidents acquired more discretion over policy and could be credited with leadership for successful trade initiatives, they could also be held accountable if their activities proved damaging. And because they too could parcel out benefits, they attracted a growing clientele. Closely watched by additional dissatisfied or greedy groups and their backers in Congress, the administration in power had to cope with rising expectations. Thus presidential policymaking on trade came to be influenced, at least in part, by incentives familiar to congressmen: the desire to retain political control but also to shed responsibility. Like the legislature, the executive developed devices to do both.

These behaviors exhibit what has been called the politics of blame avoidance.[61] They lie at the core of the growing fascination with questions of fair trade and of the tendency to administer more and more trade justice through indirect approaches: low-profile revisions of the statutes, for example, and plea bargains (so to speak) negotiated at the administrative level under congressional prodding and presidential auspices. Thus a construct that started by providing only a safety valve for protectionist sentiments became capable of generating managed trade.

60. For an excellent general analysis of the shift-the-responsibility rationale for delegation, see Morris P. Fiorina, "Group Concentration and the Delegation of Legislative Authority," in Roger G. Noll, ed., *Regulatory Policy and the Social Sciences* (University of California Press, 1985), especially pp. 186–87.

61. The definitive theoretical analysis is R. Kent Weaver, "The Politics of Blame Avoidance," *Journal of Public Policy*, vol. 6 (October–December 1986), pp. 371–98.

Remedies versus Relief

If the object of trade regulation were only to dampen protectionist demands rather than to distribute material benefits while minimizing political costs, one would expect greater reliance on the escape clause. After all, the purpose of this outlet is to accommodate the needs of industries damaged by import competition without subjecting the entire political system to their plight.[62] Industries in distress can turn to an impartial arbiter—the International Trade Commission—that determines whether imports caused or threatened them with economic injury. Only the president can approve or disapprove the ITC's recommendations. Yet since the 1970s many beleaguered industries have avoided invoking the escape clause. And this is not because important petitioners or persistent ones who elect to make use of section 201 come away empty-handed.[63] Since 1981 the president has approved relief in two-thirds of the cases in which the ITC considered an industry seriously impaired. Granted, presidents can and do rebuff ITC opinions. In instances such as the copper case in 1984, in which awarding protection would have incurred severe political or diplomatic censure, the commission's affirmative opinions have been

---

62. Robert Z. Lawrence and Robert E. Litan, *Saving Free Trade: A Pragmatic Approach* (Brookings, 1986), chap. 2.

63. The received wisdom about section 201 determinations is that presidents usually reject major petitions. But the record is less clear cut. Recent presidents have sometimes overruled the ITC but have then turned around and instructed the USTR to negotiate informal voluntary restraint agreements for the same commodities. President Reagan did just that in the case of carbon steel in 1984. Then too, some of the most important ITC petitions in recent years have been resubmissions—cases in which an industry was turned down the first time but later received a favorable ruling. For instance, though the nonrubber footwear industry failed to persuade Gerald Ford to endorse an affirmative ITC opinion in 1976, it convinced Jimmy Carter to reach restraint agreements with Korea and Taiwan a year later. The real success rate is thus higher than if the basic caseload is measured entirely as a series of discrete actions involving different complainants. In addition, the president has sometimes overridden ITC rulings against a petitioning industry. The most notorious illustration is, of course, the export restraints imposed on Japanese automobiles. In 1981, after the ITC found that the case for quotas lacked merit, the Reagan administration negotiated them anyway. Finally, scholars reviewing the record would do well to differentiate politically trivial cases from important ones; the final relief rate may appear low only because the caseload has included more small fry (clothespin manufacturers, vendors of cut flowers) than big businesses. The litmus test is whether presidents are willing to approve protection for huge industries.

rejected.[64] Congressional criticism of presidents for periodically over-ruling the ITC, however, has been disingenuous. Technically Congress has always reserved the right to reverse presidential decisions in section 201 cases, but not once has it exercised this veto.[65] To do so would be to take back full responsibility for perceptible acts of protection, something most legislators, like most presidents, would rather avoid.

The main reason for the meager application of section 201 is the greater ease and political comfort of seeking protection through alternative avenues, in particular the antidumping law. In part the bias reflects internationally accepted codes. Under article 19 of GATT, escape clause protection is permissible only if an industry can show it has been "seriously" hurt by imports. In cases seeking antidumping rulings or countervailing duties, only "material" injury—meaning merely harm that is not 'inconsequential"—needs to be proved. The easier test inevitably induces greater use. But Congress has also gradually eased access to these shelters by making small yet significant adjustments in the legal machinery for processing complaints. And presidents have abetted this shift from a system that weighed reprieves from trade pressures to one promising remedies for injustices.

Three important points about current trade policy need to be stressed. First, a preference for policy that purports to redress grievances of discontented industries rather than one that simply considers bailing them out fits modern tastes. Under the premises of the postwar trade debate, pleas for help, whatever their merits, carry greater force when they invoke fairness. Earlier in the century this was less true. Undisguised bids for protection did not suffer the stigma of special pleading: indeed, high tariffs were deemed a near-universal entitlement.[66] Crude excuses for protectionism are no longer encouraged, however, and the

64. The administration was persuaded by end users that "the number of copper fabricators' jobs that would have been placed at risk [by import protection] was six times the number of copper miners' jobs that would have been saved." Alan F. Holmer, "Congress and the President—The Issues," in Claude E. Barfield and John H. Makin, eds., *Trade Policy and U.S. Competitiveness* (Washington: American Enterprise Institute for Public Policy Research, 1987), p. 15.

65. After the Supreme Court's decision in *Immigration and Naturalization Service* v. *Chadha* (1982), Congress simply substituted a joint resolution for the newly unconstitutional concurrent resolution to override presidential determinations in section 201 cases. The change was introduced in the Trade and Tariff Act of 1984.

66. E. E. Schattschneider, *Politics, Pressures and the Tariff: A Study of Free Private Enterprise in Pressure Politics, as Shown in the 1929–1930 Revision of the Tariff* (Prentice-Hall, 1935), pp. 86, 88.

inclination now is to frame discussion in terms of polite metaphors, such as "level playing field," that implicitly appeal to a sense of equity and good sportsmanship. Those who demand and those who supply protection have learned to follow these conventions. Like the clients and custodians of farm policy, who prefer price supports to handouts, trade lobbyists and legislators assume a greater mantle of legitimacy when proposing to referee trade for the sake of fair play than when asking government just to dole out relief.

Another consideration of current policy is that members of Congress who try to obtain legislated constraints on imports that compete with industries in their districts face a Herculean task.[67] Because few industries have lobbying muscle in hundreds of congressional districts (the textile industry is perhaps the best-known exception), a legislator finds that logrolling is normally necessary to broaden the base of support for a pet trade restraint. But as the number of industries covered by the protectionist measure increases, so does the opposition. Representatives whose constituents include producers dependent on exports or on crucial imports will mobilize to defeat the bill or at least to uphold a presidential veto. Thus legislators interested in protecting favorite industries are likely to fare better by quietly amending existing laws, especially such arcane ones as the antidumping and antisubsidization statutes. The amendments are often visible only to cognoscenti, and sometimes even they do not appreciate the full implications until later. If the sleepers are spotted, their proponents cloak a particularistic intent in the language of a collective good (ridding the marketplace of discriminatory pricing, fixing distortions caused by subsidies, and so on).

Finally, although export-oriented agricultural and manufacturing lobbies worry about trade measures that could invite retribution, their support of free trade is not unconditional. Expansion in world markets has always been critical to American agriculture, but it has become an increasingly vital interest in such industries as semiconductors, telecommunications, and commercial aircraft, in which domestic consumption alone does not suffice to realize an attractive return on investment. Typical characteristics in these industries—major economies of scale, heavy R&D costs, and rapid product cycles—make securing offshore markets desirable.[68] In all three, firms have advocated

67. See Robert E. Baldwin, *The Political Economy of U.S. Import Policy* (MIT Press, 1985), pp. 49–50.

68. Helen V. Milner and David B. Yoffie, "Between Free Trade and Protectionism:

sectoral reciprocity, restricting access to the American market if foreign practices could not be altered.[69] And in at least one instance, the upshot has been an administered guarantee of market presence backed by sanctions: under the 1986 semiconductor arrangement, Japan promised U.S. chipmakers a 20 percent share of all Japanese purchases by 1991.

Thus what is called fair trade regulation can conveniently include not only trade management to aid domestic industries battered by imports but a retaliatory commercial policy to help exporters and multinationals increase their sales abroad. Why some scholars draw a fine line between remedial import controls and what I. M. Destler has called "export politics"—and why they assume that pursuit of the latter will somehow mute demands for the former—is not always easy to understand. The two kinds of regulatory endeavors are often complementary. Both entail the use of public power to advance private interests by what amounts to haggling over market shares and prices. And together they offer a basis for building coalitions that include both exporters and industries hurt by imports—at least so long as the reason for government intervention is correcting foreign foul play that undercuts the sales bases of domestic firms, as distinct from old-fashioned protectionism. Throughout the 1980s, but especially in the events leading to the 1988 trade bill, policymakers who sought to modify the rules against unfair trade, often to assist particular interest groups, attracted new allies. By packaging tighter rules against, say, industrial subsidies with provisions to broaden beachheads in various overseas markets, all in the name of a fairer playing field, they brought erstwhile skeptics on board.

Tailoring Generic Rules to Special Interests

To intensify the enforcement of trade remedies, Congress typically either legislates subtly or pretends to legislate boldly. Subtlety is usually associated with the periodic need to enact major bills to renew grants of presidential negotiating authority in multilateral trade rounds or to ratify the results of the negotiations. Flamboyant legislative moves are more often a spasmodic outburst occasioned by some sudden crisis

---

Strategic Trade Policy and a Theory of Corporate Trade Demands," *International Organization*, vol. 43 (Spring 1989), pp. 239–72.

69. Yoffie, "American Trade Policy," p. 126.

or a *grand geste* orchestrated by a few enterprising congressmen on behalf of favored constituents. Both activities have shaped U.S. policy. However, the accumulation of inconspicuous revisions to statutory rules warrants top billing. For while the technical minutiae glaze the eyes of headline writers, this is where basic, perhaps irreversible, changes in policy are codified (and where not a few special interests realize that most of their bread is buttered).

THE TRADE ACT OF 1974

Modifications of the laws had been a quid pro quo for nearly every extension of delegated negotiating authority since 1934, but the Trade Act of 1974 marked a watershed. When the Nixon administration, reeling from the Watergate scandal, requested permission to open the Tokyo round of talks on reducing nontariff barriers, Congress jumped at the chance to lace its enabling legislation with important, if obscure, legalistic refinements to "promote the development of an open, non-discriminatory, and fair world economic system."[70] The most remarkable of these turned out to be a change in the antidumping provisions. In essence, dumping—selling products abroad at a price lower than at home—was redefined to include sales at less than the cost of production. Henceforth, if investigators surmised that prices in home markets fell below fully allocated production costs for an extended period, sales would be considered abnormal even if the domestic and export price did not differ.[71] In time, more than half of all dumping cases would be brought on this more facile charge of pricing below cost.

The idea that such pricing is an actionable practice, that it somehow falls outside the ordinary course of business, is eccentric. In the 1970s it had become clear that extended sales of domestic goods below fully allocated cost but above average variable cost would not be subject to penalties under U.S. antitrust regulations. Yet with virtually no debate, Congress wrote into law an incongruent cost-based pricing standard for imported goods. How did this happen? The provision seems to have been masterminded by Russell B. Long of Louisiana, chairman of the Senate Finance Committee, who came to the rescue of Freeport Industries, a Louisiana firm that was having trouble contesting the

70. From title of Trade Act of 1974, 88 Stat. 1978.
71. Antidumping Act of 1921, sec. 205(b), as amended by Trade Act of 1974, sec. 321[d] (88 Stat. 2046-48). See, in general, Bruce Stokes, "Everybody's in the Act," *National Journal*, April 18, 1987, p. 928.

price of Canadian sulfur exports.[72] Except for a few Treasury Department specialists who eventually took part in the drafting, Long's
handiwork drew little immediate attention. Probably no one foresaw
the way the new antidumping provisions would create a trade regulator's
bazaar where imaginative Washington lawyers "forum shopped" on
behalf of clients with competitive problems (and where purveyors of
protection could fabricate "fair values" to fit political circumstances).
Certainly few legislators seem to have paused to contemplate the long-
range ramifications of section 205(b). In the face of congressional
concerns with such flagrantly protectionist projects as a proposal by
Senator Thomas J. McIntyre to effectively freeze tariffs for the benefit
of the footwear industry and a renewed attempt by Representative
James A. Burke and Senator Vance Hartke to impose rigid quotas on
all but a few imports, the reworded antidumping section slipped
through.

THE TRADE AGREEMENTS ACT OF 1979

When legislative approval was needed to implement the results of
the Tokyo round in 1979, Congress resumed fine-tuning of trade
remedies. Subsidies subject to countervailing duties were given a more
encompassing definition than in the GATT code, and a stiffer yardstick
was mandated to measure them. At the same time, the causality test
required for imposing antidumping and countervailing duties was
shaded to favor findings of injury by the ITC, as was a provision
letting tie votes by the commissioners suffice to establish injury in
cases calling for countervailing duties.[73] Proven cases of dumping or
subsidizing could now also be suspended without formal fines or duties
if the offending party agreed to rectify wrongs through negotiation.[74]
Most important, administration of antidumping and countervailing
duty petitions was transferred from the Treasury Department to the
Department of Commerce, which was operating under new guidelines:
more stringent statutory deadlines, wider public access to previously
confidential information, and a more intensive system of judicial review.

In the ensuing years each of these innovations had its intended
effect. With the Commerce Department, a client-serving agency, in

72. Interview with Donald Harrison, former counsel for Freeport Industries,
Washington, D.C., May 31, 1988.

73. Trade Agreements Act of 1979, sec. 771 (93 Stat. 176-81).

74. *Trade Agreements Act of 1979*, H. Rept. 96-317, 96 Cong. 1 sess. (GPO, 1979),
p. 54.

charge, the number of countervailing and antidumping investigations soared from 66 in 1979 to 211 in 1982. A more assertive judiciary kept the ITA and ITC in line but also at times expanded their regulatory reach. (The Court of International Trade is no bit player in shaping trade policy. In elevating the court's stature, Congress envisioned not only more opportunities for petitioners to press their claims through litigation but also a receptive adjudicator. By and large the CIT has lived up to expectations.) Finally, by legalizing negotiated resolutions of cases in lieu of highly visible penalties, Congress indirectly sanctioned a trend toward murky "voluntary" export restraints and orderly marketing arrangements. For parties on both sides, these became a preferred political mode of managing complaints—and the least efficient economically.

The customary explanation for the reforms of 1979 is that in the years following the 1974 act the antidumping and countervailing duty laws were still being inadequately enforced and hard-pressed industries were getting only slightly more support from the administrative procedures than they had before.[75] But there is some question of this. In the mid-1970s, thanks to a depreciating dollar, the U.S. trade balance in manufactured products shifted from deficit to surplus, a decline in America's portion of world trade in these goods was arrested, and foreign trade supplied a net addition to domestic output and jobs in manufacturing.[76] These were not conditions conducive to widespread calls for protection. Some would argue that the protection actually afforded between 1974 and 1979 was considerable in light of the double-digit inflation plaguing the economy. To be sure, much is made of the numerous countervailing duties waived during the Ford and Carter administrations, thereby denying successful petitioners the full remedy of the law, but until 1979 the law under which duties could be imposed lacked an injury test, which put it out of step with the emerging international code on subsidies. A discretionary waiver was temporarily indispensable if American negotiators were to pull other signatories into line. As for antidumping actions, the 1974 legislation had clearly induced an increase. A year after enactment, 75 dumping cases were being processed. By mid-1978 the number had risen to 129.[77]

---

75. *Trade Agreements Act of 1979*, H. Rept. 96-317, p. 48; and Destler, *American Trade Politics*, p. 120.

76. Lawrence, *Can America Compete?* pp. 7, 94.

77. *Administration of the Antidumping Act of 1921*, Hearing before the Subcommittee

Congress may also have revised the rules in 1979 because the revisions of 1974 had begun to pay off for a few powerful interest groups, most notably the steel industry. Although earlier attempts by American steel companies to curb imports through antidumping initiatives failed, a 1977 complaint filed by Gilmore Steel against carbon steel plate from Japan hit the jackpot, thanks to skillful exploitation of the law's dubious cost-recovery criteria. The Gilmore decision set off a blizzard of additional dumping charges, blanketing nearly $1 billion worth of steel shipments from Japan, all the major European producers, and India. The breadth of these cases eventually led the Carter administration to bar cheap imports comprehensively through an elaborate trigger price mechanism that in effect placed a floor under the price of all imported steel. In the first five months of 1978, steel imports fell from 20 percent of the market to 14 percent.[78] By 1979, however, the effectiveness of the mechanism was being undermined by shifts in exchange rates, and the U.S. industry and its allies, uncomfortable with the level of protection, lobbied for additional guarantees.[79] When exchange rate fluctuations made it harder to prove dumping, other weapons were readied—expedited procedures to offset foreign government subsidies and systemic changes that would facilitate the use of antidumping and countervailing actions for bargaining purposes. In 1982 the steelmakers again lodged boxloads of complaints against foreign (mainly European Community) suppliers. Before the ITC had ruled definitively on many of these cases, the Europeans volunteered to suppress exports in what amounted to a pretrial settlement, and the U.S. producers withdrew their petitions.

Although the 1979 act represented a major overhaul of U.S. trade laws, the final package breezed through (395–7 in the House, 90–4 in the Senate). This was not just because the skids had been greased by parliamentary procedures that barred controversial riders on the floor, but also because the would-be hitchhikers had been picked up and placated elsewhere. Late in 1978, for example, Senator Ernest F.

on Trade of the House Committee on Ways and Means, 95 Cong. 2 sess. (GPO, 1978), p. 8.

78. Walter Adams and Joel B. Dirlam, "Unfair Competition in International Trade," in *Tariffs, Quotas, and Trade: The Politics of Protectionism* (San Francisco: Institute For Contemporary Studies, 1979), pp. 103–04; and Baldwin, *Political Economy*, pp. 138, 140.

79. Barry Eichengreen and Hans van der Ven, "U.S. Antidumping Policies: The Case of Steel," in Robert E. Baldwin and Anne O. Krueger, eds., *The Structure and Evolution of Recent U.S. Trade Policy* (University of Chicago Press for the National Bureau of Economic Research, 1984), pp. 74–77.

Hollings had almost won adoption of a measure that would have disallowed all the Tokyo round's negotiated reductions in textile duties. To block that bill from resurfacing in the next session, the Carter administration offered to ration textile imports through adjustments in the Multifiber Arrangement. In the celebration at having sidetracked outright protectionist schemes, less scrutiny was given to the side deals that were cut or later to the more elliptical "process protectionism" embedded in the 1979 act.

THE TRADE AND TARIFF ACT OF 1984

Despite an explosion of successful trade cases after 1979, petitioners continued to protest the inadequacy of the regulatory statutes, protests that gained force amid the economic and political conditions of the early 1980s. Several basic industries, wracked by the 1981–82 recession, did not bounce back when the economy recovered. Renewed consumer demand and a high-flying dollar spurred competing imports that the depressed industries sought to constrict by getting the trade laws amended. And more than ever, access points and outlets in Congress abounded. Although responsibility for managing trade measures had once been concentrated in the Senate Finance and House Ways and Means committees by virtue of their primary jurisdiction over tariffs, as trade questions moved beyond tariffs and conceptions of alleged foreign malpractices changed, legislative power flowed downward to subcommittees and outward to other panels. Whereas the chairmen of the two tax-writing committees could once control the contents of trade bills, the cast of characters and their agendas now became considerably longer. Induced by the new, more complicated policy requirements, but also by increased staff support and opportunities for political aggrandizement, participation spread to include the House Energy and Commerce Committee (domestic content), the Judiciary committees (antitrust reciprocity), the Armed Service committees (procurement codes), the Banking committees (foreign investment), and so forth. Historically, trade bills were always potential legislative Christmas trees, but weaker congressional gatekeepers, multiple referrals, and new parliamentary norms that invited changes from the floor now meant that even more ornaments could be hung on them.[80]

These tendencies would be fully realized in drafting the landmark

80. See in general Pietro S. Nivola, "The New Protectionism: U.S. Trade Policy in Historical Perspective," *Political Science Quarterly*, vol. 101, no. 4 (1986), pp. 593–94.

1988 trade act, but hints of what lay ahead appeared in 1984. General trade legislation enacted that year amalgamated more than a hundred measures, many of which purported to fix deficiencies in existing law. At least three novelties had long-term significance. An industry unable to prove that any one country's dumped or subsidized exports were a source of hardship could now win its case by showing damage from the *combined* shipments of any number of foreign producers, no matter how negligible individually.[81] With this so-called cumulation proviso, a domestic complainant could persuade the ITC that, say, $250,000 worth of Canadian fresh-cut flowers caused material injury. (The ITC was required to lump in Canada's trivial flower exports with eight other countries whose annual U.S. sales totaled well over $10 million.)[82]

The Trade and Tariff Act of 1984 also made it harder for the ITC to reject requests for relief under the provisions of section 201. Earlier in the year the commission had turned down a petition by the shoemaking industry on the basis that large footwear manufacturers were operating more profitably than the manufacturing average.[83] With the welfare of shoe manufacturers in mind, Congress rewrote the law to ensure that regulators would consider factors other than mere profitability in assessing injury.[84] Finally, section 613 of the 1984 act gave the Commerce Department authority to impose countervailing duties on subsidies of components if they "bestow[ed] competitive benefits" and had "a significant effect" on manufacturing costs of final products for export. While Commerce retained discretion in making these judgments, its first decision under the provision concluded that upstream subsidies accounting for more than 1 percent of the cost of producing the export product had a "significant effect."[85]

As had been true in 1979 and 1974, technicalities like these bored most people and were inserted over few objections. If anything, the insouciance was all the greater this time because the 1984 legislation had started out larded with blunt amendments protecting carbon steel

---

81. Trade and Tariff Act of 1984, sec. 612(a)(2)(A) (98 Stat. 3033).

82. Comments by Gary N. Horlick on Murray G. Smith, "Negotiating Trade Laws: Possible Approaches," in Murray G. Smith, *Bridging the Gap: Trade Laws in the Canadian-U.S. Negotiations* (Toronto: C. D. Howe Institute; Washington: National Planning Association, 1987), p. 54.

83. U.S. International Trade Commission, *1984 Annual Report*, p. 5.

84. Trade and Tariff Act of 1984, sec. 612(a)(2)(B) (98 Stat. 3033–34).

85. "Certain Agricultural Tillage from Brazil," 50 Fed. Reg. 24270, 24274 (1985). See also Michael Sandler, "Primer on United States Trade Remedies," *International Lawyer*, vol. 19 (Summer 1985), p. 772.

and copper, ferroalloys and footwear, cloths and cow's milk, garments
and grapes, bromine and table wine, but had emerged from conference
a good deal sleeker. The *Washington Post*, which a fortnight earlier had
urged President Reagan to veto the bill, hailed the outcome as a "happy
ending" in which "most of the bad stuff got thrown out and all of the
good stuff stayed in."[86] This assessment might be valid if one took as
a serious baseline the original versions of the 1984 bill. But the original
extremes may have been partly bargaining chips or decoys behind
which other "stuff" could be unobtrusively maneuvered into position.
The story of the 1984 trade debate, in short, is not only about how
an antitrade bill was transmogrified but also how, in its final rendition,
the bill added more tiers to the fairly impressive edifice of trade
regulations already in place.

THE OMNIBUS TRADE AND COMPETITIVENESS ACT OF 1988

The script was similar for the progress of the 1988 trade bill, except
that it was played out over three years in an atmosphere highly charged
with partisan politics. The opening scene took place in east Texas on
August 3, 1985. Running for a vacant House seat, Democratic candidate
Jim Chapman fastened on trade as a "real red, white and blue issue."
Blaming Reagan administration policies for unilateral disarmament in
the war on imports and for the closing of a local steel plant, Chapman
won (by a margin of less than 2 percent) in a district that had never
sent a Republican to Congress.[87] Gearing up for the 1986 midterm
campaign, Democratic strategists chose to read the returns from the
Texas by-election creatively: stern trade proposals, which had seemed
so unpromising after Mondale's defeat a year earlier, could provide
live ammunition in the upcoming congressional contests. In the words
of Representative Tony Coelho, chairman of the Democratic Campaign
Committee, trade had become "a Democratic macho issue."[88]

To be sure, the various incarnations of the latest trade bill were
born of more than partisan calculations. In 1985, when the House
Ways and Means Committee reported out the first of a series of plans
to penalize countries that stubbornly sold more merchandise to the
United States than they bought, U.S. external deficits were hitting
new heights. The mood on Capitol Hill was that doing something

86. "On Trade, a Happy Ending," *Washington Post*, October 12, 1984, p. A22.
87. "The Bill That Came to Dinner," *Wall Street Journal*, April 26, 1988, p. 38; and
Congressional Quarterly Almanac, 1985, vol. 41 (1986), p. 5-B.
88. Quoted in *Congressional Quarterly Almanac, 1985*, p. 253.

about these deficits, even something largely ineffectual, was better than doing nothing, and that so far the administration had done nothing. The sense of urgency was genuine. Democratic lawmakers felt it, but so did some entrepreneurial Republicans, particularly in the Senate, who had been advocating a harder line on trade for years and who had left their mark on the 1984 bill.[89] Eventually the administration also joined the push for new legislation, mainly to secure reauthorized negotiating powers for the approaching Uruguay round of multilateral talks.

Still, the omnibus bill was chiefly neither a concerted effort to fix the nation's trade imbalance nor an exasperated reaction to a passive president; it remained a partisan affair. The administration's record was hardly laissez-faire, especially after September 1985, when the president announced a coordinated program of currency intervention to devalue the dollar and reaffirmed his determination not to "stand by and watch American businesses fail because of unfair trading practices abroad."[90] Yet three years later the legislative wagon continued to roll in spite of these measures. Its drivers were principally the Democratic leadership, which persevered in trying to flog a bulging trade package into law even after the October 1987 stock market crash had raised new doubts about its expediency and when the monthly trade figures began showing a torrid increase in exports.[91] For when the Democrats took control of the Senate in January 1987, adoption of the trade bill had become the party's cause célèbre, and on both sides of the Capitol a process of political mobilization got under way that could be stalled but not stopped.

The partisan maneuvering associated with H.R. 3 both delayed the bill's enactment and freighted it with politically self-serving provisions. Until the Democrats regained a majority, the Senate was unlikely to rally behind the radical measures being incubated in the Democratic House. With notable exceptions, Republicans tended to distrust the

89. Ahearn and Reifman, "U.S. Trade Policy," pp. 103–27. A leading example was Senator John C. Danforth, chairman of the Senate Finance Trade Subcommittee in the Ninety-ninth Congress, who had been urging legislation to require reciprocity in telecommunications equipment trade.

90. *Weekly Compilation of Presidential Documents*, vol. 21 (September 30, 1985), p. 1129.

91. Rose Gutfeld, "Trade Deficit for March Narrowed to $9.75 Billion, Lowest Level in Three Years, on a Surge in Exports," *Wall Street Journal*, May 18, 1988, p. 3.

House initiatives as Democratic ploys to best Reagan's economic policies with a competing economic issue. (In theory, trade policy, like Reaganomics, involved little nondefense spending and no obvious tax increases.) In the One-hundredth Congress, under unified Democratic control, the two bodies were better able to act in tandem. They were also in a stronger position to challenge the president, even strong enough to court a veto fight. That temptation became overwhelming in the spring of 1988 as the parties positioned themselves for the fall election. At the eleventh hour, after months of bargaining to reach a compromise acceptable to the administration, the congressional negotiators suddenly dug in their heels over the only remaining provision the White House had vowed to resist: a requirement that companies give advance notice of plant closings or layoffs. The Democrats, under intense pressure from organized labor to retain the stipulation at all costs, also sensed that they would enjoy a political windfall if the president carried out his threatened veto. He did, and the legislation was shelved for several more months pending resubmission of a twin version. Before recessing in the summer, however, a cloned H.R. 3 minus the plant closure clause finally cleared Congress. Satisfied, the president signed off.

The second result of partisanship was that the early drafts of the 1988 bill were stuffed with blatantly restrictive components to mollify importuning constituents and provide grist for the campaign mills of particular Democratic candidates. And because H.R. 3 was to be not just another trade act but something like a Democratic party economic program dealing comprehensively with "competitiveness," nearly two dozen congressional committees threw in more than the usual assortment of controversial items. Although as usual most of the red herrings were gutted in conference, the effect was to move the debate's center of gravity toward the bill's widening coalition of support.

During much of the debate members inserted technical provisions that conferees failed to smoke out or else regarded as moderate substitutes compared with the protectionist lightning rods attracting public attention. The clearest example was the substitution of the Senate's revision of section 301 for the Gephardt amendment. As an influential member of Ways and Means, Representative Richard A. Gephardt had managed to include a proposal requiring countries with "excessive and unwarranted" trade surpluses to make specified mandatory reductions in their bilateral deficits with the United States or face sanctions.[92] Because Gephardt was also running for president and fighting unfair trade was his main message, the amendment received a thorough inspection; the liberal trade elite, the news media, and political rivals rained opprobrium on it. Having barely squeaked by on the House floor (218–214), the proposal was generally expected to die in conference. It did; but observers paid less attention to what the conference committee put in its place. Senators Donald W. Riegle, Jr., and John C. Danforth crafted new language for section 301 requiring the U.S. trade representative to identify publicly as many as forty-two countries having "a consistent pattern of import barriers and market distorting practices."[93] If mandatory negotiations failed to remove all such practices within fifteen to nineteen months, sanctions would follow. Much like the Gephardt amendment, "Super 301" conjured up the spectacle of the world's greatest democracy regularly denouncing and punishing its allies as illicit merchants. Yet this "Brother of Gephardt," as a few attentive skeptics dubbed it, was incorporated with relatively little fuss.

As in the Gephardt amendment, retaliation under Super 301 can be waived by the president for national economic or security considerations, but conditions were added making frequent waivers difficult. Under existing law the USTR could only investigate trade complaints and make a recommendation to the president, who would decide what action, if any, to take. The new rules transfer to the trade representative the power to determine fairness and order remedial action. Although the USTR is lodged in the Executive Office of the President and remains decidedly a presidential agency, the shift of responsibilities will make it harder for the president to refuse retaliation; to do so would give the appearance of blocking the lead trade agency in the conduct of its newly mandated duties. At other times, when the White House must protect an industry (or avoid making the choice), it, like Congress, will have the added convenience of letting that decision be reached at another address.

The Riegle-Danforth "World Market Opening Initiative" is a relatively prominent element in the big trade law. There are others, however, that are buried more deeply. Section 1342 is a fundamental

92. *Congressional Record*, daily ed., April 29, 1987, pp. H2755–57.

93. *Omnibus Trade and Competitiveness Act of 1988*, Conference Report to accompany H.R. 3, H. Rept. 100-576, 100 Cong. 2 sess. (GPO, 1988), p. 576. See the critique of "Super 301" by Claude E. Barfield, "Brother of Gephardt," *Washington Post*, March 9, 1988, p. A25.

change in the procedures for protecting intellectual property rights (section 337 of the 1930 Tariff Act) that received virtually no publicity, as Corning Glass, disappointed with the rulings of the ITC and the District of Columbia Circuit Court on a patent infringement complaint, prevailed on the legislators to eliminate an injury test in ITC patent cases. Similarly, with little debate the threat of competition for Boeing and McDonnell Douglas from the European Airbus wrought new wording in the countervailing duty law: under section 1314, subsidies to international consortia, direct or indirect, are now included in calculating the duties. After heavy lobbying by the Semiconductor Industry Association, the lawmakers also authorized expedited investigations of foreigners caught dumping "short life-cycle products" (Japanese computer chips) more than once in an eight-year period (section 1323). And for the telecommunications equipment industry, section 1375 orders the USTR to negotiate suitable "market opportunities" with countries that have denied "mutually advantageous" ones to U.S. manufacturers.

By 1988 this sort of tinkering had turned the trade statutes into a regulatory patchwork—an expanding fabric of rules, with new layers stitched to older ones. The congressional urge to embroider the administrative remedies every few years has not been prompted only by actual defects in the laws (though there were plenty): the alterations have been politically profitable. Generic procedures for trade redress have frequently been reorganized or adjusted to meet the needs of specific claimants or of a wider range of commercial interests without appearing to endorse discredited policies of commercial protection and promotionalism. In almost every instance the pattern has been recognizable: groups of legislators seem to start by unfurling colorful excesses, while specialized aides and trade lawyers weave less flashy technical changes. A sober House-Senate conference then strikes the indelicacies, leaving the subtler sections intact. When the sewing is finished, the quilt is thicker, and heavier.

Good Cop, Bad Cop

Even when Congress only pretends to legislate or merely murmurs that it might, trade regulation can expand. Some of the costliest import restraints of recent years have been joint ventures, so to speak, in which the White House played more than a reactive role. Perhaps the best example was the self-administered regime governing imports of

Japanese automobiles. In 1981 President Reagan was confronted with
the possibility that Congress would mandate auto quotas if Japan did
not voluntarily restrict exports. For Congress to round up enough
votes to overcome a presidential veto of such legislation would have
been difficult in view of the president's extraordinary popularity (plus
the fact that imposing quotas would have constituted a breach of
American obligations under article 11 of GATT and article 14 of the
Japan-United States Treaty of Friendship, Commerce and Naviga-
tion).[94] But the administration genuflected anyway, not so much because
Congress was on a credible legislative warpath as because the president's
campaign statements on Japanese auto exports rendered a veto politically
awkward. Naturally, in arranging with the Japanese government to
rein in exports, it was useful to imply that Congress had forced the
president's hand and that a negotiated solution with the good cops in
the executive branch would be milder than the alternatives contemplated
by the bad cops on Capitol Hill. And by leaving an impression that
Congress had compelled the administration to act, the White House
could palm off some of the responsibility for the quota's $5 billion to
$10 billion in annual costs to consumers, or rather leave it suspended
somewhere between the two institutions, since the legislature had not
legislated and it too could dodge blame. Four years later the institutional
legerdemain became even fancier. In March 1985 the administration
formally terminated the restraint agreement. Within days an outraged
House and Senate adopted nonbinding resolutions condemning Japan.
The Japanese announced plans to keep a cap on auto exports, albeit at
a higher level. Thus, without the president's fingerprints and with no
serious legislative action, the restriction continued with no end in
sight.[95]

Presidential partnership with Congress in creating certain import
control programs may have seemed especially ironic under an administration that continually professed to prefer leaving markets to take
care of themselves. However, the practice of allowing decisions to
depend at least in part on political considerations or priorities unrelated
to trade definitely predated the Reagan presidency. In the early 1970s
the Nixon administration advanced the Multifiber Arrangement to
help clear the way for the Trade Act of 1974 (the president's efforts

94. Carl J. Green, "The New Protectionism," *Northwestern Journal of International Law and Business*, vol. 3 (Spring 1981), p. 8.
95. See William A. Niskanen, *Reaganomics: An Insider's Account of the Policies and the People* (Oxford University Press, 1988), pp. 139–41.

to limit textile imports actually began six years earlier with campaign pledges tied to his "southern strategy"). The Carter administration devised the trigger price system for steel to strengthen its 1979 omnibus trade initiative by staying one step ahead of the congressional steel caucus. The arrangement was reportedly also one of several promises corporate interests wrested from the White House when it was desperately seeking business support for its controversial energy program.[96] Moreover, the administration favored a legalistic mechanism for managing imports instead of the more overt protection afforded by quantity restraints. The engineers of the trigger price mechanism drew on accusations of unfair pricing and deployed the antidumping laws to regulate prices. Justifying this approach, Carter appeared to outdo even the fiercest congressional firebrands: he had harsh words not only for the comportment of foreign steel manufacturers but for his own Treasury Department, which he charged with "derogation of duty" in enforcement.[97]

Why does the executive occasionally act this way? A partial explanation, of course, is that sustaining the delegated power to make trade policy requires maintaining credibility with Congress. Presidents have behaved as if they needed to bank a certain amount of "vigorous and decisive" trade regulation to count on congressional cooperation when it came time to request that the delegation of power be renewed. Executive leeway on policy can thus come heavily mortgaged to preemptive pacts with various trade-sensitive factions. In a sense, executive-legislative relations have resembled an exacting marriage of convenience: the pragmatic partners periodically endear themselves, not just by reacting belatedly to each other's demands, but also by anticipating one another's wishes.

But that is only part of the answer. It may also be argued that presidential courtship of Congress is often unnecessarily solicitous, since for all their grousing many members scarcely relish the responsibility of a fully emancipated relationship. Conceivably, presidents less willing to compromise their liberal trade preferences and more willing to call Congress's bluff could hold their own. Indeed, such leaders might even be able to direct the national trade debate on their terms, rather than follow it on terms defined by others. The fact is,

96. Robert G. Kaiser and J. P. Smith, "Political Dealing Prompts Big Steel's Flip-Flop on Gas Bill," *Washington Post*, September 7, 1978, p. A2.
97. Green, "New Protectionism," p. 13.

though, that the traditional distinction between a constituent-minded Congress clamoring for import bars and a globally minded president standing steadfastly for open trade is simplistic; both dread the stain of protectionism, and neither can resist scoring points in domestic politics by departing from free trade for the sake of fair trade.

If the departures always bore clear and present political dangers, such as immediate and nondiffuse impacts at home and angry reactions abroad, presidents and lawmakers would risk them less frequently. But thanks to the way potentially explosive cases are typically handled— through bilateral executive agreements instead of legislated tariffs— the risks are greatly reduced. At home the political advantages of negotiated restraint agreements are considerable.[98] A domestic industry gets to raise prices and expand its market share. The subsidy and its cost are largely hidden. And the restraint is called "voluntary," which provides a fig leaf for government intervention and avoids the need to compensate the exporting country (as GATT would require if a discriminatory tariff or quota were imposed). A voluntary export restraint may also appeal to the foreign suppliers. Not only may it enable producers to make higher profits on the mix of merchandise sold to the restricted market, as the Japanese automakers and semiconductor manufacturers have been able to do, but it also permits dominant firms in an industry to form an export cartel, shielding themselves from the possible competition of more dynamic newcomers. Under normal circumstances such a cartel would be difficult to arrange, or if arranged would be impossible to police. It would also be vulnerable to antitrust suits. But an officially negotiated restraint can erect what amounts to a government-sponsored cartel, enforced by export licenses and safe from legal challenges since the firms can technically claim immunity under the doctrine of "sovereign" (or governmental) compulsion. To be sure, arrangements that enable foreign producers to capture the scarcity rents created by protection (instead of at least allowing the U.S. government to collect these excess profits as a straight tariff would) may appear to make little sense from the standpoint of the national economic interest. But the revenues are often willingly forgone because the immediate diplomatic advantages of voluntary restraints outweigh them, and in any event most taxpayers are unaware of the waste.

98. The discussion of voluntary export restraints draws on Jan Tumlir, *Protectionism: Trade Policy in Democratic Societies* (Washington: American Enterprise Institute for Public Policy Research, 1985), pp. 39–43.

The modern process of presidential selection may account for much of the politicization of trade policy that has extended to the White House. Seeking nominations and financing campaigns, presidential aspirants become weighted with obligations to special interests. Walter Mondale's candidacy in 1984 was perhaps the clearest illustration of this potential trap. Had Mondale won, his many understandings with organized labor and other groups experiencing troubles ascribed to trade would have forced him to deliver on much of his rhetoric. Although Reagan was not equally boxed in, neither was he wholly unencumbered. Several of the trade-managing plans initiated during his presidency could be traced in no small part to the politics of presidential elections.

Even in 1988, when candidates who talked particularly tough on trade fared poorly, the jockeying in a few pivotal primaries altered some positions. Iowa and Michigan, caucus states where candidates attempted to pitch highly parochial appeals at tiny bands of voters, elicited tougher attitudes toward trade abuses. In preparation for Michigan, Michael Dukakis, the eventual Democratic nominee, suddenly announced support for the stiffest provision in the pending trade legislation—Super 301—cosponsored by Senator Riegle of Michigan, whose endorsement he had just received.[99] Dukakis lost the Michigan caucus but remained on record in favor of Riegle's amendment for the rest of the campaign. George Bush later successfully painted the Massachusetts governor as a foreign policy neophyte with a wobbly understanding of international economics. But while Bush set off on the high road of free trade, he took a few startling detours of his own to secure key states, such as a promise, for Pennsylvania, to prolong the comprehensive restraint agreements for the steel industry. When his administration took the reins in 1989, the USTR wasted no time in enforcing Super 301; Japan soon found itself on the hit list.

How closely presidents adhere to the letter or spirit of campaign pronouncements on fair trade depends among other things on the nature and size of their electoral mandate, the strength of their party in Congress, the extent of inflationary pressures in the economy, their foreign policy, and the latitude Congress is willing to grant them in discharging delegated functions. On the whole, postwar presidents have managed to remain nimble enough at least to retreat from, if they

99. Robin Toner, "Dukakis Takes New Trade Message to North and Gephardt Cries Foul," *New York Times*, March 23, 1988, p. A21.

could not avoid, some regrettable campaign promises. But such flexibility is not unlimited, regardless of how Congress delineates presidential discretion. Presidents have often exercised their discretion politically—sometimes to gain the confidence of Congress, other times to settle their debts (preferably with a good measure of "plausible deniability"). Sometimes the White House has balanced the competing claims on trade policy with a clear sense of the public interest, and sometimes not. For the most part, presidents since World War II have striven valiantly to liberalize international commerce. But recent deviations have been serious. And recalling who did what at various other junctures of American history, one must understand that vesting powers in the executive provides no inherent guarantee of steady trade liberalization. In 1922, for example, Congress passed the Fordney-McCumber Tariff Act, giving the president authority to adjust tariff rates up or down as much as 50 percent. In the next eight years, presidents made thirty-seven changes in specific duties—of which thirty-two were increases.[100]

Some Conclusions

Enforcing rules against the commercial misdeeds of other countries has become a major emphasis of American foreign economic policy in the past decade. While the possible long-range consequences have not been adequately explored, the political dynamics have become clearer. Politicians have realized that efforts to regulate trade transgressions offer little prospect of righting economic imbalances. Jousting with the trade deficit, however, has not been their sole purpose. Moralistic pretensions aside, the objective of fair trade regulation has been the same as that of any other trade policy, here or elsewhere: to improve the competitive position of particular firms or industries against other firms or industries. Since 1980, American business interests and workers have demanded much more of this assistance, not simply because their competitive rank has slipped but increasingly because they and their advocates in government have accused international competitors of laying siege to the American economy through rapacious commercial stratagems. Cries for protective or promotional trade intervention are neither new nor unique; they have cycled through the commercial

100. Asher Isaacs, *International Trade: Tariff and Commercial Policies* (Irwin, 1948), p. 227.

histories of all the major trading nations. What seems distinctive now is the way these cries are being expressed—as requests for legal redress rather than naked redistributions of rents.

The legalistic style might be readily explained if the rest of the world's unlawful commerce were the root cause of America's trade woes. It would also befit a bureaucracy that was truly "capable of looking at the whole economic situation of the country with a dispassionate and disinterested scrutiny" and had really managed to divorce trade law enforcement "from any strong prepossession in favor of any political policy."[101] But neither proposition squares with the facts, and few politicians are cynical or naive enough to say otherwise. Macroeconomic forces—chiefly the interaction of domestic fiscal policy with interest and exchange rates, low savings levels, and possibly some productivity lags—have been the underlying sources of America's trade tribulations, not an increasingly lawless trading system in which the United States finds it hard to compete.[102] Perhaps, given the political intractability of factors such as the budget deficit, it has been natural, even cathartic, to repair to trade policy, patrolling the margins of the economic problem by prosecuting trade offenses.[103] Yet one suspects another reason for the litigation is that domestic economic and political interests have learned how to benefit from the proceedings without incurring too many conspicuous costs. While it is an exaggeration to say that trade remedies have become no more than a mask for protectionism, the regulatory program's political utility lies in supplying equivalent results without the evident negatives.

The power-sharing compact between Congress and the executive

101. President Woodrow Wilson's request to Congress in February 1916 to establish a tariff commission, quoted in John M. Dobson, *Two Centuries of Tariffs: The Background and Emergence of the U.S. International Trade Commission* (GPO, 1976), p. 87.

102. Conservative economists and liberal ones have reached virtually identical conclusions on the role of exchange rates. For a sample of opinion, compare Sven W. Arndt and Lawrence Bouton, *Competitiveness: The United States in World Trade* (Washington: American Enterprise Institute for Public Policy Research, 1987), chap. 2; and Ralph C. Bryant, Gerald Holtham, and Peter Hooper, eds., *External Deficits and the Dollar: The Pit and the Pendulum* (Brookings, 1988), chaps. 1–3. On congressional cognizance of the trade deficit's macroeconomic causes, see Raymond J. Ahearn and Alfred Reifman, "Trade Legislation in 1987: Congress Takes Charge," in Robert E. Baldwin and J. David Richardson, eds., *Issues in the Uruguay Round* (Cambridge, Mass.: National Bureau of Economic Research, 1988), p. 80.

103. Ahearn and Reifman put it more bluntly: " 'Being tough, but fair' with foreign governments on trade is much easier than raising taxes or cutting expenditures at home." "Trade Legislation in 1987," p. 79.

has reinforced this political discovery. When constituent claims are framed as trade complaints instead of rent-seeking demands, they not only enlist allies but can be addressed safely through administrative and judicial conduits. Amending the administrative procedures frequently and pressuring the administrators, members of Congress can control the flow of dispensations without being branded protectionists. Congress can have it both ways, retaining opportunities for constituent service without being directly answerable for flawed or controversial policies. Meanwhile, the executive also enjoys enough power to confer benefits while ducking blame for unfortunate consequences. The executive's authority has been sufficiently loose to design elaborate restraint agreements (where the chief architect is difficult to distinguish from other collaborators) and sufficiently hedged to permit such disclaimers as "Congress left us no choice."

The preferred administrative formulation under GATT, the escape clause, has lacked the same political charm. A section 201 petition lays no claim to fairness; it simply asks for protection. This puts policymakers on the spot. Presidents, perhaps increasingly, have their own domestic political headaches to nurse when refusing trade relief for powerful pressure groups. Still, turning thumbs up in 201 cases is incommodious: the decision may smack of pandering to special pleaders; the exporting country will demand compensation; the buck cannot disappear in a bureaucratic labyrinth but rather stops pretty much at the president's desk. The natural inclination therefore has been to invoke the escape clause sparingly and, when invoked, to obscure (or redefine) the subvention it implies.[104] As for the legislature, it gets no free ride either if the president turns thumbs down. The disappointed petitioner will run back to Capitol Hill and wonder why congressmen do not practice what they preach by flatly overruling the president's judgment with a joint resolution, as the law permits. If section 201 has fallen out of favor, it is because everyone knows that the probable political benefit-cost ratio is higher in the forum of legal remedies for unfair trade.

Because regulating pernicious trading practices, while often frustrating, is less fraught with political hazards, it no longer quells

104. The case of steel in 1984 was illustrative. The administration transformed an affirmative ITC finding—that fairly priced imports were causing serious injury—into grounds for negotiating globally comprehensive restraint agreements "in the name of rolling back 'unfairly' priced import competition." Ahearn and Reifman, "U.S. Trade Policy," p. 109.

pressures for trade management; on the contrary, it stimulates them. For every unfair practice that is attacked, several new ones pop up, summoning amendments as the definition of unfairness expands. Thus whereas dumping was once defined strictly as predatory pricing (the requisite intent on the part of the dumper being "to injure or destroy" an American industry), the antidumping law has been amended incrementally until now it engulfs pricing patterns that could be neither anticompetitive nor unreasonable.[105] Similarly, illegal subsidies were originally defined as direct "bounties or grants" bestowed by foreign governments on products imported into the United States.[106] Now the scope of the countervailing duty law has widened; today precedents exist for countervailing duties on everything from regional development programs to industrial adjustment payments.[107] Since the 1988 trade bill became law, the number of commercial practices deemed iniquitous has grown to encompass such novelties as export targeting (even in forms currently allowed by GATT) and violations of workers' rights (even though the United States has not signed the international agreement that defines these rights).[108]

One way to interpret this seeming reductio ad absurdum is by considering the futility of controlling unfair trade in the absence of better multilateral covenants. The national trade balance sheets barely budge under the unilateral rules, so the rulemakers redouble their efforts, tightening the regulations, filling in gaps. Such an interpretation is too simple, however; for while the regulation of unfair trading may be largely ineffective at the macroeconomic level, it promises micro-economic advantages. It is perceived to provide security or support for particular firms or industries. That perception too might be mostly wishful thinking (in the long run protected industries still tend to falter), but not entirely.[109] The system has delivered enough immediate rewards to keep participants, if not wholly satisfied, keenly interested.

105. Smith, "Negotiating Trade Laws," p. 11.

106. "An Act to provide revenue for the Government and to encourage the industries of the United States," 1897, sec. 5 (30 Stat. 151, 205). (Readers may notice an admirable candor in this title.)

107. *ASG Industries, Inc.* v. *United States* (1979), discussed in Peter D. Ehrenhaft, "The 'Judicialization' of Trade Law," *Notre Dame Lawyer*, vol. 56 (April 1981), p. 600; and *British Steel Corp* . v. *United States* (1985), discussed in Sandler, "Primer on United States Trade Remedies," p. 770.

108. *Business Week*, May 23, 1988, p. 57.

109. Robert Z. Lawrence and Paula R. DeMasi studied sixteen American industries that received some type of import protection between 1954 and 1988 and found that

And Policy Implications

To say that litigating foreign trade abuses is less hazardous in contemporary domestic politics than providing old-style tariff protection is not to suggest that it will necessarily remain more benign in economic terms and in terms of sound international relations. The web of voluntary export restraints spun around goods such as steel and semiconductors has posed all the predictable economic problems of protectionism with none of the fiscal silver lining. For example, voluntary restraints have reduced consumption of carbon steel from already depressed levels and induced shortages of semifinished slab needed by the industry's small specialized producers.[110] If the import controls have saved some steelworkers' jobs, it has been at a cost to the economy of $113,600 per job saved, according to a study by the Federal Trade Commission.[111] At the same time, since negotiated export restraints by definition levy no official fee or charge on the imported product, none of the shortage-induced proceeds of protection are being captured by the U.S. Customs Service, a curious choice in the age of structural budget deficits.

The outcomes of the microchip restraint accord with Japan appear to have been even more perverse.[112] Under the terms of the agreement the Japanese government has been able to cartelize its producers and impose production quotas. The resulting shortage in dynamic random

---

only one—the bicycle industry—expanded after it received protection. Lawrence and Litan, *Saving Free Trade*, p. 71. Likewise, a Congressional Budget Office study of the footwear, automobile, steel, and textile industries found that in each case protection has failed to significantly increase their international competitiveness. Daniel P. Kaplan, *Has Trade Protection Revitalized Domestic Industries?* (Congressional Budget Office, November 1986), p. 101.

110. Jonathan P. Hicks, "A Steel Quota Divides the Industry," *New York Times*, May 19, 1988, p. D1.

111. David G. Tarr and Morris E. Morkre, *Aggregate Costs to the United States of Tariffs and Quotas on Imports: General Tariff Cuts and Removal of Quotas on Automobiles, Steel, Sugar, and Textiles* (Federal Trade Commission, December 1984), cited in Gary Clyde Hufbauer, Diane T. Berliner, and Kimberly Ann Elliott, *Trade Protection in the United States: 31 Case Studies* (Washington: Institute for International Economics, 1986), p. 179.

112. The problems are neatly summarized by Kenneth Flamm, "U.S. Memory Chip Makers: In a Fix," *Washington Post*, March 1, 1988, p. A19. See also Eugene Volokh, "The Semiconductor Industry and Foreign Competition," *Policy Analysis*, no. 99 (Washington: CATO Institute, January 28, 1988).

access memories (DRAMs) doubled their retail price from $2.50 in early 1986 to more than $5.00 by the spring of 1988. The increased prices have not much inconvenienced the Japanese electronic equipment giants, who largely build their own DRAMs, but they have hurt U.S. computer manufacturers, who are highly dependent on open-market chip purchases. Moreover, with Japan already accounting for 90 percent of world commodity chip sales, the price hikes have mainly translated into higher profits for Japanese competitors of the two American companies still making DRAMs, Texas Instruments and Micron Technology. That only leaves Japanese producers in a stronger position to research and develop future generations of memory devices. An explicit duty or tariff on Japanese semiconductors would at least have diverted some revenues to the U.S. government, rather than mostly into the pockets of Toshiba, Hitachi, Fujitsu, and NEC. But such a clear tariff would have mobilized opposition, not only from the Japanese but by domestic chip users, who would have discerned the cost implications of the import restriction instantly (instead of nearly two years later, as has happened under the negotiated settlement).

The foreign policy repercussions of fair trade regulation have been, until now, less pronounced, partly because other countries do not always wind up big losers. (Initially the Japanese protested the computer chip action, but soon they were crying all the way to the bank.) Nonetheless, there are signs that a crusade for fairness, pursued without consent from the international community, can antagonize or bewilder allies. Accurately or not, they perceive the United States as browbeating others about commercial improprieties while overlooking comparable practices of its own. Europeans, for instance, cannot understand why Americans passionately disapprove of loans to the Airbus consortium while the U.S. aeronautics industry is cross-subsidized through military contracts.[113] The Japanese hear themselves scolded about their restrictive policy on rice imports by a formidable adversary whose sugar import program is equally indefensible—and possibly more harmful

113. The European Airbus consortium has estimated that the U.S. government provided $23 billion in identifiable direct and indirect financial support "of a subsidy nature" to Boeing and McDonnell Douglas through various governmental and quasi-governmental agencies between 1978 and 1987. Airbus Industrie, "Government Funding of Boeing and McDonnell Douglas Civil Aircraft Programs" (Blagnac, France, March 14, 1988), p. iii. See also "European Aircraft Industry Charges U.S. Companies Received $23 Billion in Subsidies," *International Trade Reporter*, vol. 5 (March 23, 1988), p. 394.

to the rest of the world, since it keeps the Philippines and struggling countries in the Caribbean from selling sugar to a vast market.[114]

So long as countries consider that fairness in international trade is largely in the eye of the beholder, a righteous policy launched unilaterally with escalating threats and sanctions can become an irritant. Tensions may rise as more of America's commercial neighbors adopt adversarial policies. In recent skirmishes Canada has mimicked the style of U.S. antisubsidy suits by slapping harsh duties on subsidized American corn exports. More ominously, the capricious appearance of some U.S. countervails—on lumber, for example—probably fanned the inflammatory rhetoric of Canadian politicians opposed to the U.S.-Canada trade treaty. (For a time during the parliamentary election of 1988, Canadian voters seemed fearful that the United States would declare open season on every manner of subsidy from old-age pensions to medical insurance.) In Europe the adoption of legislation mirroring section 301 means that more American companies can expect to be legally harassed, much as foreign firms claim to be under the U.S. trade rules. And increasingly the current artillery of trade war—weapons such as the EC's "new commercial policy instrument"—may be trained on those U.S. rules, heightening mutual recriminations.[115] At a time when the United States can no longer rely on expansionary fiscal policy and must count increasingly on export-led economic growth facilitated by friendly foreign governments, developments like these can complicate matters. Worse, the U.S. offensive may reignite (or provide a pretext for) anti-American sentiment and contribute to political instability, as in South Korea.[116]

When the long-term economic and diplomatic costs of the evolving American commercial policy come to light, they may still prove

114. James Fallows, *More Like Us: Making America Great Again* (Houghton Mifflin, 1989), p. 41.

115. "On the Strengthening of the Common Commercial Policy with Regard in Particular to Protection Against Illicit Commercial Practices," *Council Regulation* (EEC), no. 2641/84, September 17, 1984. For example, after a 1986 investigation using this instrument, the European Commission concluded that U.S. application of section 337 of the 1930 Tariff Act constituted "an illicit commercial practice" in excluding from the U.S. market aramid fibers manufactured by AKZO, a Dutch synthetic fiber manufacturer. Commission of the European Communities, "AKZO: The Commission Decides to Initiate a Consultation and Dispute Settlement Procedure in GATT," Press Release, Brussels, March 20, 1987.

116. Susan Chira, "In South Korea, Anger at U.S. Spreads," *New York Times*, June 3, 1988, pp. A1, A12.

politically acceptable. Defenders could posit that in time the gains for the nation and the world economy will exceed the drawbacks. Alternatively, they could claim that the interests of certain domestic groups are well served and worth serving, even at the expense of some national and global welfare. Or the proponents might even be able to demonstrate that vigorous defense of fair trade must be a matter of principle—that no society can afford to be taken for a sucker, regardless of whether the strenuous remedy leaves it better off.

Whatever the case, the underlying questions of fact and value in a policy dialogue of such importance ought to be spelled out more plainly through the policymaking institutions. So far this has not occurred. The three-year legislative colloquy on the 1988 trade bill was not an elevating experience. The combatants spent months bickering over peripheral concerns such as the bill's plant-closing provision while ignoring core issues: what, precisely, does a "level" playing field *mean* in the global economic context?[117] Is it feasible for America to officiate alone? And in the end, what difference will it make? Instead, buzzwords—"reciprocity," "symmetrical access," "competitiveness"—were bandied about as if their meaning and implications were self-explanatory.

To sharpen public debate on the future of American trade policy, it may become necessary to clarify who is responsible for the policy. Interestingly, one way for this to happen might be for Congress to repossess more of its constitutional prerogatives. This unconventional notion warrants more study than can be offered in these pages, but a mental experiment provides a starting point: what would the trade policy process be like today if the balance of power reverted unambiguously to the legislature? In the worst case, Congress, more decentralized and desultory than in 1930, would abandon all restraint and reenact the functional equivalent of Smoot-Hawley. The chances of such legislation becoming law, however, seem remote. Smoot-Hawley protectionism is still anathema. And much more than in 1930, the stakes would be enormous. Economic interests with a lot to lose could

---

117. Maybe one reason this question is seldom asked is that it is so hard to answer. The tendency is to apply intuitive standards of fairness to international commerce much as is done to the domestic economy. In doing so one risks vitiating the entire rationale for international trade: that nations trade with one another because transactions based on their differences can enhance mutual welfare, often regardless of whether they are "fair." See Robert Z. Lawrence, comments on paper by Paul R. Krugman, *BPEA*, *1:1984*, p. 128.

not afford to sit on the sidelines; they would hurl themselves into the fray. Legislators would have to face these and other counterweights under an added constraint of institutional learning from past mistakes.

More likely than an extensive trade wall would be attempts to legislate industry-specific quotas. These schemes would also have difficulty overcoming presidential vetoes (the failures of the 1985 and 1988 textile quota bills are illustrative), but some might slip through. Whether the world would look altogether different if these measures were enacted is hard to say. Would the cost of imported Japanese cars have been much higher in the first half of the decade if statutory quotas or tariffs rather than a voluntary export restraint had been imposed in 1981? Perhaps the chief contrast would not have been the steeper prices, but that Congress would have had to explain those prices to the voters. The uproar that would surely ensue in GATT could ultimately prove chastening to some congressional trade hawks. At a minimum, it would flush their designs into the open and subject them to recorded roll calls.

The most probable behavior would be for Congress to try to restore the former status quo, redelegating authority to the executive while clinging to a good deal of indirect control. One could expect renewed efforts to empower such administrative go-betweens as the USTR or Commerce and to enrich their regulatory functions. This would present the presidency with three choices: continue to oblige Congress in the customary fashion, laying an uneasy hand on the steering wheel while it remains a vigorous backseat driver; drive a harder bargain by insisting on greater autonomy; or decline to accept. A reluctant administration, or one holding out for more autonomy, would annoy the legislators and could risk a loss of coveted powers, including reduced ability to lead foreign trade negotiations credibly. An intransigent or aloof administration might also face more frequent showdowns with Congress over disruptive trade bills. And because incentives to avoid blame are potent in both branches, for Congress to grant the executive carte blanche in trade decisions would be a reform as imperfect as it is implausible: the trend toward orderly marketing agreements and voluntary restraint agreements would not abate.

Yet the traditional compromise—arranging institutional roles so that the lines of responsibility for policy remain blurred—now seems unsatisfactory because it permits policymakers to keep drifting toward regulated trade without adequately exposing their work to rigorous cross-examination. That such an arrangement will always be preferable to the alternatives is no longer obvious. If the executive has not always charted a wise course for American economic policy, neither does the modern Congress incorrigibly champion protectionism. That at least seems particularly true when the the members are less free to cast easy votes. Viewed this way, it becomes possible to understand how, within a two-month span, the same lawmakers who wrought the Omnibus Trade and Competitiveness Act of 1988 endorsed overwhelmingly one of the more enlightened trade initiatives of the postwar period: the free trade agreement with Canada. In the first instance the potential for mischief could be concealed; in the second it could not. Facing a choice over, say, a new section 780(a) requiring more monitoring of imports incorporating dumped or subsidized components, most in Congress found it irresistible to vote yea. But confronted with the do-or-die decision to support open trade with Canada or go on record to kill the accord, only one legislator in nine found it expedient to vote like a "protectionist."

What these vagaries may suggest is that when Congress makes trade policy, the stakes are best kept high and clear, not low-grade or uncertain. Choices should be delineated starkly, forcing participants to choose sides. Structuring legislative life this way will not be easy, especially since Congress makes its own decision rules. But Congress has altered its ways of doing business in the past, sometimes opting for closed rules, "fast tracks," and other constructive procedures in trade debates, and responsible reformers could do so again.

Index

255